PUBLIC HEALTH HUMANITARIAN RESPONSES TO NATURAL DISASTERS

The pressure of climate change, environmental degradation, and urbanisation, as well as the widening of socio-economic disparities have rendered the global population increasingly vulnerable to the impact of natural disasters. With a primary focus on medical and public health humanitarian response to disasters, *Public Health Humanitarian Responses to Natural Disasters* provides a timely critical analysis of public health responses to natural disasters.

Using a number of case studies and examples of innovative disaster response measures developed by international agencies and stakeholders, this book illustrates how theoretical understanding of public health issues can be practically applied in the context of humanitarian relief response. Starting with an introduction to public health principles within the context of medical and public health disaster and humanitarian response, the book goes on to explore key trends, threats and challenges in contemporary disaster medical response.

This book provides a comprehensive overview of an emergent discipline and offers a unique multidisciplinary perspective across a range of relevant topics including the concepts of disaster preparedness and resilience, and key challenges in human health needs for the twenty-first century. This book will be of interest to students of public health, disaster and emergency medicine and development studies, as well as to development and medical practitioners working within NGOs, development agencies, health authorities and public administration.

Emily Ying Yang Chan is a professor and assistant dean at The Chinese University of Hong Kong (CUHK) Faculty of Medicine and visiting professor of public health medicine at the Oxford University Nuffield Department of Medicine. She is also associate director at CUHK JC School of Public Health and Primary Care, centre director at Collaborating Centre for Oxford University and CUHK for Disaster and Medical Humanitarian Response (CCOUC), director at CUHK Centre for Global Health, visiting scholar at the Harvard University FXB Center for Health and Human Rights, senior fellow at Harvard Humanitarian Initiative, fellow at Hong Kong Academy of Medicine, member of The Asia Science Technology and Academia Advisory Group of the United Nations Office for Disaster Risk Reduction (UNISDR ASTAAG) and co-chairperson of World Health Organization Thematic Platform for Health Emergency & Disaster Risk Management Research Group.

Routledge Humanitarian Studies Series

Series editors: Alex de Waal and Dorothea Hilhorst
Editorial Board: Mihir Bhatt, Dennis Dijkzeul, Wendy Fenton, Kirsten Johnson, Julia Streets, Peter Walker

The Routledge Humanitarian Studies series in collaboration with the International Humanitarian Studies Association (IHSA) takes a comprehensive approach to the growing field of expertise that is humanitarian studies. This field is concerned with humanitarian crises caused by natural disaster, conflict or political instability and deals with the study of how humanitarian crises evolve, how they affect people and their institutions and societies, and the responses they trigger.

We invite book proposals that address, amongst other topics, questions of aid delivery, institutional aspects of service provision, the dynamics of rebel wars, state building after war, the international architecture of peacekeeping, the ways in which ordinary people continue to make a living throughout crises, and the effect of crises on gender relations.

This interdisciplinary series draws on and is relevant to a range of disciplines, including development studies, international relations, international law, anthropology, peace and conflict studies, public health and migration studies.

The New Humanitarians in International Practice
Emerging actors and contested principles
Edited by Zeynep Sezgin and Dennis Dijkzeul

Natural Hazards, Risk and Vulnerability
Floods and slum life in Indonesia
Roanne van Voorst

UNHCR and the Struggle for Accountability
Technology, law and results-based management
Edited by Kristin Bergtora Sandvik and Katja Lindskov Jacobsen

Australia's Foreign Aid Dilemma
Humanitarian aspirations confront democratic legitimacy
Jack Corbett

Public Health Humanitarian Responses to Natural Disasters
Emily Ying Yang Chan

People, Aid and Institutions in Socio-economic Recovery: Facing Fragilities
Gemma van der Haar, Dorothea Hilhorst, and Bart Weijs

PUBLIC HEALTH HUMANITARIAN RESPONSES TO NATURAL DISASTERS

Emily Ying Yang Chan

LONDON AND NEW YORK

from Routledge

First published 2017
by Routledge
2 Park Square, Milton Park, Abingdon, Oxon OX14 4RN

and by Routledge
711 Third Avenue, New York, NY 10017

Routledge is an imprint of the Taylor & Francis Group, an informa business

British Library Cataloguing-in-Publication Data
A catalogue record for this book is available from the British Library

Library of Congress Cataloging-in-Publication Data
Names: Chan, Emily Ying Yang, author.
Title: Public health humanitarian responses to natural disasters / authored
    by Emily Ying Yang Chan.
Description: Milton Park, Abingdon, Oxon ; New York, NY : Routledge,
    [2017] | Series: Routledge humanitarian studies
Identifiers: LCCN 2016036341 | ISBN 9781138953680 (hbk) |
    ISBN 9781138953703 (pbk) | ISBN 9781315667218 (ebk)
Subjects: LCSH: Disaster medicine. | Medical assistance. | Disaster relief. |
    Humanitarian assistance.
Classification: LCC RA645.5 .C43 2017 | DDC 363.34/8—dc23
LC record available at https://lccn.loc.gov/2016036341

ISBN: 978-1-138-95368-0 (hbk)
ISBN: 978-1-138-95370-3 (pbk)
ISBN: 978-1-315-66721-8 (ebk)

Typeset in Bembo
by Apex CoVantage, LLC

Printed and bound by CPI Group (UK) Ltd, Croydon, CR0 4YY

Dedicated to Eric, Ellie and Ernest
and
to those who risk their lives in the remote corners of our
world to make it healthier and more humane

CONTENTS

ILLUSTRATIONS

Figures

Tables

BOXES

Case boxes

Knowledge boxes

CONTRIBUTORS

Author

Emily Ying Yang Chan, MBBS (HKU), BS (Johns Hopkins), SM PIH (Harvard), MD (CUHK), DFM (HKCFP), FFPH, FHKAM (Community Medicine), FHKCCM, is a professor and assistant dean at The Chinese University of Hong Kong (CUHK) Faculty of Medicine and visiting professor of public health medicine at the Oxford University Nuffield Department of Medicine. She is also associate director at CUHK JC School of Public Health and Primary Care, centre director at the Collaborating Centre for Oxford University and CUHK for Disaster and Medical Humanitarian Response (CCOUC), director at CUHK Centre for Global Health, visiting scholar at the Harvard University FXB Center, senior fellow at Harvard Humanitarian Initiative, fellow at Hong Kong Academy of Medicine, member of The Asia Science Technology and Academia Advisory Group of the United Nations Office for Disaster Risk Reduction (UNISDR ASTAAG) and co-chairperson of World Health Organization Thematic Platform for Health Emergency & Disaster Risk Management Research Group. She received academic training at Johns Hopkins University, Harvard T.H. Chan School of Public Health, University of Hong Kong, CUHK and London School of Hygiene and Tropical Medicine. Her research interests include disaster and humanitarian medicine, health needs and programme impact evaluation of evidence-based medical and public health interventions in resource-deficit settings, climate change and health, global health, and violence and injury epidemiology. She also has rich medical and public health frontline experience and won a myriad of awards. Mostly recently, she was recognised as National Geographic Chinese Explorer for her frontier works.

Case contributors

Ali Ardalan, MD, PhD, is a pioneer in disaster risk management in Iran and the Middle East and North Africa (MENA) region who was the driving force behind the creation of MPH and PhD training programmes in disaster health studies. He is an associate professor and director of Disaster and Emergency Health at Tehran University of Medical Sciences, an adviser to the deputy minister of health and director of the Disaster Risk Management Office at I. R. Iran Ministry of Health and Medical Education. Dr Ardalan is a member of WHO/EMR Health Emergency Advisory Group and a member of the UNISDR Asia Science, Technology and Academic Advisory Group (ASTAAG). Dr Ardalan serves WHO/EMR as a consultant and collaborates with WHO/Geneva on advocacy of "disaster risk reduction for health" and "hospitals safe from disasters" in line with SFDRR and the Bangkok Principles on implementation of health aspects of SFDRR. Dr Ardalan is the representative of Central Asia region in the International Board of Global Network of Disaster Reduction (GNDR). He was a nominee for the 2015 UN Sasakawa Award. Since 2012, he has been a visiting scientist at Department of Global Health and Population at Harvard School of Public Health, and a senior fellow at Harvard Humanitarian Initiative. Dr Ardalan is author and co-author of over 70 articles in English and Persian peer-reviewed journals and contributed to the 2009 UNISDR Global Assessment Report and 2013 IFRC World Disasters Report. He was a guest researcher at the Karolinska Institute, and remains an active contributor to the Disaster Supercourse based in Pittsburgh University.

Christy Oi Yan Jing Catrina Chan, BA (Psyc. Biol.), MPH, was a research assistant at the Collaborating Centre for Oxford University and CUHK for Disaster and Medical Humanitarian Response (CCOUC). She obtained a dual degree in Psychology and Biology at the College of St. Benedict and St. John's University, USA, where she worked as a health advocate and peer educator, promoting physical, mental and social wellbeing among the college population. She has participated in overseas service projects and research-based missions in Tanzania and rural China.

Gloria Kwong Wai Chan, BSSc (CUHK), MSSc (CUHK) is a professional journalist by training. After spending years in political news reporting in Hong Kong, she joined the international medical humanitarian organisation Médecins Sans Frontières as the Director of Communications for the organisation's communication effort in Hong Kong, China and Southeast Asia. Her expertise was employed in the frontline of a number of emergencies over the world. Before joining the Collaborating Centre for Oxford University and CUHK for Disaster and Medical Humanitarian Response (CCOUC), she was the Chief Executive of the Hong Kong Medical Association. Ms Chan is currently a Board Member of Médecins Sans Frontières Hong Kong and serves as Assistant Director of CCOUC.

Mayling Chan, PhD, was raised in Hong Kong and received her higher education in the UK and Cuba. Her thematic expertise includes food security and national policy for both rural and urban sectors; sustainable systems of food production and livelihood, including sustainable management of natural resources and adaptation and mitigation of impacts of climate change. Her latest publications include *Unfinished Puzzle, Cuban Agriculture: The Challenges, Lessons and Opportunities* (Food First, USA, March 2013) and 古巴農業改革 *(Rural Reforms in Cuba)* (China, June 2013). She had held various management positions with international non-governmental organisations and she is currently the international programme director at Oxfam Hong Kong.

Eliza Cheung, MSSc in Clin. Psy., Reg. Psychol (Clin. Psych), PhD, specialises in disaster mental health and psychological first aid for her clinical practice, field work and research. She completed her professional training in clinical psychology and obtained her doctor of philosophy degree in public health at The Chinese University of Hong Kong. Dr Cheung currently serves as a clinical psychologist at Hong Kong Red Cross, and is a master trainer and roster member of the International Federation of Red Cross and Red Crescent Societies (IFRC). She has thus far trained over 2,000 disaster first responders and trainers in psychological first aid and psychosocial support from all over the world, including those from the Auxiliary Medical Service, Civil Aviation Department and Department of Health of the Hong Kong SAR government. In 2014 and 2015, she served as an IFRC psychosocial delegate in Liberia during the Ebola virus outbreak and in Nepal after the earthquake. She also worked with the World Health Organization in the review, translation and adaptation of some leading psychosocial support guidelines in emergency, including *Psychological First Aid: Guide for Field Workers* and *Psychological First Aid during Ebola Virus Disease Outbreaks*.

Cecilia YS Choi, MBBS (Sydney), MPH (CUHK), BSc (CUHK), was a graduate fellow at the Collaborating Centre for Oxford University and CUHK for Disaster and Medical Humanitarian Response (CCOUC) in 2011–12. She has worked on the CCOUC disaster case study series.

Janice Ying-En Ho is a PhD student in the School of Public Health and Primary Care at The Chinese University of Hong Kong. She is interested in the interactions between climate change, environment and health. A graduate from the University of Michigan with a degree in environmental sciences and psychology, she previously worked at the Collaborating Centre for Oxford University and CUHK for Disaster and Medical Humanitarian Response (CCOUC) as a research project officer.

Kevin KC Hung, MBChB, MRCSEd, MPH, EMDM, FHKCEM, FHKAM(EM), FRCEM, is an assistant professor in emergency medicine at The Chinese University of Hong Kong. Dr Hung is an emergency medicine specialist with vast experience in conducting rural health needs assessment in the Asia-Pacific region with various NGOs and humanitarian initiatives. He was the founding executive director of Hong Kong Jockey Club Disaster Preparedness and Response Institute (HKJCDPRI). Dr Hung is also a Hong Kong Red Cross volunteer and had served as a community health delegate of Japanese Red Cross Society Basic Health Care Emergency Response Unit.

Rinzin Jamtsho was Head Deputy Secretary at the Public Grievance Redressal Office and a Political Secretary at the Prime Minister's Office in the Kingdom of Bhutan (2008-2013). He was a Regional Fellow of the Collaborating Centre for Oxford University and CUHK for Disaster and Medical Humanitarian Response

(CCOUC) from April to August 2012 and completed a project on glacier lake outburst flood disaster mitigation.

Levina Chandra Khoe, MD, MPH, is currently teaching at the Department of Community Medicine, Universitas Indonesia. She received her Master in Public Health at The Chinese University of Hong Kong, focusing on public health disaster. She was also a CCOUC regional fellow (2013-2014), working on CCOUC disaster case study series. Before joining the university, she has been working with the Indonesian Ministry of Health on projects related to the implementation of Universal Health Care. She is also working as clinician and researcher, mainly in community health, public health in natural disasters, migrant health, health economics and policy.

Eva Chor-chiu Lam, BPharm, RPh, MPH, is a registered pharmacist and holds a master's degree in public health, specialising in the global health sector. She is currently director of the Hong Kong Jockey Club Disaster Preparedness and Response Institute (HKJCDPRI). Over the eight years before she joined HKJCDPRI, she worked for Hong Kong Red Cross, the International Federation of Red Cross and Red Crescent Societies in Kuala Lumpur, Malaysia, and has been involved in the frontline coordination or fieldwork of various emergencies in China, Nepal, Pakistan, Haiti, West Africa, Vietnam, Japan and so forth.

Poyi Lee, RN, MPH, completed her professional training in nursing and obtained her Master of Public Health degree in Hong Kong. She worked as a clinical nurse before joining the Collaborating Centre for Oxford University and CUHK for Disaster and Medical Humanitarian Response (CCOUC) in 2011. Ms Lee served as a Project Manager at CCOUC until 2015, and was mainly responsible for coordinating research and teaching activities. Her research interests include climate change and health, disaster and humanitarian medicine, health needs assessment, public health interventions and programme evaluation in resource deficit settings.

Donald KT Li, SBS, OStJ, JP, MBBS, FHKCFP, FRACGP, FHKAM, FHKDS, FFPH, FAFPM, FACP, FRCPT, FAMS, is a specialist in family medicine and president-elect of World Organization of Family Doctors (WONCA). Dr Li is also immediate past president of the Hong Kong Academy of Medicine and censor of the Hong Kong College of Family Physicians. Dr Li is the chairman of the HKJDPRI Governing Board. Dr Li graduated with his first degree (BA) in 1975 from Cornell University, USA, and second degree (MBBS) in 1980 from the University of Hong Kong. He is an honorary fellow of the Hong Kong College of Family Physicians, fellow of the Hong Kong Academy of Medicine, honorary fellow of the Hong Kong College of Dental Surgeons, honorary fellow of the Royal Australian College of General Practitioners, fellow of the Faculty of Public Health, honorary fellow of the Academy of Family Physicians of Malaysia, honorary fellow of the Academy of American College of Physicians, honorary fellow of the Royal College of Physicians of Thailand and fellow of the Academy of Medicine, Singapore. He is a registered medical practitioner in mainland China.

Sharon Tsoon Ting Lo, MA (University of St Andrews, Scotland), is a Project Officer at the Collaborating Centre for Oxford University and CUHK for Disaster and Medical Humanitarian Response (CCOUC), where she coordinates their engagement with various UN-related international platforms pertaining to health and disaster risk reduction, and at the CUHK Centre for Global Health where she supports the Centre's operation and activities, particularly through the CGH Sustainable Development Goals Series. She is also a Regional Focal Point at the UN Major Group for Children and Youth (UN MGCY), coordinating youth engagement in various UN processes under the 2030 Agenda for Sustainable Development. She founded Youth Empact, an ethnic minority youth empowerment platform, under the Clinton Global University Initiative in January 2016. She won the Collaborating Centre for Oxford University and CUHK Outstanding Disaster Project Award in 2016.

Anne Yan-yan Lung, BA, graduated from the Faculty of Arts at the University of Hong Kong. She joined Médecins Sans Frontières (MSF) in 1997 and specialises in research and advocacy. She is currently the manager of programme development of the Operational Support Unit of MSF in Hong Kong.

Makiko Kato MacDermot, RN, MSc (LSHTM), DLSHTM, completed a BSc Psychology (Hons) at Middlesex University and subsequently gained an MSc Global Health Policy at London School of Hygiene & Tropical Medicine to further her career in the field of global health. She is also a registered nurse in Japan and the UK, as a senior intensive care nurse. She joined the JC School of Public Health and Primary Care as a research fellow in 2014 and was involved in various research activities. Her areas of interests are health system strengthening, disaster risk reduction for health, urban city planning, and climate change and health.

Carman Ka Man Mark, BSc (University of Essex), MPH (CUHK), obtained her bachelor's degree in Health Studies at the University of Essex in UK and received her Master of Public Health from The Chinese University of Hong Kong in 2014, majoring in Population and Global Health. She won the Collaborating Centre for Oxford University and CUHK Outstanding Disaster Project Award in 2014. Carman is now a Graduate Fellow at the Collaborating Centre for Oxford University and CUHK for Disaster and Medical Humanitarian Response (CCOUC).

Provash Mondal, MA, PhD, holds BA in economics, BA in law, MA in economics specialising in rural development, and PhD in disaster management. Dr Mondal works as a humanitarian coordinator for Oxfam in Laos. He specialises in project and programme cycle management, managing emergency preparedness and developing contingency plans, emergency relief and rehabilitation, disaster risk reduction, climate change adaptation, livelihoods and Watsan projects. He joined Oxfam in 2000, and has worked in Bangladesh, India, the Philippines, Viet Nam and Laos. Dr Mondal worked initially with GUP, a national NGO in Bangladesh, and Action-Aid UK, MSF-Holland, EU and Bangladesh government bilateral projects.

Elizabeth Newnham, MPsych, PhD (W.Aust.), is a research fellow at the University of Western Australia, and research associate at the Harvard T.H. Chan School of Public Health. Dr Newnham has published broadly in the fields of trauma, global mental health and humanitarian emergencies, and is the recipient of a number of research grants and awards, including a National Health and Medical Research Council of Australia Early Career Fellowship. Dr Newnham conducted her postdoctoral training at Harvard University and the University of Oxford, held a CCOUC regional fellowship at the Chinese University of Hong Kong, and has acted as a consultant to the World Bank.

Satoko Otsu, MD, MPH, DTMH Team leader of Japanese Red Cross Society Basic Health Care Emergency Response Unit, is the director of the Infectious Disease Department and assistant director of the International Medical Relief Department, Japanese Red Cross Society. Dr Otsu was involved in the Red Cross medical relief operations since 2001 and deployed to more than 15 missions, including Afghan refugees in Pakistan and Indonesia tsunami operations. In addition, she has worked for WHO since 2007 and just returned from Vietnam as the team leader for Emerging Disease Surveillance and Response Unit.

Carol Ka Po Wong, BSSc (CUHK), MIPA (HKU), is a journalist by training and has acquired a Master's Degree in International and Public Affairs. She has years of project management experience in NGOs in Hong Kong and overseas, with a focus on public health and disaster managements. Before joining the Collaborating Centre for Oxford University and CUHK for Disaster and Medical Humanitarian Response (CCOUC), Ms Wong was stationed in the Philippines for more than two years, where her work in the field particularly focused on slum health, disaster preparedness and health in resource deficit settings.

Chi Shing Wong, MSc (LSE), has a background in journalism and communication. He received his master's in comparative politics at the London School of Economics and Political Science, focusing on democratisation, ethnic politics and nationalism, with regional foci in China and Southeast Asia, and researched on political identity at the University of Oxford afterwards. Mr Wong has worked in various teaching, research and administrative positions in universities. Working at the Collaborating Centre for Oxford University and CUHK for Disaster and Medical Humanitarian Response (CCOUC), he is also the copy editor of this book.

Crystal Yingjia Zhu, MPH, received her bachelor's degree in Biomedical Engineering from Zhejiang University of China. She worked at the Collaborating Centre for Oxford University and CUHK for Disaster and Medical Humanitarian Response (CCOUC) from 2011-2015 as a project officer, focusing on rural projects in China to promote disaster preparedness and key health messages. She has conducted research about rural health, climate change and waste management.

FOREWORD

By Professor Joseph J. Y. Sung

From the South-East Asian earthquake and tsunami in 2004, Sichuan earthquake in 2008 and Sendai tsunami in 2011 to the recent earthquake in Nepal in 2015, there is no shortage of major natural disasters in Asia. Professor Emily Chan has often reminded both clinical and non-clinical colleagues that natural disasters of various kinds are increasing in frequency and intensity with the dynamics of climate change, and making sense of how they can be responded to cost-effectively by employing public health principles is as important and as urgent a medical response to the post-disaster humanitarian crises as clinical treatment of disaster victims.

As the world leaders reached a global agreement on climate change at the Paris Climate Conference by the end of 2015, health has been brought into the centre of the respective agendas of the Sendai Framework for Disaster Risk Reduction 2015–2030, endorsed in the United Nations Conference on Disaster Risk Reduction earlier in March, and the new global Sustainable Development Goals (SDGs) adopted at the United Nations in September of that year. The publication of this book is very timely to take stock of the public health principles relevant for responses to natural disasters, in particular those exacerbated by climate change, and the implications of these responses for development.

Professor Chan is to be congratulated for coming up with this very useful collection of the knowledge and experience she has acquired and accumulated in her years of teaching, research, knowledge transfer and consultancy activities locally, nationally, regionally and internationally, with the strong support of the Collaborating Centre for Oxford University and CUHK for Disaster and Medical Humanitarian Response (CCOUC). As a staunch believer and supporter of the Centre on both academic and humanitarian fronts, I am very glad that this collaboration between the two universities has been fruitful in moving forward this worthy discipline of disaster and medical humanitarian response, particularly in mainland China and the wider Asian region. It is also a reiteration of CUHK's aspiration of promoting humanistic values through cooperating and exchanging with world-renowned academic institutions.

Covering the major topics in this emergent discipline of medical humanitarian response, this book is supplemented with well-known case studies of recent disasters resulting from natural hazards in Asia and Africa as well as innovative disaster response measures developed by international agencies. It introduces readers to the disaster-relevant basic public health concepts and the unique human health impact of various natural hazards, like earthquakes, volcanic eruptions, tropical cyclones, floods, droughts and famines, heat waves and cold waves, as well as the needs of vulnerable groups, including women, children and the elderly, to be responded to in disasters. This book is also unique in highlighting the importance of preparedness and resilience in disaster response, which form the core of both the passing and coming international frameworks for disaster risk reduction – namely the Hyogo Framework of Action and the Sendai Framework. I believe that this book will help readers develop insights in understanding, mitigating and reducing disaster risk and disaster impact by employing the prisms provided by relevant public health theories and principles.

As a clinician myself, I share the vision of Professor Chan and CCOUC in raising the awareness and knowledge of disaster response and preparedness among the local community, across the Asian region and further afar in the globe. I recommend this book as an important resource for disaster response students and practitioners of health and non-health backgrounds alike, and an essential reading for anyone seeking to understand health impact of and public health response to disasters.

Professor Joseph J.Y. Sung
Vice-Chancellor and President
The Chinese University of Hong Kong
2010–present

FOREWORD

By Professor Andrew Hamilton FRS

Looking back over my vice-chancellorship of the University of Oxford I can see many highlights of the last six years or so. One of the most treasured is the establishment in 2011 of the Collaborating Centre for Oxford University and CUHK for Disaster and Medical Humanitarian Response. The short history of CCOUC itself contains many milestones, punctuating an extremely impressive range of activities. These include, just to give a few simple examples, the establishment of the Croucher Summer Courses, fellowship programmes for NGOs, conference presentations and a number of important and timely publications.

Professor Emily Chan's outstanding leadership of CCOUC has been instrumental to its success, and this latest publication, *Public Health Humanitarian Responses to Natural Disasters*, is indicative of the high-quality fieldwork and research that have been undertaken by the Centre since its inception. Publication of this book could not be timelier, given the recent history of natural disasters that have taken place across the planet. Mankind's response to such events is critical, and publications such as this are vital to how relief work and humanitarian aid are organised and implemented.

So it is with great pride and considerable pleasure that I write this foreword, as CCOUC approaches its fifth anniversary. CCOUC will be, I hope, one of the enduring achievements of the relationship between the University of Oxford and the Chinese University of Hong Kong. But I hope even more that the natural disasters which its research and teaching address so comprehensively will over time have a less and less devastating impact on those caught up in them.

Professor Andrew Hamilton FRS
Vice-Chancellor
University of Oxford
2009–2015

FOREWORD

By Professor Virginia Murray

Exacerbated by climate change and urbanisation, the mounting intensity, frequency and diversity of natural hazards worldwide has been resulting in significant negative impact on all people's health globally. Meanwhile, the awareness and recognition of the importance of promoting health as a major goal of disaster risk reduction has been growing in the global community. Most recently, health was referenced throughout the 2015 UN Landmark agreement, the Sendai Framework for Disaster Risk Reduction 2015-2030, which is a key international policy document in this area for the coming 15 years.

The accelerating pace of formulating and implementing international and local policies to mitigate and adapt to the health impact of natural disasters heightens the urgency for wise use of scarce resources. Hence, scientific approaches to build relevant research methods are increasingly important in supporting an evidence-based approach to disaster risk reduction efforts in general and, in particular, evidence-based public health and global health which are pivotal in foregrounding health amidst disaster risk reduction and management. These are the core of the emerging field of Emergency and Disaster Risk Management for Health (EDRM-H).

Professor Chan's new book Public Health Humanitarian Responses in Natural Disasters is a timely and valuable scholarly contribution to this very important up-and-coming field by summarising what is already known and what are the newly developing areas of concern. As a long-time collaborator of her in this field, including our latest partnership of the co-chairpersonship of the WHO Thematic Platform for Health Emergency & Disaster Risk Management Research Group, I am delighted that Professor Chan and her team are ensuring disaster risk management for health is part of the global, national and local agendas by formulating, testing and providing evidence for public health disaster ideas and good practices which can have international and local policy implications and impact. Thus this book is an important contribution by providing perspectives to understand the key public health concepts and trends of disasters, their impacts, response, preparedness and resilience via a rich collection of cases. Indeed many of the case studies shared in this book have rarely been reviewed in previous publications.

I believe that this book will serve as an important resource to inform practitioners and policy makers on the key principles on how public health might contribute in emergency and disaster medicine, disaster risk reduction, humanitarian response and health systems. These concepts are important as public health calls for strengthening advocacy and catalysing actions for Emergency and Disaster Risk Management for Health, as well as inspiring early-career and experienced researchers alike in these fields to continue their research for evidence-based ways to reduce the health risk our world is facing as a result of disasters.

Professor Virginia Murray
Public Health Consultant in Global Disaster Risk Reduction,
Public Health England
Vice-Chair Scientific and Technical Advisory Group,
United Nations Office for Disaster Risk Reduction (UNISDR)

ACKNOWLEDGEMENTS

This work originates from my teaching and research at the JC School of Public Health and Primary Care (JCSPHPC), Faculty of Medicine, The Chinese University of Hong Kong, and the Collaborating Centre for Oxford University and CUHK for Disaster and Medical Humanitarian Response (CCOUC) in the past decade. I am indebted to the tremendous and incessant trust extended by the two universities and their vice-chancellors, Professor Andrew Hamilton and Professor Joseph Sung, the former and incumbent deans of CUHK Faculty of Medicine, Professor Tai-fai Fok and Professor Francis Chan, the former and incumbent deans of JCSPHPC, Professor Sian Griffiths and Professor Eng-kiong Yeoh, director of the Wellcome Trust, Professor Jeremy Farrar, associate head of Oxford University Nuffield Department of Medicine (NDM), Mr Darren Nash, and vice-chair of UNISDR Scientific and Technical Advisory Group, Professor Virginia Murray. This field of study would never have been able to flourish without their belief in and vision of the importance of humanitarian studies in the twenty-first century.

I gratefully acknowledge the meticulous assistance of Mr Chi Shing Wong for preparing the manuscript for submission and the patience of Ms Helena Hurd, Ms Helen Bell, Ms Khanam Virjee and their colleagues at Routledge as well as Ms Kerry Boettcher at Apex CoVantage. I also wish to thank Professor Samuel Yeung-shan Wong, Professor William B. Goggins III, Professor Colin A. Graham, Professor Jean H. Kim, Professor Peter Horby, Dr Elizabeth Newnham, Ms Janet Yiu-wai Chow, Ms Christy Oi-yan-jing Chan, Ms Gloria Kwong-wei Chan, Ms Queenie Wei-ngan Chan, Dr Calvin Ka-yeung Cheng, Dr Eliza Yee-lai Cheung, Dr Cecilia Yuen-see Choi, Dr Wenwen Du, Dr Xue Gao, Ms Hale Hay-lam Ho, Ms Janice Ying-en Ho, Mr Zhe Huang, Professor Kevin Kei-ching Hung, Dr Levina Chandra Khoe, Ms Christine Pui-yan Ko, Ms Karen Wing-tung Kwok, Ms Teresa Po-lam Lee, Ms Po-yi Lee, Ms Agatha Kit-ying Lin, Ms Cherry Lee-yung Lin, Mr Kelvin Wai-kit Ling, Mr Kevin Sida Liu, Ms Sharon Tsoon-ting Lo, Mr Jonas Lossau,

Ms Carman Ka-man Mark, Ms Jamie Rose Rodas, Dr Andrew Darby Smith, Dr Rosamund Southgate, Dr Greta Chun-huen Tam, Dr Alvin Ho-cheuk Wong, Ms Carol Ka-po Wong, Mr Terry Wong, Ms Nicole Yan, Professor May Pui-shan Yeung, Ms Tiffany Lok-yan Yeung, Ms Janice So-kuen Yue, Dr Tony Ka-chun Yung, Ms Crystal Yingjia Zhu, Ms Elizabeth Deacon, Ms Caroline Dubois, Ms Karen Valentine, Ms Tracy Chin-wai Lai, Mr Elgar Chung-po Lam, Dr Johnson Chun-hong Lau, Ms Holly Lai-ho Li, Ms Rebecca Siu-kam Tsui, Professor Chok-wan Chan, Mrs Irene Che-yun Yau Lee, Ms Winnie Chan, Ms Jennifer Ma, family and all friends who have assisted in the publication of this manuscript for their valuable assistance at various points in this book project. Further thanks go to colleagues and students at JCSPHPC and CCOUC for their friendship and the joyful memories of fieldwork. Last but not least, special thanks must go to Eric Yau and our children, Ellie and Ernest.

Emily Ying Yang Chan
Hong Kong, November 2016

ABBREVIATIONS

ADRC	Asian Disaster Reduction Center, Japan-based
AIDS	Acquired immune deficiency syndrome
AMS	Auxiliary Medical Service, Hong Kong SAR Government
APA	American Psychiatric Association
APFM	Associated Programme on Flood Management, World Meteorological Organization
BHC ERU	Basic Health Care Emergency Responses Unit, International Federation of the Red Cross and Red Crescent Societies
BHW	Barangay/Neighbourhood health worker
BMJ	British Medical Journal
BNPB	Badan Nasional Penanggulangan Bencana/National Disaster Management Authority, Indonesia
CATS	Community approaches to total sanitation
CBDRM	Community-based disaster risk management
CBM	Christoffel-Blindenmission, Germany-based
CBR	Community-based rehabilitation
CBRN	Chemical, biological, radiological and nuclear
CCOUC	Collaborating Centre for Oxford University and CUHK for Disaster and Medical Humanitarian Response, Hong Kong-United Kingdom
CDC	Centers for Disease Control and Prevention, United States
CFS	Child-friendly space
CIDA	Canadian International Development Agency
CIFOR	Council to Improve Foodborne Outbreak Response, United States
CMR	Crude mortality rate
CPIA	Country policies and institutional performance assessment
CRED	Centre for Research on the Epidemiology of Disasters, Université catholique de Louvain, Belgium

CRISE	Centre for Research on Inequality, Human Security and Ethnicity, University of Oxford, United Kingdom
DALY	Disability-adjusted life year
DEWA	Division of Early Warning and Assessment, United Nations Environment Programme
DFID	Department for International Development, United Kingdom
DG SANCO	Health and Consumers Directorate General, European Commission
DPRK	Democratic People's Republic of Korea
DRI	Disaster Risk Index
DRR	Disaster risk reduction
EM-DAT	Emergency Events Database, Centre for Research on the Epidemiology of Disasters, Université catholique de Louvain, Belgium
EMHP	Ethnic Minority Health Project, Collaborating Centre for Oxford University and CUHK for Disaster and Medical Humanitarian Response, Hong Kong-United Kingdom
ENP	European Neighbourhood Policy, European Commission
ERC	United Nations Undersecretary General for Humanitarian Affairs and Emergency Relief Coordinator/Head of United Nations Office for the Coordination of Humanitarian Affairs
EWS	Early warning system
FAO	Food and Agriculture Organization of the United Nations
FEMA	United States Federal Emergency Management Agency
GAIN	Global Alliance for Improved Nutrition, United Nations
GAM	Global acute malnutrition
GAVI	Global Alliance for Vaccines and Immunizations, Switzerland–United States–based
GDP	Gross domestic product
GFATM	Global Fund to Fight AIDS, Tuberculosis and Malaria, Switzerland-based
GFDRR	World Bank Global Facility for Disaster Reduction and Recovery
GHC	Global Health Cluster, World Health Organization
GHG	Greenhouse gas
GHI	Global Hunger Index
GLOF	Glacial lake outburst flood
GNH	Gross national happiness
GVP	Global Volcanism Program, Smithsonian Institution, United States
HFA	Hyogo Framework for Action
HIV	Human immunodeficiency virus
HKJCDPRI	Hong Kong Jockey Club Disaster Preparedness and Response Institute
HKRC	Hong Kong Red Cross
HKSAR	Hong Kong Special Administrative Region, People's Republic of China

HPA	United Kingdom Health Protection Agency
HPG	Humanitarian Policy Group, Overseas Development Institute, United Kingdom
IAEA	International Atomic Energy Agency
IASC	United Nations Inter-Agency Standing Committee
ICRC	International Committee of the Red Cross
IDA	International Development Association, World Bank Group
IDP	Internally displaced person
IFAD	International Fund for Agricultural Development, United Nations
IFFN	International Forest Fire News, United Nations Economic Commission for Europe (UNECE) Timber Committee and the FAO European Forestry Commission
IFPRI	International Food Policy Research Institute, United States-based
IFRC	International Federation of the Red Cross and Red Crescent Societies
IHR	International Health Regulations
ILO	International Labour Organization, United Nations
IMF	International Monetary Fund
IOTWS	Indian Ocean Tsunami Warning and Mitigation System, Inter-governmental Oceanographic Commission of United Nations Educational, Scientific and Cultural Organization
IPCC	Intergovernmental Panel on Climate Change, United Nations Environment Programme and World Meteorological Organization
JRCS	Japanese Red Cross Society
KAP	Knowledge, attitude and practice
LGU	Local government unit
LICUS	Low-income countries under stress
MDG	Millennium Development Goal
mHealth	Mobile health
MISP	Minimum Initial Service Package
MPRA	Munich Personal RePEc (Research Papers in Economics) Archive, Munich University Library, Germany
MSF	Médecins Sans Frontières/Doctors without Borders
Munich RE	Munich Reinsurance, Germany
MVC	Measles vaccination coverage
NCD	Non-communicable disease
NDMC	National Disaster Management Centre, Brunei
NGO	Non-governmental organisation
NHFPC	National Health and Family Planning Commission, People's Republic of China
NIH	National Institutes of Health, United States Department of Health and Human Services
NISEE	National Information Service for Earthquake Engineering, Pacific Earthquake Engineering Research (PEER) Center, University of California, Berkeley, United States

NRH	Nutritional Rehabilitation Home, Nepal
NTU	Nephelometric turbidity unit
OCHA	United Nations Office for the Coordination of Humanitarian Affairs
ODF	Open-defecation-free
ODI	Overseas Development Institute, United Kingdom
OHCHR	Office of the United Nations High Commissioner for Human Rights
ORS	Oral rehydration solution
PAHO/WHO	Pan American Health Organization/Regional Office for the Americas of the World Health Organization
PEER	Pacific Earthquake Engineering Research Center, University of California, Berkeley, United States
PFA	Psychological First Aid
PRC	People's Republic of China
PSS	Psychological Support Service, Hong Kong Red Cross
PTSD	Post-traumatic stress disorder
SACOSAN III	Third South Asian Conference on Sanitation
SARS	Severe acute respiratory syndrome
SERI	Sustainable Europe Research Institute, Austria
SLTS	School-led total sanitation
STI	Sexually transmitted infection
TSF	Télécoms Sans Frontières/Telecoms without Borders
TSP	Total suspended particles
U5MR	Under-5 mortality rate
UN	United Nations
UNAIDS	Joint United Nations Programme on HIV/AIDS
UNDCP	United Nations Drug Control Programme
UNDESA	United Nations Department of Economic and Social Affairs
UNDG	United Nations Development Group
UNDP	United Nations Development Programme
UNEP	United Nations Environment Programme
UNESCO	United Nations Educational, Scientific and Cultural Organization
UNFPA	United Nations Population Fund
UN-Habitat	United Nations Human Settlements Programme
UNHAS	United Nations Humanitarian Air Service
UNHCR	Office of the United Nations High Commissioner for Refugees
UNICEF	United Nations Children's Fund
UNIDO	United Nations Industrial Development Organization
UNIFEM	United Nations Development Fund for Women
UNISDR	United Nations Office for Disaster Risk Reduction
UNRWA	United Nations Relief and Works Agency for Palestine Refugees in the Near East
UN-Water	United Nations Water

USAID	United States Agency for International Development
USGS	United States Geological Survey
WASH	Water supply, sanitation and hygiene promotion
WEDC	Water, Engineering and Development Centre, Loughborough University, United Kingdom
WFP	World Food Programme, United Nations
WHI	Women's Health Initiative, United States Department of Health and Human Services
WMO	World Meteorological Organization, United Nations
WHO	World Health Organization, United Nations
WHO/EHA	World Health Organization Department of Emergency and Humanitarian Action
WHO-EMRO	World Health Organization Regional Office for the Eastern Mediterranean
WHO-WPRO	World Health Organization Regional Office for the Western Mediterranean
WIPO	World Intellectual Property Organization, United Nations
WTO	World Trade Organization

INTRODUCTION

Asia is the most natural disaster-prone continent globally. With the pressure of climate change, environmental degradation and urbanisation as well as the widening of socio-economic disparities, people everywhere experience increasing vulnerabilities and exposures to the impact of natural disasters. To safeguard community well-being, the ability to understand, analyse and address the health needs of populations affected by natural disasters is pertinent.

This book intends to serve as a reference book for students and practitioners to obtain an overview of the applications of public health principles in the practice of disaster and humanitarian medicine. Lessons learnt from previous disasters and medical humanitarian reliefs globally are used to illustrate how theoretical understanding of the public health issues might be related to actual practices. Specifically, the author attempts to draw case examples from the Asia-Pacific region as far as possible. The book will help readers to:

1   Understand and discuss the public health needs and gaps in disaster preparedness and response, specifically in the context of the Asia-Pacific region;
2   Systematically formulate key guiding questions during pre- and post-disaster phases to drive evidence-based disaster mitigation action; and
3   Select and consult relevant and credible databases, guidelines and documents to address the foregoing issues.

This book aims to introduce how public health principles may be applied during humanitarian contexts and responses to natural disasters. It also focuses on how some essential public health tools and processes can be put into practice. Case studies in this book provide its readers a range of Asian disaster preparedness and medical humanitarian response examples which are currently lacking in academic literature despite the prevalence of natural disasters in the region. Relevant terminologies, indicators and working tools in assessment of needs for action and interventions are also introduced. Disaster as an emergency situation means that taking no action to wait for a perfect solution is not an option.

This book is divided into nine chapters. Chapter 1 describes the various public health approaches and principles that are relevant to the understanding of medical and public health disaster and humanitarian response. Chapter 2 explores the key concepts and trends of disasters and their implications for the twenty-first century. Chapter 3 discusses the general impact of disasters and Chapter 4 examines the human health impact of common natural disasters. Chapter 5 provides an overview of how health-related survival needs in natural disasters may be addressed, and Chapter 6 explores the public health threats and challenges for disaster medical response in the twenty-first century. Chapter 7 examines the role of key stakeholders and the challenges in public health response to disasters post-millennium. Chapter 8 discusses public health emergency preparedness and Chapter 9 concludes the themes throughout the book. Each of these chapters is embedded with case studies which will illustrate the application of key concepts.

1

KEY PUBLIC HEALTH CONCEPTS OF DISASTER PREPAREDNESS AND RESPONSE

Public health is a multidisciplinary subject that concerns the health of a population. Its practitioners, composed of doctors, nurses, pharmacists, lawyers, educators, policymakers and researchers, aim to prevent diseases, promote health and prolong life through the organised efforts of society. This subject draws on a wide variety of disciplines and has developed tools which can allow practitioners to describe, analyse, manage and respond to problems that threaten the health and well-being of a society and community group. This chapter will introduce fundamental principles of public health and their applications to the study and understanding of disasters and medical humanitarian assistance. Basic terminology definitions and theories of public health will also be covered in this chapter.

Historical background of how public health is involved in disaster response

A brief review of the history of this field of study demonstrates the rapid development of the public health approach to medical disaster and humanitarian response. Although most disasters are natural phenomena, their impact is often defined by human consequences. Historically, major disasters were documented from the perspectives of how human communities might be affected and how systems were destroyed and subsequently improved after these natural calamities.

The application of public health principles in studying disasters and their public health and medical humanitarian responses can be useful in mitigating and understanding the human impact of these disasters. Early papers published about the public health impact on disaster management can be dated back to the early 1970s. Results of health surveys related to a tropical cyclone hitting the coast of Bangladesh in 1970 with over 250,000 deaths demonstrated the complicated matrix of needs and risks faced by different stakeholders in disaster situations. The publication highlighted the "value of early on-the-spot assessments" in providing valid and timely

CASE BOX 1.1   TSUNAMI WARNING AND MITIGATION FOR THE INDIAN OCEAN REGION

The Indian Ocean Tsunami in 2004 caused major human losses and rampant destruction. The root causes for such massive damage are not only the rapid expansion of coastal communities but also the hampered translation of knowledge of tsunami science into practice.

Soon after the Indian Ocean Tsunami, scientists and policy makers teamed up to form an international commitment – the Indian Ocean Tsunami Warning and Mitigation System (IOTWS). The IOTWS is dedicated to issuing tsunami advisories to all National Tsunami Warning Centres of the Indian Ocean rim countries. With the establishment of IOTWS, all the country members in the Indian Ocean could receive early warnings. Warnings can thus now reach the millions of people who did not receive any warning prior to 2004 and the system also enables tsunami hazard mapping and evacuation planning for coastal communities.

In April 2012, an offshore earthquake of magnitude 8.5 struck Sumatra, Indonesia. Specifically, in Banda Aceh, one of the hardest hit regions in the Indian Ocean Tsunami 2004, over 75% of the population managed to evacuate soon after the strike of the earthquake. This example demonstrates clearly the significance of an early warning system together with physical defence and evacuation procedures in enhancing disaster preparedness and preventing the loss of life.

data for disaster relief (Sommer & Mosley, 1972, p. 7759). Publications following the Guatemala earthquake that caused an estimated 23,000 deaths in Guatemala illustrated how significant *logistical challenges and deficiencies* in the international relief system might affect human toll and health outcomes of a natural disaster (de Ville de Goyet, del Cid, Romero, Jeannee, & Lechat, 1976; Spencer et al., 1977). These early examples illustrated the plausible use of disaster research methodology in *identifying risk factors* associated with specific negative health outcomes linked to the disaster, and hence the possible implementation of effective and targeted interventions as a means of health protection (Glass et al., 1980) (see Case Box 1.1).

Concepts of health and public health

The World Health Organization has defined **health** as "a state of complete physical, mental and social well-being and not merely the absence of disease or infirmity" (Constitution of the World Health Organization, 1946, p. 1). It is important to point out that this definition encompasses a wide range of outcomes from **physical**, **mental** and **social** well-being. It includes both negative and *positive aspects* of health. It implies that action should aim not only to minimise diseases but also to *maximise* attainment of potential health. Although this definition has been criticised for over 60 years since its enforcement in 1948, and alternative proposals have been published, it remains the working definition of health internationally.

CASE BOX 1.2   SCHOOL-IN-A-BOX BY UNICEF

Psychosocial interventions in the post-impact phase of disasters and crises are useful for creating a supportive environment and restoring a sense of normalcy for the affected people. For example, for the child population, being able to return to school is very important for their psychosocial health. In the 1990s, the United Nations Children's Fund (UNICEF) developed the "School-in-a-Box" programme for children in disaster-affected situations. It is literally a box containing supplies and basic materials that can be used to support the teaching of 40 students for approximately three months; temporary classrooms can be set up within 72 hours after a disaster. Further information can be found in this video: http://www.unicef.org/supply/kits_flash/schoolinabox.

Public health has been defined as "the science and art of preventing disease, prolonging life and promoting health through organised efforts of society" (Acheson, 1988, p. 1; World Health Organization [WHO], 2004, p. 32). Unlike **clinical medicine**, where physicians and allied health professionals focus on treating diseases and managing the health of individuals, public health professionals focus on optimising the health of *populations*. The field of public health comprises evidence-based methods, decision-making and the application of theories in society. Effective public health practice is a multidisciplinary effort to make health a priority for all by understanding the determinants of health, addressing health disparities, identifying disease risk factors and implementing preventive strategies.

In the context of disaster preparedness, response and management, the definition of health implies the importance of addressing all three fundamental components of health: the physical, social and mental well-being of a population. Although health and medical disaster response programmes tend to focus heavily on safeguarding physical health (e.g. injury management, communicable disease control, food access), an effective health response should consider the mental and social health aspects as well as activities which lead to health improvements instead of focusing only on physical dimensions (see Case Box 1.2).

Scope of the field of public health: three domains of public health

Public health is a multidisciplinary field in medicine that utilises epidemiology, clinical trials, biostatistics, laws and ethics to protect health, improve health and secure the provision of health services. The various components of public health practice can be grouped into three widely accepted domains of public health: **health protection, health improvement** and **health services** (Griffiths, Jewell, & Donnelly, 2005). The **three domains of public health** illustrate the multidisciplinary nature of this field and its potential applications in the development of evidence-based medical and humanitarian response in disasters.

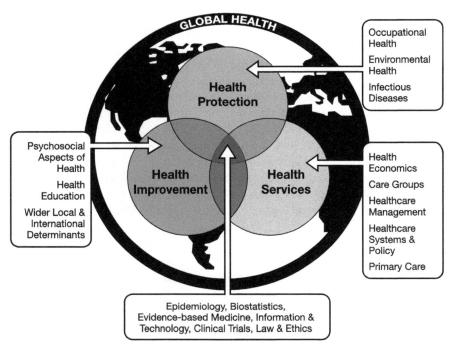

FIGURE 1.1 Three domains of public health

Figure 1.1 shows the anatomy of public health. The three domains include health protection, health improvement and health services, with global health encompassing, and some common tools supporting, all the domains.

Health protection involves the prevention, control and response to outbreak of infectious diseases, the regulation of occupational hazards, the monitoring of environmental health hazards, such as air, water and food quality, and response to chemical or technological emergencies (e.g. bioterrorism and radiation disasters). **Health improvement** involves actions to improve outcomes and health determinants and to reduce health inequalities in a population. This area of work combines different sectors (e.g. housing and education) to ensure that policies and health promotion and education activities at the population level will empower and support individuals to make informed lifestyle choices. **Health service and management** focuses on the policies and delivery of health services. It promotes evidence-based clinical practices, governance and resource allocation. Of note, the three domains of public health are not mutually exclusive to each other; these subjects overlap and are often interdependent. These domains are commonly applied in general public health practice.

Epidemiology, biostatistics, clinical trials, and law and ethics are overlapping public health skill sets that serve as foundation tools for public health practice. They provide common technical approaches to support the knowledge-based domains, as illustrated at the centre of the Venn diagram (Figure 1.1). **Epidemiology** is the branch of medicine studying the distribution and determinants of health-related states. **Biostatistics** is the application of statistical techniques to research related to the health field. **Clinical trials** are a specific type of clinical research that conducts comparisons between treatments/intervention options and serves three major purposes: confirming the safety of treatment, identifying side effects and comparing the effect of a new treatment with the existing standard procedure. This type of research produces evidence-based interventions in disaster response. **Law and ethics** provide frameworks for decision making. Specifically, public health law is the study of the legal power and hence the duties of the state in providing conditions where people remain healthy. Ethics provides a guiding principle for deciding what is right and wrong. In health care, it is also related to how professionals behave, based on professional bodies' definition of what is right, fair and just when serving the general community (Griffiths, Jewell, & Donnelly, 2005).

In public health- and medical-related disaster studies, epidemiology and biostatistics can provide the technical tools to assess and evaluate the impact and outcomes of disasters. Health policy and service analysis can support service emergency preparedness and training planning, and disaster response management. Health protection actions, such as outbreak and infection control, environmental health assessment and protection, and psychological first aid to support the mental health of responders and affected community, are important activities to protect the community from the secondary impact of a disaster. Health promotion, nutritional programmes, health risk communication, resource mobilisation and technical capacity building (e.g. human resources development and disaster response team building) might not only support a disaster-affected community but also improve its underlying resilience in its health systems and technical capacity and, ultimately, safeguard the health and well-being of the community.

Measuring health

There are four major ways to measure health. Firstly, it can be measured by **consequences**, such as mortality, morbidity, economic implications and so forth. Secondly, it can be assessed by targeting **population subgroups**. The health impact of an incident toward children, women, older people or those with chronic diseases may vary within the same context. Health outcomes may thus be categorised according to the specific characteristics and needs of each of these subgroups. Thirdly, health might be measured by **frequency**. Incidence, prevalence, mortality rates and ratios are examples of metrics by which one can quantify health outcomes. Last but not least, **disease severity** might differentiates a person's experiences in health. For example, someone who has early asymptomatic stage of diabetes mellitus might experience a different quality of life when compared with someone who has a severe diabetic condition which requires dialysis or diabetic foot-related amputation.

In a disaster, the actual health impact may be difficult to quantify. Available information (e.g. mortality data and hospitalisation information) might allow only a partial overview of the actual health implication of a situation. Figure 1.2 shows that unless

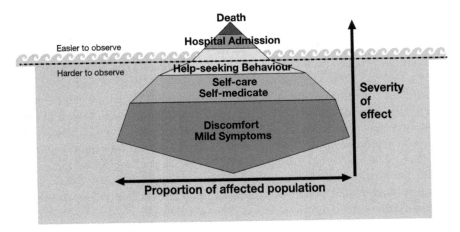

FIGURE 1.2   An iceberg of health outcomes

specific effort is dedicated to examine the overall real impact of an incident or disaster, most reports provide only a specific and partial perspective toward the true impact.

In order to build responsible and evidence-based disaster preparedness and response programmes, it is important to choose the relevant and appropriate metrics to quantify health impacts, assess needs, plan programmes, track intervention programmes and evaluate the effectiveness of activities in a post-disaster context.

Disaster epidemiology

Epidemiology is the study of how disease/health outcome is distributed in populations and the factors that influence or determine this distribution. The underlying principle of this technical discipline assumes adverse health outcomes do not occur randomly within a population but follow a predictable pattern. Thus, although a population might be exposed to health risks or environmental hazards, not everyone will be affected equally by disasters or suffer from their adverse impact to the same extent. For example, if someone lives in a well-engineered, earthquake-resistant concrete building, the risk of this individual being injured by the building collapsing during an earthquake is likely to be lower than for those who live in makeshift shelters built of lumber and bricks.

Epidemiologic methodologies applied to the disaster context are useful to measure and describe the adverse effects of disasters on human populations. Through epidemiological analysis, risk factors may be identified to explain why certain people are more prone to the negative health impact of disasters and protective measures may be developed to protect people before a disaster strikes. Publications about the public health impact of disasters using epidemiological methodologies were significant because their focus was on finding ways to prevent and mitigate the impact of future disasters. The development of the Interagency Emergency Health Kit 2011 is an example of applying research to maximise the effectiveness of medical and relief efforts (see Case Box 1.3).

CASE BOX 1.3 HOW DOES DISASTER EPIDEMIOLOGY BENEFIT A DISASTER-AFFECTED POPULATION?

One significant milestone in disaster response that illustrates the applications of disaster epidemiology studies is the application of research findings for the development of standardised evidence-based protocols.

Emergency Health Kit

Standardised lists of essential drugs, medical supplies and relief-equipment are developed to address humanitarian needs post-disaster. These lists were usually compiled after rounds of rigorous field-testing and modifications. The WHO, Office of the United Nations High Commissioner for Refugees (UNHCR) and the London School of Hygiene and Tropical Medicine co-developed one such list, naming it the "Emergency Health Kit" in 1984. The kit evolved into the "New Emergency Health Kit" in 1990 and later again into the "New Emergency Health Kit 98" in 1998 (WHO, 1998). The **"Interagency Emergency Health Kit 2011"** is the current version of the kit, which was devised by multiple UN agencies and international NGOs, such as Médecins Sans Frontières and the International Federation of Red Cross and Red Crescent Societies. In general, the kit includes medicines, disposables and instruments that meet the primary health needs of 10,000 people for three months. The kit is not designed for immunisation programmes, cholera, meningitis or specific epidemics, but is primarily intended for displaced populations without medical facilities. It can also be used as the initial supply of primary health care facilities where the normal system of provision has broken down (WHO, 2011). Disaster epidemiology studies, however, continue to drive research and debates about the content of the Emergency Health Kit. In fact, the Emergency Health Kit is only one example. The preparation and modification of similar "disaster response units" for immediate deployment by international relief organisations are also a result of the relief workforce's appreciation of evidence-based disaster response.

Another important disaster response development with the support of disaster epidemiology is "The Sphere Project", which was initiated in 1997 and is currently one of the most widely known and internationally recognised sets of common principles and universal minimum standards in disaster and medical humanitarian response. As a result of lessons learnt from the emergency plan in response to the genocide in Rwanda in 1994, major international humanitarian organisations co-founded The Sphere Project in 1997. Headquartered in Geneva, Switzerland, it advocates the Humanitarian Charter. It also established a set of standards now widely adopted for humanitarian assistance around the world. The standards encompass aspects of water supply, sanitation and hygiene, food security and nutrition, shelter, and medical care.

Although every disaster has its unique context and circumstances, commonalities exist and relief/medical supplies could be prepared in advance for dispatch in times of crisis. In addition, while major disasters were often followed by generous donations of relief items from the international community, the logistical challenges and the lack of rapid on-the-ground needs assessments meant that many of these items could not benefit the disaster-affected population. As a result, aid-responders and beneficiaries might be supplied with inappropriate donation items.

Determinants of health

The socio-ecological approach in public health connotes health is governed by many external factors, not just individual biological make-up or lifestyle choices. This framework proposes that other social, economic, political and environmental factors are all important **determinants of health** as well, which are the "things that make people healthy or not" (WHO, 2014a).

Figure 1.3 illustrates the determinants of health organised according to the level of control an individual has over them. At the centre of the diagram are largely **non-modifiable** biological factors, such as the age, sex and genetic make-up of a person. The second ring beyond the centre includes a person's individual lifestyle choices, such as dietary habits and activity level. Both the biological and

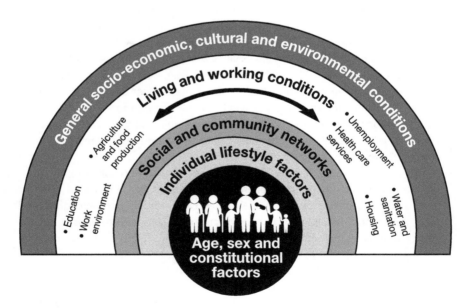

FIGURE 1.3 Determinants of health

Source: Adapted from Dahlgren and Whitehead (1991).

individual lifestyle factors make up the **intrapersonal-level determinants**, which are mostly within the control of an individual. The third ring includes a person's **social capital**, which refers to the social network among which he/she lives, works and interacts. **Interpersonal-level determinants** involve the impact on health of primary social relationships surrounding an individual, such as friends, family and co-workers. In principle, greater support from families, friends and communities tends to link to better health. In addition, culture, customs and traditions of family and community all impact on the context and how an individual may thrive and live healthily. The fourth ring refers to the wider socio-economic conditions of a person and the society in which he/she resides. Factors including education, work environment, housing and health systems constitute the **community/institutional-level determinants** that are likely to determine individuals' material access through income and social status. The outermost ring refers to the general socio-economic, cultural and environmental conditions of the society. Policies, regulations and programmes may affect access to basic services, such as health care and education, and opportunities to thrive socially and economically in society. These are collectively known as **macro/public policy-level determinants** (McLeroy, Bibeau, Steckler, & Glanz, 1988).

In the context of a disaster, although an individual may be free of physical and mental health symptoms, the socio-ecological approach conceptualises health outcomes of individual or population subgroups as varying according to how disaster impacts and alters the various levels of health determinants. For example, a disaster might cause the partial or complete breakdown of transportation networks that limit access to health services. The absence of social services (such as police or fire stations) or the closure of important facilities (such as banks and hospitals) will also pose an indirect impact on health outcomes and general well-being.

Life-course approach

An individual's behaviour, socio-economic disadvantages and health disadvantages will accumulate over time, creating ever more daunting constraints on a person's ability to be healthy. Social advantages and health risks will be presented across lifetimes and generations. Thus, the **life-course approach** takes age into consideration and how past experiences shape future health risks or status. The life-course approach examines the impact of **time** and human behaviour from both past and present experiences, as well as **across generations** to identify the current impacts on health. It emphasises how early life intervention shapes health in later life and potentially across generations. Figure 1.4 illustrates how the obstacles to health are passed on from generation to generation.

The life-course approach includes two key concepts: first, that intervention in early life is important as it influences the future of one's health, and second, that different life stages reflect different needs, and therefore require different approaches. Many studies have confirmed the importance of early life intervention. Barker

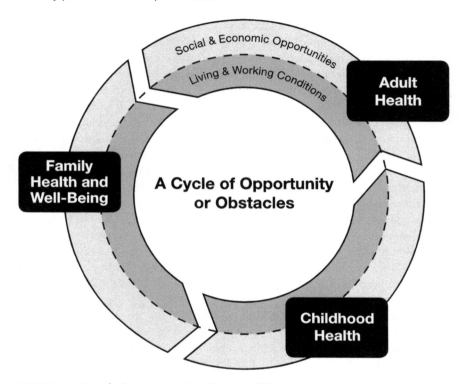

FIGURE 1.4 Social advantages and health across lifetimes and generations

hypothesised that metabolic syndromes in adulthood, such as cardiovascular disease, diabetes mellitus and hypertension, are associated with inadequate nutrition during foetal and infant growth (Barker, 2003). An adult's mental health may also be related to early trauma (Anda et al., 2006). The Dutch famine provides evidence of undernutrition effects in the period of gestation: babies exposed to famine were lighter, shorter and thinner than unexposed babies (Roseboom et al., 2001; Roseboom, de Rooij, & Painter, 2006). The study also found an association between early undernutrition and the development of diseases in adult life, such as increased risk of chronic heart disease and increased prevalence of obstructive airway disease (Lopuhaa et al., 2000; Roseboom et al., 2000).

Different life stages have different needs. Maternal nutritional deprivation in different pregnancy trimesters implies different effects on the *in utero* growth. Foetal length is mostly gained in the second trimester, while weight is mainly in the third trimester. These concepts have implications for action taken in disaster response. For instance, the nutrition provided for infants, pregnant women, children, adults and the elderly should be adjusted according to their particular needs.

The life-course argument proposes important criteria and considerations in prioritisation of intervention in population subgroups in a resources-deficit environment such as that of disaster and humanitarian crisis (see Case Box 1.4).

CASE BOX 1.4   THE DUTCH FAMINE TRAGEDY

The Dutch Tragedy started when the embargo on transport in the Netherlands was imposed in October 1944 during the Second World War. This embargo resulted in extreme hunger because of declining food supplies and the severe winter. About 10,000 people died because of the famine. Adults lost 15–20% of their weight on average. The intake of calories dropped to only 400 per day (pregnant women normally require 2,500 calories per day). In early May 1945, the Netherlands was liberated by the Allied Army and food supplies arrived. Conditions quickly improved but more than 40,000 babies were born during the hardship.

During the famine, Dutch women's fertility was impaired as they did not have enough body fat to support conception and the conception rate declined to one-third of normal. Infant mortality rate also increased if the babies were exposed to food insecurity during famine. Foetuses exposed to famine in their third trimester suffered from low birth weight, while foetuses exposed in the first and second trimesters could maintain normal birth weight. However, the negative impact of famine on these babies did not stop at their early life. Recent findings showed that women who were exposed to famine as foetuses in the first and second trimesters gave birth to underweight babies. In short, babies were affected by the starvation their grandmothers experienced many decades earlier (Diamond, 2004).

Epidemiologic and demographic transitions in the global burden of diseases

Epidemiology is the study of disease distribution in a population, and the factors affecting the distribution and progression of diseases. Demography is the study of population structures that might be affected by birth, death and migration. Over the past decades, the demographic structure of many countries has changed considerably. Changes in demographic and epidemiological profiles pose impact on public health and health service needs.

Age structure: demographic transition

In simple terms, the theory of demographic transition states that "[d]uring the transition, first mortality and then fertility declines, causing population growth rates first to accelerate and then to slow again, moving toward low fertility, long life and an old population" (Lee, 2003, p. 167). This transition was first observed in Europe in 1800. During the pre-transition period, life was short, with a high birth rate and death rate (Wahdan, 1996).

The second stage of demographic transition in the classic model involves the decrease of population mortality. As a result, there is population growth as mortality decreases but fertility remains high. This is a stage in transition as the growth in population cannot be sustained in a society with limited resources and is constrained by the cost of raising a family. When family size begins to grow, it becomes more costly to maintain a household. Social development, in particular the advancement in technology, also plays a role in increasing the opportunity cost of rearing children (Kirk, 1996). Although it remains debatable, the availability of contraceptive methods may also facilitate the transition of this demographic stage to the next (Kirk, 1996). Of note, prior to this stage of transition, most people die at a young age. The initiation of this transition stage is reflected in the presence of older people in the population and a higher dependency ratio. As mortality declines, more infants survive through childhood while there is persistent high fertility. There are more children per household. At this stage of transition, young people still make up a large proportion of the population.

The beginning of the third stage in transition is marked by a decrease in fertility. Families begin to have fewer children as the conditions for child development improve and child mortality declines. Markets and government policies also contribute to diminishing the value of children as the opportunity cost increases when technological development makes labour more productive (Lee, 2003). Mortality may continue to decrease with continual advancements in medical technology. When the reduction in fertility reaches equilibrium with mortality, population growth stabilises back to a constant level. The population growth usually continues to rise for a period of time due to the lag time between the drop in mortality and fertility. If fertility drops to a low level (e.g. below the replacement level) while life expectancy increases, the population shifts to an older average with slow replacement from the young generation.

Beginning around 1800, the transition began in Europe with declining mortality, which was helped by reductions in infectious diseases and improvements in nutrition (Kirk, 1996). The transition did not start in many low-income countries until the twentieth century, but with better public health infrastructure, nutrition and technology, many of these developing countries had a shorter period to progress their demographic transition by the end of the twentieth century.

Disease pattern: epidemiological transition

Epidemiological transition is usually referred to as "[t]he general shift from acute infectious and deficiency diseases characteristic of underdevelopment to chronic non-communicable diseases characteristic of modernisation and advanced levels of development" (Wahdan, 1996, p. 9). It can generally be observed when non-communicable, chronic conditions become the predominant disease profile as development evolves. Specifically, in this transition process, there is a period when a country is still being burdened with communicable diseases, while non-communicable, chronic conditions begin to climb.

In general, for the twenty-first century, western developed countries have a much larger proportion of deaths from chronic illness than communicable diseases and injuries. On the other hand, the communicable diseases category makes up the largest proportion in the cause of death in the WHO African region, which is the only WHO region with a higher proportion of death from the communicable diseases category than non-communicable conditions. The second largest burden of communicable diseases category is to be found in the WHO Eastern Mediterranean region and WHO South-East Asia region. Injuries, on the other hand, have less variation across the WHO regions, and are responsible for approximately 10% of the world's mortality. Although disease burden in developed countries is mainly from chronic NCDs, more than 80% of the deaths caused by chronic diseases happened in low-income and middle-income countries (Abegunde, Mathers, Adam, Ortegon, & Strong, 2007).

Over the next decades, the burden of NCDs is predicted to be an increasing trend with ageing populations, urbanisation and the growing prevalence of behavioural health risk factors in many developing countries (Beaglehole, Ebrahim, Reddy, Voute, & Leeder, 2008). The age-standardised death rates for chronic diseases in the selected 15 low- and middle-income countries were higher than those in high-income countries (Abegunde et al., 2007). In spite of the general trend in the change of disease patterns, it is important to note that the transition is not time-bound and unidirectional but a dynamic process, integrated by changes and the interactions between demographic, socio-economic, environmental and biological factors (Abegunde et al., 2007). For example, although the classic epidemiologic transition progresses with the decline of infectious diseases and the rise of non-communicable/degenerative diseases, the large burden of chronic communicable diseases such as AIDS and the re-emergence of evolving drug-resistant TB also pose significant health threats to many developing countries and even developed countries.

There are many ways in which disasters might affect populations with chronic conditions. In order to effectively respond to needs after disasters, responders and policy makers should have a good overview of the demographic and disease patterns underlying the disaster-affected countries. For the first decade post-millennium, four out of five of the world's most populous countries (China, India, Indonesia and Pakistan) are also disaster-prone, middle-income developing countries in Asia. These countries have entered into demographic and epidemiologic transitions and their health needs have changed accordingly. Not only are they experiencing population ageing, but also the health care systems of these countries are often faced with the need to manage and cater for populations that have a double-disease burden of both infectious diseases and chronic illnesses. As NCDs are the most important cause of mortality and morbidity in the twenty-first century, there is an imperative to respond to NCDs if the disaster response involves medical and health interventions.

Global population ageing and epidemiological transitions of the global burden of disease are occurring in this century (Abegunde et al., 2007; WHO, 2015). Researchers in the United States have suggested about 80% of older adults have at least one chronic condition and many also have some level of disability (Aldrich & Benson, 2008). As illustrated by various studies, in the twenty-first century, with the global population ageing and the increasing burden of non-communicable, often chronic diseases, there is a need to rethink how to provide for post–natural disaster medical and health care needs (Chan, 2008; Chan & Griffiths, 2009; Chan & Kim, 2010, 2011). Of note, despite the changes in underlying health and medical needs in these communities, international post-disaster medical humanitarian aid practices and policies are built upon assumptions that are based on conflict settings of a couple of decades ago (Chan & Sondorp, 2007; Spiegel, Hering, Paik, & Schilperoord, 2010).

Pathway of care

Pathway of care is a concept that illustrates how health needs may be addressed over the span of an individual's health journey for a condition or a disease. As shown in Figure 1.5, for any health-related risk or condition, an individual will begin by experiencing activities/interventions that address "health protection", "disease prevention" and "health promotion" to try to keep him/her free from diseases. His/her disease or health experiences will then be followed by diagnosis, treatment and rehabilitation, and finally palliative care if he/she is in the terminal stage of a disease. In public health, an emphasis on prevention in all aspects of the pathway of care model will demonstrate how comprehensive health care services might be possible even under limited resources.

It is important to highlight once again that the management of medical conditions involves a spectrum of services that range from disease prevention/protection to health promotion, diagnosis, treatment, rehabilitation and palliative care. Heath responses after a disaster will focus on diagnosis and treatment of clinical conditions. Medical relief groups and health respondents who might have limited technical capacity and resources could consider technical knowledge transfer and community capacity training of local staff so as to ensure the possibility of clinical case follow-up. Community partnerships and collaborations that promote local ownership and technical transfer would be essential for the sustainability of service beyond the disaster relief period. Even if medical and health relief programmes do not include the provision of chronic

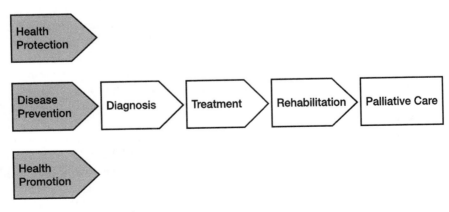

FIGURE 1.5 Pathway of care

disease treatment, agencies could consider: (1) providing health education and promotion information that are relevant to protect patients with knowledge to enhance well-being and to reduce potential disease complications, (2) identifying potential referral where relevant services and clinical management support may be provided, (3) facilitating referral with good clinical record keeping, and (4) coordinating with other domains of relief services (e.g. food and nutrition-based assistance groups to provide a nutritionally appropriate diet for a medical disease affected population, such as a low-salt, low-sugar diet) to minimise avoidable clinical disease complications. At the very least, relief groups and respondents might consider documenting the key disease burdens among the disaster-affected population so as to highlight health gaps that need to be addressed in the post-disaster rebuilding phase.

Hierarchy of prevention

"Prevention is better than cure" is one of the most commonly known principles in public health. There are three levels of health prevention – namely primary, secondary and tertiary (Leavell & Clark, 1958). **Primary prevention** concerns measures that prevent the onset of disease. Strategies may include health protection and health promotion. Health protection can be carried out through the establishment of health policies, regulations and vaccinations, while health promotion mainly involves health education. **Secondary prevention** refers to stopping the progression of disease after it occurs. It aims to detect disease early, thus increasing the opportunity for intervention to prevent its progression and the emergence of symptoms. Screening is one classic example of secondary prevention. **Tertiary prevention** focuses on the rehabilitation of patients with an established disease to minimise residual disabilities and complications. It aims to restore bodily functions that have been impaired by the disease. Services in this category include treatment, rehabilitation and palliative care. The application of these prevention concepts in establishing disaster mitigation strategies, response programmes and post-disaster recovery policies may enhance individual survival and protect communities from adverse health outcomes in natural disasters (Leavell & Clark, 1958; Hong Kong Special Administrative Region [HKSAR], 2008).

Figure 1.6 displays the hierarchy of prevention related to disasters. In disasters, primary prevention is at the lowest level of the pyramid, covering the largest proportion of preventable health impact. This is because primary prevention is targeted at the wider community. Secondary prevention is targeted at smaller populations which are affected by the disaster. Tertiary prevention focuses only on people who have already sustained the health impact of the disaster, which constitute a small portion of the affected population.

Disaster prevention refers to "[t]he outright avoidance of adverse impacts of hazards and related disasters... through actions taken in advance" (United Nations Office for Disaster Risk Reduction [UNISDR], 2009, p. 22).

The public health approach of prevention may apply in disaster prevention.

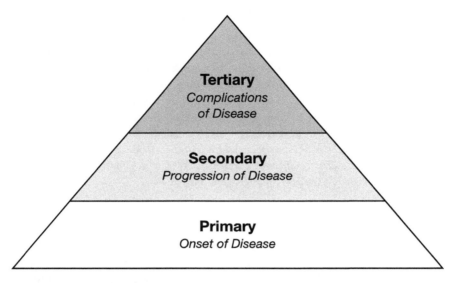

FIGURE 1.6 Hierarchy of prevention pyramid

Primary prevention is concerned with measures that prevent the onset of disease. In the context of disaster preparedness, primary prevention proactively addresses the potential health risk associated with disasters before the incident. In flood-prone areas, it is known that heavy rainfall might lead to stagnant water that can be major breeding sites for mosquitoes, therefore increasing the potential for vector-borne diseases, such as malaria, dengue fever and West Nile fever (World Health Organization Regional Office for the Eastern Mediterranean [WHO-EMRO], 2005). Primary prevention activities include the promotion of building structures that prevent water traps and the accumulation of stagnant water, as well as the promotion of community awareness of disease risks. In other disaster-prone areas, design and building codes of disaster-resistant hospitals are examples of primary prevention to minimise the impact of calamities (World Health Organization (WHO), United Kingdom Health Protection Agency (HPA), & partners, 2011). The World Health Organization has recognised the role of hospitals in a disaster and made specific guidelines to create safe hospitals (World Health Organization Regional Office for the Western Mediterranean [WHO-WPRO], 2010).

Secondary prevention refers to blocking the spread of diseases and/or their adverse impact after disasters. It is implemented after a disaster to prevent potential health impacts. For instance, to avoid an increased burden of clinical consultations after the occurrence of a disaster, the health-related needs of people with underlying chronic disease conditions (e.g. drugs, specific food requirements) should be attended to in order to avoid medical complications of their underlying conditions due to lack of management. Another classical example is that when nuclear reactor accidents occur, radioactive materials may be released into the environment. Due to

KNOWLEDGE BOX 1.1   PRIMARY PREVENTION IN COMMUNICABLE DISEASES

Primary prevention of infections includes interventions such as **avoidance of exposure**. In a health care setting, hand hygiene, food hygiene, environmental hygiene, wearing face masks and targeting behavioural-related risk factors are typical examples. **Community restrictions** are another subset of avoidance strategy in primary prevention. **Social distancing** (measures for limiting the duration/space whereby people come together) as an avoidance strategy focuses on the setting rather than specific individuals (e.g. quarantine/isolation). Some examples of social distancing measures are travel restriction, school closures, workplace closure and suspension of group events. Primary prevention also includes the **provision of prophylaxes** such as chemoprophylaxis and immune-prophylaxis. Chemoprophylaxis is the prescription of medicine to prevent infection following exposure and immune-prophylaxis refers to induction of immunity before exposure. Commonly this can be in the form of active immunisation to transfer immunity. Post-exposure vaccination is also being carried out for other conditions such as rabies, hepatitis A and tetanus. Last but not least, prevention programmes may be **organised for different target groups**. They can be organised for the general population, at-risk/vulnerable population or infectious diseases–affected population.

concerns over thyroid cancer as a result of radioactive contamination in food and water, the World Health Organization developed guidelines for iodine prophylaxis during nuclear accidents and recommended that iodine tablets should be given to the affected population to minimise the potential harm (WHO, 1999).

Tertiary prevention is the rehabilitation of patients with established diseases to minimise residual disabilities and complications. In a disaster context, tertiary prevention aims to minimise the impact and damage after a disaster. Tertiary prevention is targeted specifically at people who have already suffered from the impact of the disaster. For example, after an earthquake, patients might suffer from orthopaedic trauma and require operations. While rapid clinical operations could save lives, it is also important to offer early post-operational physiotherapies to maximise functional recovery potential of the patients (e.g. amputees).

As discussed in previous sections, even with limited resources and capacity in post-disaster settings, there are always ways to support populations with chronic conditions after disasters. For example, giving health advice will incur almost no operation cost but have potential long-term implications for disease prevention. Not only can smoking cessation advice prevent potential adverse clinical outcomes, such as heart diseases, stroke and cancer, but also such health advice may reduce spending on cigarette consumption. In order to implement meaningful preventive-based relief programmes, however, it is pertinent to emphasise the need to collect relevant demographic profiles, health information, knowledge, attitudes and behaviour information during needs assessment so as to design and implement relevant programmes according to the project needs.

Principles of health protection

Infectious diseases are an important emergency medical risk and the control of communicable diseases is a core technical competency area for practitioners who might be interested in disaster response. In infectious disease control, four major core knowledge areas involve natural science, epidemiology, behavioural science and education as well as risk management and communications. The principle of **control of infections** includes (1) protecting the host, such as enhancing an at-risk person's immunity through the provision of prophylactics, vaccinations and preparing the patient before operations; (2) modifying environmental reservoirs – that is removing sources of infection by sterilising, disinfecting and cleaning contaminated materials and services, and pest control to reduce viral load; and (3) interrupting transmissions – that is blocking the route of transmission. Examples of such work include developing the appropriate infrastructure and functions, relevant guidelines and protocols, education programmes, surveillance programmes, and quality improvement and assessment programmes.

Infectious diseases prevention applies prevention concepts to develop its approaches. Primary prevention refers to activities practised before the biological origin of diseases and can be regarded as exposure prevention (see Knowledge Box 1.1). Secondary prevention means prevention of disease development in an infected person, which also means infection prevention. Tertiary prevention is the prevention of a negative impact, such as clinical complications, which means disease prevention.

Disasters of different types affect health to different degrees. While an outbreak of communicable disease is not inevitable in the affected area, if the public health system is defective in the beginning and a disaster has increased the system's burden, an outbreak can cause a surge in morbidity and mortality. In the cholera outbreak ten months after the 2010 Haiti earthquake, 700,000 people were infected and 8,540 died. The outbreak was still not under complete control three years later. The consequences were devastating.

Principles of health promotion

The definition of health promotion as adopted in the 1986 Ottawa Conference, the first ever international conference on health promotion, is as follows:

> Health promotion is the process of enabling people to increase control over, and to improve, their health. To reach a state of complete physical, mental and social well-being, an individual or group must be able to identify and to realise aspirations, to satisfy needs, and to change or cope with the environment.
>
> *(WHO, 1986)*

The Ottawa Charter for Health Promotion specified ways in which action could be taken to achieve "health for all" around the world. Some basic prerequisites for this included: creating supportive environments, enabling community participation, developing personal skills for health, reorienting health care services towards prevention and health promotion, and building wide-ranging public policies that protect the environment and promote health. There are many theories conceptualising health promotion. As an example, Tannahill (1985) described three overlapping spheres of activities in health promotion – namely disease prevention, health education and health protection. These activities are usually more cost-effective when compared with treatment-based health promotion. In recent years, there are emphases in health literacy and social marketing approaches in health promotion efforts.

Health promotion efforts have important implications in disaster preparedness, response and reconstruction. It is important to harness the opportunity and resources available during disaster relief and response to maximise the health gain possibility of a disaster-affected community.

Overview of a health system

According to the definition of the WHO, "**health system**" includes all units, individuals and behaviours that aim to improve, resume and maintain the health of the population. Conceptually, there are six main components in a health system. The first building block of the system is **leadership and governance**, which concerns the oversight, coalition, regulation and policy of a country's or a region's health system. The second essential component is related to the **health care financing structure**. This component concerns the appropriate collection, allocation and utilisation of resources as well as risk management, which are important to a well-functioning health system. The third essential element is the **health workforce**. Health care workers specialising in different duties, including doctors, nurses, pharmacists, physiotherapists and nutritionists, are required to fulfil the health care needs of the community. The fourth core component is **medical product and technology**, which includes medical products, vaccines, medical technologies, and safety protocols and guidelines that ensure quality, effective and safe medical care. The fifth area is related to **information and research**. In this era of technology and innovation, the exchange and management of information, as well as the application of new findings in medical science, can improve people's health. A smoothly run health system can disseminate reliably and effectively any timely information and results of scientific research relevant to determinants of health, health impacts and health systems, thus enhancing health in the community. Last but not least, the sixth element of a health system is **service delivery**. A quality health system can provide appropriate and comprehensive health care services, ranging from primary care and specialist treatment to recovery. In conclusion, the objectives of a health system are to improve health in society, respond to the needs of society in terms of health care ensure that health care does not become a huge financial burden to patients, and increase the efficacy of services. The ultimate target is to achieve full coverage of health care and medical services, and enhance the health of the entire population.

Disasters may affect a medical system by destroying infrastructure, injuring medical staff and obstructing normal operation of regular and emergency services. In addition to increase of patient load resulted from direct trauma, destruction of lifeline infrastructure and collapsed or destroyed houses are all examples of disaster impact that aggravate victims' living conditions and sanitation, thereby increasing the health risks of the general public indirectly. Of note, health risks of some disasters may last for a long time, even across generations. These pose a medical burden on the health system of the affected community. For example, during nuclear disasters, victims are exposed to radiation and their offspring thus suffer from an increased risk of developing cancers and a defective reproductive system.

Ethics and decision-making in public health

Public health ethics are guiding principles and ethical frameworks that help establish consistent and fair resources allocation, minimising legal liability for service providers and improving service quality and management quality.

Ethical principles are an important cornerstone to support decision-making in disasters and humanitarian crises when there may be competing priorities, such as who is to be rescued and who should receive health care in a limited-resources environment, the protection and response mandate of emergency responders, the need to give the public timely information and the challenges of public communication with incomplete information, the lack of evidence-based support and resource allocation with multiple constraints. As highlighted by *Principles of the Ethical Practice of Public Health* (Public Health Leadership Society, 2002), important guiding principles for decision-making during disasters include: reasonableness, responsiveness, fairness, respect for persons, solidarity and accountability based on openness and transparency (Landesman, 2012).

When rescuers provide humanitarian aid to those affected by disasters, diseases and starvation, their foremost priority is, in addition to providing for basic human needs, to ensure they live with dignity, and everything is done to relieve their pain.

In cases of disasters and emergencies, humanitarian principles are ethical codes involved in saving lives and relieving pain. The United Nations advocates four key humanitarian principles: (1) **humanity**: human suffering must be addressed wherever it is found and the purpose of humanitarian action is to protect life and health, and ensure respect for human beings; (2) **impartiality**: humanitarian action must be impartial, and carried out on the basis of needs alone, making no distinctions on the basis of nationality, race, gender, class, religious belief or political opinions; (3) **independence**: humanitarian action must be autonomous from the political, economic, military or other objectives wherever it takes place; and (4) **neutrality**: humanitarian actors must not take sides in controversies of a political, racial, religious or ideological nature.

The *Humanitarian Charter* (The Sphere Project, 2011), initiated in 1997 by a group of non-governmental organisations (NGOs) and the International Red Cross and Red Crescent Movement for disaster relief, declares that all human beings are born free and equal in dignity and rights. All humanitarian action should be taken based on this fundamental principle. Rescuers are to be impartial and to offer assistance based only on needs, so that disaster victims are not discriminated against due to their gender, race, political affiliation or religion.

The primacy of the **humanitarian imperative** is that "action should be taken to prevent or alleviate human suffering arising out of disaster or conflict, and that nothing should override this principle" (The Sphere Project, 2011, p. 20). Under the **principle of right to receive humanitarian assistance** in *Humanitarian Charter*, people affected by conflicts are entitled to an adequate standard of living, including adequate food, water, clothing, shelter and the requirements for good health. Governments and non-governmental individuals should all respect humanitarian organisations' impartiality, independence and **non-partisanship**, assist them in eliminating any unnecessary restrictions, both legal and non-legal, and secure their safety during operations. Humanitarian organisations should also be allowed to give prompt and continuous assistance to any affected parties of conflicts who are in need of help. At the same time, the **principle of impartiality** and the **principle of non-discrimination** should be adhered to: humanitarian assistance (including medical humanitarian aid) is to be offered only on the basis of need and irrespective of the victims' background.

In addition to ensuring unobstructed and fair provision of humanitarian assistance, the *Humanitarian Charter* also includes the **principle of the right to protection and security**, which states that the safety and security of people in situations of conflict are of particular humanitarian concern. This principle is rooted in the provisions of international law, in resolutions of the United Nations and other intergovernmental organisations, and in the sovereign responsibility of states to protect all those within their jurisdiction. Women and the young are particularly vulnerable to injury in conflicts, and thus should be given special protection and assistance.

Conclusion

This chapter has described the key public health concepts and theories that are relevant to the understanding of disasters. To put together relevant and evidence-based public health interventions to support humanitarian public health action, stakeholders need to consider: demographic and epidemiological factors, potential health determinants and risk factors that lead to disparities, issues of life course, health literacy and health promotion, health service provision, various levels of prevention strategy, approaches such as population-wide versus individual, pathway of care and ethics related to decision-making process.

References

Abegunde, D. O., Mathers, C. D., Adam, T., Ortegon, M., & Strong, K. (2007). The burden and costs of chronic diseases in low-income and middle-income countries. *The Lancet*, *370*(9603), 1929–1938.

Acheson, D. (1988). *Public health in England: The report of the Committee of Inquiry into the Future Development to the Public Health Function.* London, UK: Her Majesty's Stationery Office.

Aldrich, N. & Benson, W. F. (2008). Disaster preparedness and the chronic disease needs of vulnerable older adults. *Preventing Chronic Disease, 5*(1), A27.

Anda, R. F., Felitti, V. J., Bremner, J. D., Walker, J. D., Whitfield, C., Perry, B. D., . . . Giles, W. H. (2006). The enduring effects of abuse and related adverse experiences in childhood: A convergence of evidence from neurobiology and epidemiology. *European Archives of Psychiatry and Clinical Neuroscience, 256*(3), 174–186.

Barker, D. (2003). The midwife, the coincidence, and the hypothesis. *British Medical Journal, 327*(7429), 1428.

Beaglehole, R., Ebrahim, S., Reddy, S., Voute, J., & Leeder, S. (2008). Prevention of chronic diseases: A call to action. *The Lancet, 370*(9605), 2152–2157.

Chan, E. Y. (2008). Why are older peoples' health needs forgotten post-natural disaster relief in developing countries? A healthcare provider survey of 2005 Kashmir, Pakistan earthquake. *American Journal of Disaster Medicine, 4*(2), 107–112.

Chan, E. Y. & Griffiths, S. (2009). Comparison of health needs of older people between affected rural and urban areas after the 2005 Kashmir, Pakistan earthquake. *Prehospital and Disaster Medicine, 24*(5), 365–371.

Chan, E. Y. & Kim, J. J. (2010). Characteristics and health outcomes of internally displaced population in unofficial rural self-settled camps after the 2005 Kashmir, Pakistan earthquake. *European Journal of Emergency Medicine, 17*(3), 136–141.

Chan, E. Y. & Kim, J. (2011). Chronic health needs immediately after natural disasters in middle-income countries: The case of the 2008 Sichuan, China earthquake. *European Journal of Emergency Medicine, 18*(2), 111–114.

Chan, E. Y. & Sondorp, E. (2007). Natural disaster and medical intervention: Missed opportunity to deal with chronic medical needs? An analytical framework. *Asia Pacific Journal of Public Health, 19*, 45–51.

Constitution of the World Health Organization, July 22, 1946, T.I.A.S. No. 1,808.

de Ville de Goyet, C., del Cid, E., Romero, A., Jeannee, E., & Lechat, M. F. (1976). Earthquake in Guatemala: Epidemiologic evaluation of the relief effort. *Bulletin of the Pan American Health Organization, 10*(2), 95–109.

Dahlgren, G., & Whitehead, M. (1991). *Policies and strategies to promote equity in health* (Working Paper). Stockholm, Sweden: Institute for Further Studies.

Diamond, J. (2004). War babies. In S. J. Ceci & W. M. Williams (Eds.), *The nature-nurture debate: The essential readings* (pp. 11–52). Malden, MA: Wiley-Blackwell.

Glass, R. I., Craven, R. B., Bregman, D. J., Barbara, J. S., Horowitz, N., Kerndt, P., & Winkle, J. (1980). Injuries from the Wichita Falls tornado: Implications for prevention. *Science, 207*(15), 734–738. doi:10.1126/science.207.4432.734

Griffiths, S., Jewell, T., & Donnelly, P. (2005). Public health in practice: The three domains of public health. *Public Health, 119*(10), 907–913.

Hong Kong Special Administrative Region (HKSAR), Department of Health. (2008). *Promoting health in Hong Kong: A strategic framework for prevention and control of non-communicable diseases* [Internet]. Retrieved from http://www.change4health.gov.hk/filemanager/common/image/strategic_framework/promoting_health/promoting_health_e.pdf

Kirk, D. (1996). Demographic transition theory. *Population Studies, 50*(3), 361–387.

Landesman, L. Y. (2012). *Public health management of disasters: The practice guide* (3rd ed.). Washington, DC: American Public Health Association.

Leavell, H. R. & Clark, E. G. (1958). *Preventive medicine for the doctor in his community: An epidemiologic approach* (2nd ed.). New York: McGraw-Hill.

Lee, R. (2003). The demographic transition: Three centuries of fundamental change. *The Journal of Economic Perspectives, 17*(4), 167–190.

Lopuhaä, C. E., Roseboom, T. J., Osmond, C., Barker, D.J.P., Ravelli, A.C.J., Bleker, O. P., . . . van der Meulen, J.H.P. (2000). Atopy, lung function, and obstructive airways disease after prenatal exposure to famine. *Thorax, 55*(7), 555–561.

McLeroy, K. R., Bibeau, D., Steckler, A., & Glanz, K. (1988). An ecological perspective on health promotion programs. *Health Education Quarterly, 15*(4), 351–377.

Public Health Leadership Society. (2002). *Principles of the ethical practice of public health* (Version 2.2) [Internet]. Washington, DC: American Public Health Association. Retrieved from http://www.apha.org/~/media/files/pdf/about/ethics_brochure.ashx

Roseboom, T. J., de Rooij, S., & Painter, R. (2006). The Dutch famine and its long-term consequences for adult health. *Early Human Development, 82*(8), 485–491.

Roseboom, T. J., van der Meulen, J.H.P., Osmond, C., Barker, D.J.P., Ravelli, A.C.J., Schroeder-Tanka, J. M., van Montfrans, G. A., Michels, R.P.J., & Bleker, O. P. (2000). Coronary heart disease in adults after prenatal exposure to the Dutch famine, 1944-45. *Heart, 84*(6), 595–598.

Roseboom, T. J., Van Der Meulen, J. H., Ravelli, A. C., Osmond, C., Barker, D. J., & Bleker, O. P. (2001). Effects of prenatal exposure to the Dutch famine on adult disease in later life: An overview. *Molecular and Cellular Endocrinology, 185*(1), 93–98.

Sommer, A. & Mosley, W. H. (1972). East Bengal cyclone of November, 1970: Epidemiological approach to disaster assessment. *The Lancet, 1*(7759), 1030–1036. doi:10.1016/S0140–6736(72)91218–4

Spencer, H. C., Romero, A., Feldman, R. A., Campbell, C. C., Zeissig, O., Boostrom, E. R., & Long, E. C. (1977). Disease surveillance and decision-making after the 1976 Guatemala earthquake. *The Lancet, 2*(8030), 181–184. doi:10.1016/S0140–6736(77)90193–3

The Sphere Project. (2011). *Humanitarian charter and minimum standards in humanitarian response* (3rd ed.) [Internet]. Retrieved from http://www.spherehandbook.org/en/the-humanitarian-charter/

Spiegel, P. B., Hering, H., Paik, E., & Schilperoord, M. (2010). Conflict-affected displaced persons need to benefit more from HIV and malaria national strategic plans and Global Fund grants. *Conflict and Health, 4*(2), 1–6.

Tannahill, A. (1985). What is health promotion? *Health Education Journal, 44*(4), 167–168. doi:10.1177/001789698504400402

United Nations Office for Disaster Risk Reduction (UNISDR). (2009). *2009 UNISDR terminology on disaster risk reduction* [Internet]. Retrieved from http://www.unisdr.org/files/7817_UNISDRTerminologyEnglish.pdf

Wahdan, M. H. (1996). The epidemiological transition. *Eastern Mediterranean Health Journal, 2*(1), 8–20.

World Health Organization (WHO). (1986). *Health promotion: The Ottawa Charter for Health Promotion* [Internet]. Retrieved from http://www.who.int/healthpromotion/conferences/previous/ottawa/en/

World Health Organization (WHO). (1998). *Standard Health Kits – New Emergency Health Kit 98* [Internet]. Retrieved from http://www.who.int/hac/techguidance/ems/new_health_kit_content/en/

World Health Organization (WHO). (1999). *Guidelines for iodine prophylaxis following nuclear accidents: Update 1999* [Internet]. Retrieved from http://www.who.int/ionizing_radiation/pub_meet/Iodine_Prophylaxis_guide.pdf

World Health Organization (WHO). (2004). *World report on knowledge for better health* [Internet]. Retrieved from http://www.who.int/rpc/meetings/world_report_on_knowledge_for_better_health.pdf?ua=1

World Health Organization (WHO). (2011). *The Interagency Emergency Health Kit 2011: Medicines and medical devices for 10,000 people for approximately three months* [Internet]. Retrieved from http://whqlibdoc.who.int/publications/2011/9789241502115_eng.pdf?ua=

World Health Organization (WHO). (2014). *The determinants of health* [Internet]. Retrieved from http://www.who.int/hia/evidence/doh/en/

World Health Organization (WHO). (2015). *World report on ageing and health* [Internet]. Retrieved from http://apps.who.int/iris/bitstream/10665/186463/1/9789240694811_eng.pdf?ua=1

WHO Regional Office for the Eastern Mediterranean (WHO-EMRO). (2005). *Vector-borne diseases: Addressing a re-emerging public health problem* (Technical Report). Retrieved from http://apps.who.int/iris/bitstream/10665/122334/1/EM_RC52_3_en.pdf?ua=1

WHO Regional Office for the Western Mediterranean (WHO-WPRO). (2010). *Safe hospitals in emergencies and disasters: Structural, non-structural and functional indicators*. Retrieved from http://www.wpro.who.int/emergencies_disasters/documents/SafeHospitalsin EmergenciesandDisastersweboptimized.pdf

World Health Organization (WHO), United Kingdom Health Protection Agency (HPA), & partners. (2011). *Safe hospitals: Prepared for emergencies and disasters* [Disaster Risk Management for Health Fact Sheet]. Retrieved from http://www.who.int/hac/events/drm_fact_sheet_safe_hospitals.pdf

2
DISASTER CONCEPTS AND TRENDS

The previous chapter highlighted public health concepts and theories relevant to an understanding of disaster and their practices. This chapter will discuss some key concepts about disasters.

Characteristics of disasters

Depending on the academic discipline, definitions of **disaster** differ according to the emphasis of the field of study (e.g. engineering, sociology). In the health sector, there are three major definitions.

Definition 1 from The United Nations Office for Disaster Risk Reduction (UNISDR, 2009, 9): "A serious disruption of the functioning of a community or a society involving widespread human, material, economic or environmental losses and impacts, which exceeds the ability of the affected community or society to cope using its own resources."

Definition 2 from World Health Organization (WHO): "A disaster is an occurrence disrupting the normal conditions of existence and causing a level of suffering that exceeds the capacity of adjustment of the affected community" (World Health Organization, Emergency and Humanitarian Action [WHO/EHA], 2002, p. 3).

Definition 3 from Centre for Research on the Epidemiology of Disasters (CRED, 2009) specifically for the study of disaster in the discipline of epidemiology: A disaster is "[a] situation or event, which overwhelms local capacity, necessitating a request to a national or international level for external assistance; [a]n **unforeseen and often sudden event** that **causes great damage, destruction and human suffering**."

Three elements of disaster are of particular concern for this book's purpose: (1) *Human impact of the event:* disasters and catastrophes must have an impact on human lives. For example, an earthquake that occurs in the middle of the Indian Ocean where there are no human inhabitants would not be considered a disaster, but a natural phenomenon. (2) *Temporal characteristics of the event:* while unpredictability is a characteristic of disasters, associated human health outcomes are known. With technological advancements, the occurrences of certain disasters, such as droughts, famines and cyclones, are predictable and their potential adverse health outcomes can be prevented. Instead of passively responding, disaster preparedness (which will be discussed in later chapters) comprises action that can be taken before disasters to protect the health of populations. (3) *Need for external assistance:* in disasters, populations often require help beyond existing infrastructure and systems to cope.

Anatomy and structure of disaster

Most disasters can be understood in three phases – namely (1) pre-impact phase, (2) impact phase, and (3) post-impact phase. The **pre-impact phase** is the period of time before the onset of a disaster. During this phase, there is the greatest potential for preventing the negative health impact of disasters. Two key concepts are involved in this phase – namely disaster preparedness and mitigation. **Disaster preparedness** refers to activities taken by health care and public health professionals to ensure that timely and efficient response systems are in place in times of disaster. It also includes action taken at the community and individual levels to protect against and minimise physical and emotional damage resulting from disasters. **Mitigations** are measures taken to reduce the health risk to the population posed by hazards. Both the natural and built environment can turn a natural hazard into disaster if appropriate measures are not taken to protect the population from being exposed.

The **impact phase** is the period of time during and immediately after a disaster, when rapid needs assessment and search-and-rescue relief work take place. **Disaster response** is the action taken in reaction to an emergency or disaster. These actions include initial assessments as well as search and rescue immediately after the disaster. The **post-impact phase** is the period of time after the impact of a disaster when the relief effort has reached equilibrium, or stabilised. During this phase, efforts are focused on long-term rehabilitation and recovery. **Disaster recovery** covers the measures taken by national leaders and community stakeholders to help the population return to their "normal" state before the disaster struck. Mitigation measures may also be taken at this phase to reduce the health risk of the population posed by the hazard. Figure 2.1 illustrates the interface between the three phases of disasters and another key concept, the disaster response cycle.

Disaster response cycle

Disaster response cycle is an important concept in disaster-related medical response. In principle, disaster response should be planned and implemented according to the stages of the disaster and its associated needs, taking into account the principles and public health approach discussed previously. The disaster response cycle is shown in the outer ring of Figure 2.1, where there are five phases where decision-making can happen in a disaster scenario.

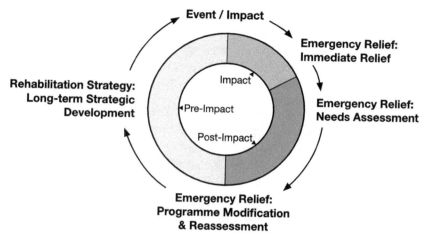

FIGURE 2.1 Five phases of disaster

These phases include (1) non-disaster or normal state before event or impact, (2) immediate relief after event or impact, (3) needs assessment, (4) programme modification and reassessment and (5) long-term strategic development. The entire process should be implemented and monitored with universally accepted guiding frameworks and indicators such as the Sphere guidelines to ensure effectiveness, accountability and enhancement of response are achieved (The Sphere Project, 2011).

The first phase is **non-disaster or normal state**. Disaster risk reduction and preparedness programmes are key activities during this phase. Community-based strategies play a vital role in all phases of a disaster, including preparedness, protection and response. Contributing health and medical actors include community health care workers, trained volunteers, local organisations and key players from different sectors (e.g. water, shelter, education). **Immediate relief** as the second stage of the disaster cycle is characterised by the event itself and the immediate interventions and relief carried out by local response units. At this stage of the emergency, due to the immediate surge of emergency cases, mortality cases and the destruction of health services, both government and relief agencies are strapped for resources. Provision of services is usually limited to essential life-saving procedures. In developing context, poor baseline population health profile and limited available resources could further hamper response capacity and health outcomes. The third stage of the disaster cycle involves **needs assessment** to facilitate evidence-based **reorganisation of health services**.

In the fourth stage of the disaster cycle, the emergency relief efforts focus on **programme modifications and rehabilitation planning** of the affected system. Health needs assessments that support the earlier stage of intervention planning might often use simple measures, such as mortality, rather than more relevant health determinants that contribute to mortality and morbidity figures. Such over-simplistic indicators are not sufficient for the purpose of capturing all possible solutions to address real needs. Since ill health can be caused by multiple factors, relief operation recommendations drawn from single sector assessments are inadequate to meet all aspects of underlying health needs. In developing countries, a myriad of underlying issues can hinder good health and they need to be taken into consideration in order to set up effective programmes.

The fifth stage of the disaster cycle requires activities that mainly address and support **rehabilitation and long-term rebuilding efforts** in a community. Due to the target-oriented and short-term nature of most interventions, an exit strategy should always be planned. Community participation and collaboration are thus essential to the sustainability of post-disaster efforts of a non-acute nature.

Myths and facts about disasters

There are many myths regarding the impact of disasters in human life and its related responses. In an exploratory study of disaster myths based on an earlier study by the Pan American Health Organization (1982), Alexander (2007) identified 19 common myths about disasters and disaster responses perpetuated in the news and entertainment mass media. In Alexander's study, involving 218 university students in the United States and 87 trainee emergency workers and managers in Italy, it was found that the myths regarding the prevalence of panic and looting and the health hazards of unburied bodies were strongly upheld by all respondents, that the need to donate used clothes to disaster victims was strongly upheld by university students, while those about the irrelevance of socio-economic status in disaster fatalities, the flight of people from a disaster area, the prevalence of epidemics and the usefulness of any aid were somewhat agreed by both groups. Table 2.1 lists some of these myths and the corresponding facts grouped according to the general nature of disasters, casualties in disasters, health hazards post-disasters and survivor behaviours, as well as aid and resources.

Debunking these disasters myths is important for preparedness, response and management of the disaster relief efforts. These misconceptions may hamper relief efforts and the efficiency of post-disaster rehabilitation.

Classification of disasters

One of the key components for the definition of disaster is *the nature of the "situation or event" (ecological breakdown)*. The classification of disasters will provide public health practitioners a good structure for potential disaster response and preparedness planning. Epidemiological approaches in analysing health needs in disaster settings can provide information for the specific **patterns of health outcomes** associated with specific disasters. *The purpose of classifying disasters is to mitigate the negative consequences of disasters by revealing the unique health patterns associated with various types.*

TABLE 2.1 Myths and facts about disasters

Myths	Facts
I. General Nature of Disasters	
1 Exceptionality: *Disasters are exceptional events.*	Disasters are part of everyday life and occur often.
2 Unmanageable disasters: *Disasters cause chaos and cannot be managed systematically.*	Disasters can be managed, after much research has been done to provide understanding of how disasters function in general.
3 Importance of technology: *Technology is the saviour in disasters.*	Problems caused by disasters usually require social more than technological solutions. Technological resources are often poorly distributed and ineffectively used.
II. Casualties in Disasters	
4 Deathly earthquakes: *Earthquakes are the direct cause of the deaths of large numbers of people.*	Most earthquakes do not cause high death tolls directly. Buildings collapsing in earthquakes do. Since earthquakes cannot be eliminated, the loss can only be alleviated by building seismic-resistant buildings and formulating effective earthquake evacuation plans in advance.
5 Irrelevance of socio-economic status in disaster fatalities: *Disasters kill people regardless of socio-economic status.*	Compared to the middle class or the rich, the poor are more vulnerable to disasters.
6 Long survival time: *People can survive for many days when trapped under the rubble of a collapsed building.*	Most people brought out alive from the rubble are saved within 24 hours of impact.
III. Health Hazards Post-Disasters	
7 The health hazards of unburied bodies: *After every disaster, even one not caused by infectious diseases, the unburied dead bodies left in the disaster area pose a health hazard to survivors.*	Unburied dead bodies usually do not cause a health hazard, even if the bodies decompose rapidly. Rather, hasty and improper and indiscriminate burial demoralises survivors and hinders arrangements for death certification, funeral rites and autopsy.
8 Prevalence of disease epidemics: *Epidemics always follow disasters.*	Whether there is an epidemic post-disaster depends on the actual situation of the disaster-affected area but epidemiological surveillance mechanisms and health care services in the area are usually sufficient to handle any potential epidemics.
IV. Survivor Behaviours	
9 Fleeing of people from a disaster area: *Large numbers of affected people flee from the area struck by disasters.*	Usually, there is a "convergence phenomenon" in a disaster-affected area: people rush into a disaster area to help. Few disaster survivors leave and evacuations are usually temporary. These create an overcrowded living environment which leads to other public health problems.

(Continued)

TABLE 2.1 (Continued)

Myths	Facts
10 Panic survivors: *Panic is a common reaction of survivors to disasters.*	Most disaster survivors behave calmly and rationally, while panic is rare.
11 Dazed and apathetic survivors: *Having experienced a disaster, survivors tend to be dazed and apathetic.*	Usually, survivors rapidly start reconstruction. Activism is much more common than fatalism (i.e. the formation of a "therapeutic community"). Only a small portion of the population is affected psychologically.
12 Prevalence of looting: *Looting is common post disaster.*	Post-disaster looting is relatively rare and mostly happens in specific communities facing acute pre-existing social polarisation or other problems.
13 Prevalence of antisocial behaviour: *Disasters usually lead to antisocial behaviour.*	Disasters usually result in greater social solidarity, generosity, self-sacrifice and even heroism.
V. Aid and Resources	
14 Usefulness of any aid: *Any kind of aid and relief is useful post disaster.*	Hasty and ill-considered relief initiatives tend to create chaos instead. Only certain types of assistance, goods and services are essential in the disaster-affected area.
15 Acceptance of any aid: *Aid of all forms should be accepted.*	Only goods and services that are needed in the disaster area should be accepted.
16 The need to donate used clothing to disaster victims: *People should donate used clothing to disaster victims.*	Garments may not be suitable for the victims and their distribution creates pressures on the logistics management in the disaster-affected area. When the garments are not suitable, it may also lead to the accumulation of a huge quantity of unwanted clothes.
17 The need of medicines: *Any kind of medicine is needed in disaster-affected areas.*	Medicine should not be taken casually. Health care needs in the disaster-affected areas should be assessed first and then needed medicines be transported to these areas by health care organisations.
18 Resource shortage: *Resource shortage usually hinders the effective management of disasters.*	Resource shortage is rare and very temporary, while the proper deployment and efficient use of resources and the oversupply of certain types of resource more often pose bigger problems.
19 Generous donors: *Commercial corporations, non-commercial associations and governments are very generous when invited to send aid and relief to disaster areas.*	Some donors may be generous, but some dump outdated medicines, obsolete equipment and unusable goods in disaster areas.

Source: Pan American Health Organization (1982) and Alexander (2007).

In general, disasters can be classified into three broad categories based on the cause: natural disasters, human-caused disasters and an additional subgroup known as complex emergencies.

Natural disasters are disastrous events that result from phenomena of natural origin, where human activities are not directly involved in triggering such events. **Human-caused disasters** are disastrous events that occur due to human-related causes, whether unintentional (e.g., nuclear explosions and chemical spills) or intentional (e.g., war and terrorism). **Complex emergencies**, that involve multifaceted humanitarian crises, are usually classified as the third type of disasters, with their own distinct sets of characteristics.

CRED classifies natural disasters into six major subcategories (see Figure 2.2):

- **Geophysical:** Events originating from solid earth
- **Meteorological:** Events caused by short-lived/micro-scale atmospheric processes
- **Hydrological:** Events caused by deviations in the normal water cycle and/or overflow of bodies of water caused by wind
- **Climatological:** Events caused by long-lived/meso- to macro-scale processes
- **Biological:** Disasters caused by the exposure of living organisms to germs and toxic substances
- **Extraterrestrial:** A hazard caused by asteroids, meteoroids and comets as they pass near earth or strike earth, or any changes in interplanetary conditions that affect earth's magnetosphere

Climatological, hydrological and meteorological disasters may be grouped together as hydro-meteorological disasters. Together with biological disasters, they are natural disasters with direct associations with the climate system; their occurrence and intensity are affected by global climate change.

The second type of disaster classified by cause is *human-caused* or *man-made disasters*. Depending on discipline, a human-caused disaster is defined as "[disaster] created by man, either intentionally or by accident" (United States Federal

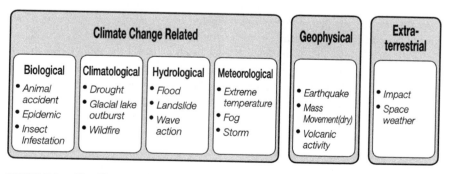

FIGURE 2.2   Classification of disasters

Source: Adapted from Below, Wirtz, and Guha-Sapir (2009).

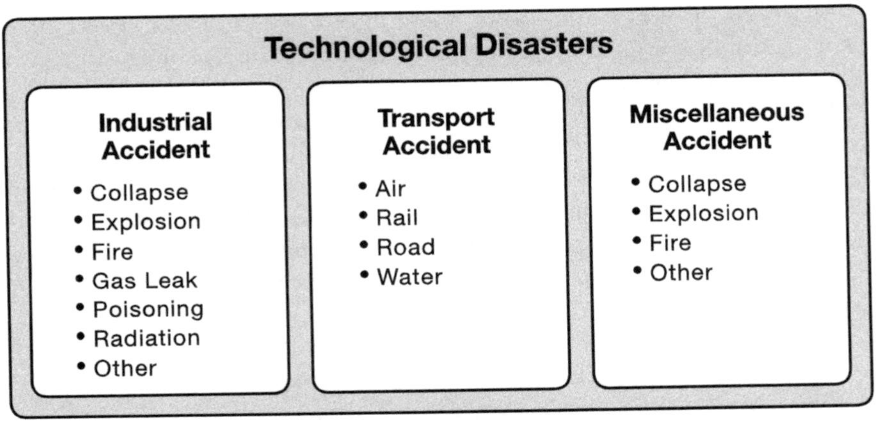

FIGURE 2.3 An example of categorising technological disasters

Source: Adapted from Below, R., Wirtz, A., and Guha-Sapir, D. (2009).

Emergency Management Agency [FEMA], 2008, D-32). Human-caused disaster is a broad category that is characterised by the presence of human factors as a cause of the event. It ranges from technological disasters to bioterrorism, famine, complex emergencies and others. Technological disasters include disasters that result as a consequence of human error or breakdown of technological systems, which can be further categorised into: (1) *industrial accidents*, (2) *transport accidents* and (3) *miscellaneous accidents*.

Figure 2.3 shows an example of how technological disasters might be categorised into industrial, transport and miscellaneous accidents. Under industrial accidents, there are collapse, explosion, fire, gas leak, poisoning, radiation and others. Transport accidents can be subdivided into four types: rail, road, water and air. Under miscellaneous accidents, the subcategories include accidents that involve collapse, explosion and fire (see Case Box 2.1).

Natural and human factors are two broad categories of factors that affect the severity and human outcomes in technological disasters. The natural factors are predominantly uncontrollable and/or unpredictable. These factors include the location, the trigger (e.g., a forest fire triggered by extreme temperature and low humidity) and the type/nature of the technological failure itself. Human-related factors include those at the individual level (such as lack of skill and training in machine operations, fatigue and performance instability), occupational hazards, as well as systems, policies and law at the societal level (see Case Box 2.2).

To protect the community, specific guidelines and training should be implemented in industries. For example, to prepare for a chemical release in chemical incidents or radiation emergencies, these guidelines and training should cover scenario analyses and impact assessment, planning for training and exercising the response, and training and equipping responders to deal with loss of containment (WHO, 2011a). For radiation emergencies, monitoring of the environment and high-risk groups should be applied (WHO, 2011c).

CASE BOX 2.1   1986 CHERNOBYL ACCIDENT, FORMER SOVIET UNION

On 26 April 1986, reactor number 4 of the Chernobyl nuclear power plant in Ukraine, then part of the former Soviet Union, exploded and released radioactive materials over the then Soviet Union member republics of Ukraine, Byelorussia (now Belarus), Russia (now Russian Federation) and several other European countries. The reactor contained about 190 metric tons of uranium dioxide fuel and fission products, of which up to 30% escaped into the atmosphere. The plant after the incident can be seen from afar in Figure 2.4.

FIGURE 2.4   The nuclear power plant at Chernobyl in Ukraine

Source: Photo by Jason Minshull/Public Domain (https://en.wikipedia.org/wiki/Chernobyl_disaster#/media/File:View_of_Chernobyl_taken_from_Pripyat.JPG).

Immediate impact

About 350,000 people helped clean up the 30 km radius ground surrounding the reactor. A total of 134 workers were diagnosed with acute radiation sickness and 28 people, including staff of the nuclear plant and emergency relief workers, died within four months.

Long-term consequences

A decade later, over 2,000 cases of thyroid cancer were observed among young people who were exposed to the nuclear accident during childhood and adolescent years. Many attribute these "unexpected" cases of thyroid cancer to the Chernobyl accident and increases in other cancer types are expected, but there is no consensus over the extent of such increases. It was suggested that radioactive material contaminated dairy products through cattle pastures. However, morbidity and mortality patterns in the affected areas have remained the same as other parts of the country. In 2006, of the five million people living in Belarus and Ukraine, 270,000 people were living in the strictly controlled zones. The community reports a higher prevalence of alcohol and tobacco abuse and addiction, potentially as a result of increased stress and anxiety levels and being stigmatised as "exposed persons". For people who were evacuated from their homes and resettled, many expressed difficulties in adapting to their new circumstances and continued to report high levels of stress associated with unemployment and lack of control over their lives. When compared with evacuees, people remaining in the affected areas reported a lower level of stress, but higher concerns about raising their children in contaminated zones.

Long-term economic consequences

The Chernobyl accident has had a profound effect, immediate and long-term, on the economy of the surrounding areas. The accident imposed a heavy burden on the national budgets through the cost of clean-up, compensation and recovery. A total of up to seven million people receive Chernobyl-related welfare benefits of one kind or another. The emigration of the skilled workforce from the affected areas has hindered industrial recovery and deterred investment. For families that rely on food production and food processing as the staple sources of income, radioactive contamination has reduced the potential for income generation.

(Gray, 2002; Bennett, Repacholi, & Carr, 2006)

The third type of disaster categorised by cause is *complex emergencies*. A complex emergency is "[a] multifaceted humanitarian crisis in a country, region or society where there is a total or considerable breakdown of authority resulting from internal or external conflict and which requires a multi-sectoral, international response that goes beyond the mandate or capacity of any single agency and/or the ongoing UN country programme" (OCHA, 2003, p. 9).

Complex emergencies often occur in settings where there have been protracted disruptions to livelihoods (e.g. threats to life produced by warfare, civil disturbance and large-scale movements of people). In these settings, the fragile or failing economic, political and social institutions fuel violations of **human rights**. Many people leave their homes to seek safety and shelter to escape from complex emergencies, the destruction of their homes, hunger, disease and persecution. These people become refugees or internally displaced persons (IDPs). Complex emergencies may emerge and be sustained over a period of time, sometimes exacerbated by natural disasters (Wisner & Adams, 2002) (see Case Box 2.3).

CASE BOX 2.2 2015 INDUSTRIAL ACCIDENT IN TIANJIN, CHINA

Industrial disasters are often associated with illegal and unethical industrial and commercial practices. In 2015, a warehouse explosion caused 158 deaths and left 698 hospitalised in Tianjin, the fourth most populated city in the People's Republic of China and the major seaport to the capital Beijing 120 km away (People's Republic of China [PRC] State Council, 2015, August 31). Post-disaster investigations at the explosion site found the warehouse had been illegally storing 2,500 tonnes of dangerous chemical substances with 1,300 tonnes of oxide and nitrate compounds; 500 tonnes of inflammable materials and 700 tonnes of highly toxic substances (mainly sodium cyanide) (PRC State Council, 2015, August 20). Not only had the blast taken a heavy toll of human lives and imposed adverse mental health impacts on survivors, the chemical pollutants were also posing immediate health risks such as fire (burns), explosion (mechanical injuries) and toxicity (ranging from asphyxiation to neurotoxicity). Long-term environmental hazards to air, soil, water and food production may affect the well-being of the neighbouring residential areas for years.

A coordinated emergency response and prevention effort is vitally important to protect a community from such disasters. For the Tianjin incident, the Chinese government was able to mount an efficient response. Although the explosion occurred around midnight, over 1,000 clinical staff were deployed and 10 emergency shelters were set up within four hours after the blast (PRC State Council, 2015, August 14). At the national level, the National Health and Family Planning Commission (NHFPC) sent at least 66 medical rescue experts to support the Tianjin blast relief within the first 72 hours (PRC Public Health Emergency Command Center, National Health and Family Planning Commission [NHFPC], 2015, August 15).

During 1995–2005, industrial accident–based disasters occurred mainly in economic and heavy industrial areas (Feng & Wang, 2008; Chan, Hung, & Cai, 2011) and the human toll tended to involve a poor vulnerable population engaging in high-risk occupations (e.g. miners) with the minimum safety protection in exchange for a basic livelihood. In the past decade, instead of being concentrated in industry-heavy, suburban communities, major industrial accident disasters were also commonly reported in urban middle-class communities. The explosion and fire in Changchun City in Jilin Province (2013), the oil spill fire and explosion in Qingdao City, Shandong Province (2013), and the factory blast in Kunshan City in Jiangsu Province (2014) were urban-based disasters that resulted in over 100 casualties, affected thousands of habitants and caused economic loss amounting to millions of renminbi (PRC State Administration of Coal Mine Safety, State Administration of Work Safety, 2013). Death patterns have also changed from predominantly industrial-based workers to disaster responders such as firefighters and policemen (PRC State Council, 2015, August 31).

Source: Chan, Wang, Mark and Liu (2015).

However, countries at war or with chronic conflict situations may or may not be reported as in complex emergencies. Classifying disasters by *cause* is a method of disaster categorisation used by the Emergency Events Database (EM-DAT). Other disaster categorisation mechanisms exist and often depend on the purpose of devising such systems. Some classifications may include "psychological events" as a category, such as the Disaster Database Project, which includes "vampire" and "witchcraft"-related phenomena under this grouping. The case ahead will illustrate the difficulties of classifying every disaster by *natural* or *man-made* causes.

CASE BOX 2.3   MINDANAO ARMED CONFLICT, THE PHILIPPINES

In Mindanao, the large island in the south of the Philippines, the government has fought insurgency groups since the 1970s. The conflict in Mindanao is rooted in many issues including poverty, poor governance, inequitable policies, and the marginalisation of the Muslim population and indigenous people in a country with a Catholic majority. More recently, the government's "all-out war" against insurgency groups in 2000 resulted in the displacement of more than 400,000 people in 2003. An estimated two million people were displaced by conflict and associated human rights violations in the Philippines between 2000 and 2007. Low intensity fighting continues and displacement is common (United Nations Office for the Coordination of Humanitarian Affairs [OCHA], 2012). Figure 2.5 shows the training of Philippine Marines who have been heavily involved in the conflict.

Health impact

The protracted conflict has led to millions of internally displaced persons (IDPs) and had devastating effects on the economy, development, livelihoods, and health of the population. Long-term programmes addressing the needs of the people have had a difficult time providing even the basic needs due to the ongoing conflict, mobility of the internally-displaced population, a draining of resources, a highly volatile timeframe, and non-reliable figures.

Many health service and system deficiencies are the result of the toll that the conflict has had on resources, the health care workforce, and the highly mobile population. The demographic and epidemiological profiles show that the population is mainly young and disproportionately female, with high excess mortality and poor access to services. Apart from the psychological and reproductive health issues stemming from violence, infectious diseases might also

FIGURE 2.5   Mindanao armed conflict

Source: Photo by Sgt Marc Ayalin, U.S. Marine Corps/Public Domain (http://en.wikipedia.org/wiki/Philippine_Marine_Corps#/media/File:PMC_BAlikatan_Exercise.jpg).

be a significant burden depending on the localities and the endemic diseases. The challenge for the medical organisations and responders is to provide the essential health services despite poor accessibility and other barriers to health services. There is also the issue of mental health from the child protection point of view. An important health agenda to push forward will be the integration of chronic disease management within the traditional aid programmes, as this has been largely ignored in the past. The issue of providing equitable care for vulnerable populations should also be addressed.

In addition to extensive loss of life, widespread damage to societies and economies and the need for large-scale and multi-faceted humanitarian assistance, the key features of complex emergencies not necessarily found in natural disasters include **massive displacement of people, hindrance or prevention of humanitarian assistance by political and military constraints and significant security risks for humanitarian relief workers in some areas** (Bureau for Crisis Prevention and Recovery, 2004). In the case of the Mindanao armed conflict, tens of thousands of people were displaced from their homes, and the armed conflict created a real and threatening security risk for humanitarian relief workers. The case highlights constraints for humanitarian assistance, which are commonly observed in the case of conflict, war and other crises occurring in **fragile states** (CCOUC, 2012).

KNOWLEDGE BOX 2.1   FRAGILE STATE: COMPLEX EMERGENCIES

There are many definitions of **fragile states**. It is defined by the UK Department for International Development (DFID) as a situation where "the government cannot or will not deliver core functions to the majority of its people, including the poor", where core functions include service entitlements, justice, and security (2005b, p. 7). A fragile state is highly susceptible to crisis in one or more governing systems. It is also highly vulnerable to internal and external shocks, as well as domestic and international conflicts. Because of this, fragile states are often characterised by a higher mortality rate and chronic need for international assistance.

The World Bank identifies fragile states by weak performance on the Country Policy and Institutional Assessment (CPIA), which share two characteristics: "State policies and institutions are weak in these countries: making them vulnerable in their capacity to deliver services to their citizens, to control corruption, or to provide for sufficient voice and accountability [; and] They face risks of conflict and political instability." (2005, p. 1)

In recent years, the World Bank employed an operational definition of "fragile situations" as "countries or territories with (i) a harmonised CPIA country rating of 3.2 or less, and/or (ii) the presence of a UN and/or peacekeeping or political/peace-building mission during the past three years." (Piffaretti, Ralston, & Shaikh, 2014, p.3)

The United States Agency for International Development (USAID) uses the term "fragile states" to cover a broad range of failing and recovering states, including non-conflict countries which are failing to ensure service entitlements to poor people. It further classifies fragile states as "**vulnerable states**" and "**states in crisis**". **Vulnerable states** are "those states unable or unwilling to adequately assure the provision of security and basic services to significant portions of their populations and where the legitimation of the government is in question." A **state in crisis** is one where "the central government does not exert significant control over its own territory or is unable or unwilling to assure the provision of vital services to significant parts of its territory where the legitimacy of the government is weak or non-existent, and where violent conflict is a reality or a great risk" (USAID, 2005, p. 1).

There are overlapping areas in the definition of fragile states by different organisations. A summary of these definitions are provided in Table 2.2. Afghanistan, with a weak central government after years of civil war, arguably fits all these definitions and the turmoil civilians suffered is illustrated in Figure 2.6. **Fragility** involves countries which are failing or at high risk of failing, and there are three dimensions that define the term failing: **authority failure, service failure**, and **legitimacy failure**.

- **Authority failure:** Failure due to a state lacking the authority to protect its citizens from interpersonal violence of various kinds.
- **Service failure:** Failure of the state to provide and ensure access to the basic services for all citizens, including delivery of health services, basic

TABLE 2.2 Comparison of some definitions of fragile states

Agency	Authority failure	Services failure	Legitimacy failure
United Kingdom Department for International Development (DFID)	Instrumental for service entitlements: "government cannot deliver core functions"	Prime emphasis: "service entitlements"	Emphasis on justice: "justice, and security"
United States Agency for International Development (USAID)	"does not exert significant control"	"provision of vital services"	"legitimacy . . . weak"
World Bank	Emphasis on high conflict risk: "They face risks of conflict and political instability."	Emphasis on institutional capacity: "State policies and institutions are weak."	Including voice and accountability: "to provide for sufficient voice and accountability."

Source: DFID (2005b), USAID (2005) and World Bank (2005).

FIGURE 2.6   Fragile state: Afghanistan – Kabul in April 2004

Source: Photo by Mark Knobil/mknobil / CC BY 2.0 (https://www.flickr.com/photos/ knobil/64544891/sizes/o/; https://creativecommons.org/ licenses/by/2.0/).

education, water and sanitation, basic transportation and energy infrastructure, and reduction in income poverty.
* **Legitimacy failure:** Identified as the state's lack of legitimacy, reflected by very minimum support from the people, typically undemocratic, media-controlling, absence of civil and political liberties and often characterised by the military ruling or dominating the government (Stewart & Brown, 2010).

Challenges in classification

Disaster classifications may suffer major shortfalls. Some common issues include the following: (1) Disaster types may not be easily categorised, as natural phenomena can initiate man-made technological disasters, and vice versa. (2) Chronic situations, such as famine or drought, are difficult to capture as disasters or complex emergencies due to their gradual onset and challenges in associating the human impact/suffering with the "natural" or "man-made" cause. The lack of evidence-based precautionary measures and understanding of them is the major "man-made factor" that "causes" the human suffering in every disaster (see Case Box 2.4).

CASE BOX 2.4   THE SIDOARJO MUDFLOW INCIDENT IN INDONESIA

By Levina Chandra Khoe and Emily Ying Yang Chan

Background

On 29 May 2006, a large hot mudflow erupted from the ground in Sidoarjo District, East Java Island, Indonesia. The volume of mudflow reached its peak at about 100,000 cubic metres per day during 2007 from the initial 180 cubic

FIGURE 2.7 Sidoarjo mudflow in Indonesia

Source: Photo by Hugh e82/CC BY-SA 3.0 *(https://en.wikipedia.org/wiki/Sidoarjo_mud_flow#/media/File:Mud_hole_opening.JPG; http://creativecommons.org/licenses/by-sa/3.0/).*

metres, and as of 2014, the flow volume stabilised at 15,000 cubic metres per day, seven years after the initial eruption. Geologists from around the world estimated that the mudflow could last for over 25 years. The mudflow has buried more than 600 hectares of land, displacing close to 40,000 people and submerging three sub-districts, 12 villages, over 10,000 buildings and 362 hectares of rice fields. Figure 2.7 shows the extent of the mud hole.

Is it natural or man-made?

The cause of the Sidoarjo mudflow was a controversy. In 2007, the Supreme Court of Indonesia ruled that the Indonesian oil and gas company Lapindo Brantas Inc. was not guilty, and that the mudflow disaster was the result of natural causes. The oil company blamed the incident on the magnitude 6.3 Yogyakarta earthquake that occurred two days before the initial mudflow eruption with the epicentre only 250 kilometres away. Geologists at the 2008 Conference of the American Association of Petroleum Geologists in Cape Town, South Africa, considered Lapindo Brantas to be responsible for triggering this rare incident because it ran high pressure drilling explorations in Sidoarjo without sufficient protective casing (Nurhayati, 2007, August 16; Satriastanti, 2008; Tampubolon, 2013, March 5).

Despite the pitfalls mentioned earlier, there is much value in classifying disasters. The objective of classification in the public health context usually includes facilitating policy and response planning to assist humanitarian action at both national and international levels, providing a rational basis for disaster preparedness decision-making and providing an objective basis for vulnerability assessment and priority setting (Below et al., 2009). In summary, classifying disasters by cause is imperfect but it serves to foster systematic understanding and recording of disaster events such that key stakeholders can thereby make informed decisions about humanitarian action and take appropriate disaster preparedness measures during non-disaster phases.

Emerging trends of disasters: risk and why?

Post-millennium, there are a general increasing number of disasters globally. From 1976 to 2005, Asia (with China, India and Indonesia being among the most populous countries in the world) was the most disaster-prone continent in terms of number of deaths and number of people affected: 62.5% of the global deaths and 89.7% of the victims of disasters were from Asia. It had twice as many earthquakes as other continents, and within the region, China experienced the three most lethal

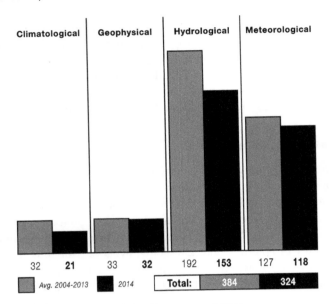

FIGURE 2.8 Natural disaster trends by disaster type (2014)

Source: Guha-Sapir, Hoyois, and Below (2015).

earthquakes of the twentieth century (the 1976 Tangshan earthquake, the 1920 Haiyuan earthquake and the 1927 Gulang earthquake).

Considering the number of natural disasters with reference to the economic development level, middle-income countries always faced the most natural disasters between 1961 and 2010 (Guha-Sapir & Hoyois, 2012). It was estimated that the cost burden of natural disasters during 1990–2000 constituted between 2% and 15% of an exposed country's annual GDP (DFID, 2005a). Among the various natural disasters, floods are the most common globally and they account for 43% of global natural disasters and affected nearly 2.5 billion people (55% of the total number affected) between 1994 and 2013 (CRED, 2015, 18–19). In 2014, hydrological disasters accounted for 58.7% of deaths and 30% of the total number of people affected by natural disasters, while flooding alone was responsible for 99% of the total number affected in this type of disaster in that year (Guha-Sapir, Hoyois, & Below, 2015, 22) (see also Knowledge Box 2.2).

In general, the rise in climate-related disasters was much higher than that of geophysical disasters during the past decades (see Figure 2.8). Climate-related disasters include floods, storms/cyclones, mass movements (wet), such as mudslides, and droughts. Such weather-related disasters represent over 80% of all disasters, over 70% of economic losses and over 20% of mortality between 2000 and 2010. As a trend in the coming decade, more people will be exposed to climate-related hazards. Out of 33 rising cities that will be inhabited by at least 8 million people in 2015, 21 are located in coastal areas, where coastal flooding is expected to increase due to a rise in the sea level. These disaster incidents have caused great loss and damage to health and social and economic conditions. In addition to climate change–induced meteorological disasters, civilians' health risk exposure to chemical, biological and radiological agents also increased (WHO, 2011a, 2011b, 2011c). Low-income countries are particularly vulnerable to disasters (see Case Box 2.5). For details of factors that contribute to emerging trends of disaster, refer to Chapter 7.

A well-managed disaster database could serve the following purposes: (1) assisting humanitarian actions at both national and international levels; (2) rationalising decision-making for disaster preparedness; and (3) providing an objective basis for vulnerability assessment and priority setting (Guha-Sapir, Below, & Hoyois, n.d.).

KNOWLEDGE BOX 2.2   MEGA-DISASTERS

Mega-disasters pose a great threat to the overall structure and functioning of society. Although mega-disasters exhibit a spectrum of different characteristics, the impact intensity is comparable across these mega-disasters. Recent cases of mega-disasters include the tsunami in Japan (2011), the Wenchuan earthquake in China (2008) and the cyclone in Myanmar (2013).

One of the major obstacles to mitigating the impact of mega-disasters is the failure to apprehend disaster risk. Hence, multi-sectoral involvement across different levels is required. A preparedness culture must be cultivated and all the vulnerable should be engaged. One successful case is the Kamaishi Miracle during the 2011 tsunami in Japan. The regular evacuation drill and other disaster preparedness education minimised child mortality after the tsunami. It perfectly exemplifies the sustained effort to instil a culture of preparedness with continuous training and community education.

Another challenge is to ensure there is coherence in the implementation of local disaster risk reduction and international disaster risk reduction. The applications of scientific knowledge and improvement in disaster risk reduction legislation and policies are crucial for success. Taking one example from the 2011 tsunami in Japan: since the system was able to capture an early sign of ground movement, all the Shinkansen high-speed trains managed to stop safely without any casualties. This case clearly illustrates the effectiveness of the dissemination and application of technology in disaster risk reduction.

Sources: UNISDR (2014, 2015a, 2015b), World Bank Global Facility for Disaster Reduction and Recovery (GFDRR) (2014, 2015).

CASE BOX 2.5   WHAT MAKES LOW-INCOME COUNTRIES PARTICULARLY VULNERABLE TO DISASTERS?

As highlighted earlier, low-income countries will face the highest burden of hazards and disasters in the 21st century. The following discusses the main reasons for such vulnerabilities.

Frequency of disasters

Globally, the number of natural disasters is increasing and developing countries are usually disproportionately affected. Furthermore, many developing countries are subject to seasonal events such as floods, droughts and tropical storms. With the increasing frequency of meteorological disasters due to climate change, the patterns of large-scale emergency events will leave a smaller window of opportunity between events to prepare for disasters. As a result, the resilience of communities can decrease.

Baseline health and livelihood status of the population

Developing countries are usually afflicted by widespread factors that generate a poor baseline health status of the population even during times of non-disaster. Some of the leading factors linked to poor health in these countries include physical factors (inadequate sanitation, water, waste disposal and housing) and behavioural factors (sexual behaviour, alcohol abuse and smoking). People in poverty are further exposed to vulnerabilities due to a lack of access to health services, safe environments, proper education and information. As a result of these factors and the vulnerabilities they create, developing countries are disproportionally affected by the health and economic losses brought about by disasters.

Demographic and epidemiological transitions

In simple terms, the theory of demographic transition states that societies that experience modernisation progress from a pre-modern regime of high fertility and high mortality to a post-modern one in which both are low. An increase in life expectancy and the ageing of populations may also lead to an epidemiological transition that is shifting the disease profile from communicable diseases to non-communicable diseases (NCDs) in many countries. For many low-income countries, this presents a double burden of disease which poses a major public health challenge during disasters. Specifically, in this transition process, there is a period when a country is still being burdened with communicable diseases, while non-communicable, chronic conditions begin to spread. The Sphere standards highlight the need to address the exacerbation of chronic health conditions during disasters. However, due to limited resources, many aid agencies overlook this issue and consider it as secondary to more acute problems. As a result, people do not have access to therapies and medicines that may reduce morbidity and mortality caused by complications of their chronic conditions.

The non-communicable disease burden in developing countries

Globally, over 60% of all deaths in 2005 were caused by chronic NCDs such as hypertension and diabetes mellitus. Although these chronic NCDs constituted the most significant disease burden in developed countries, more than 80% of the NCD-related deaths occurred in low-income and middle-income countries. With ageing populations and the increasing behavioural health risk factors associated with rapid urbanisation and lifestyle modernisation in many developing countries, the mortality and disease burden in developing countries will continue to shift from communicable disease–based to predominantly NCD-related in the coming decades.

Health systems

Health systems govern health care accessibility and availability. Well-built health care systems can better absorb the impact of disasters and respond more efficiently and the robustness of a health care system will demonstrate resilience in stress/crisis such as natural disasters. Disaster preparedness plans for the health system should include supportive policies, allocated resources, risk analysis and contingency plans. Physical measures such as the reinforcement of health infrastructure and the construction of safer facilities can mitigate the damage during a disaster to ensure that basic services will continue when they are needed most. Unfortunately, in developing contexts, limited resources, inequitable health care the low provision of public health programmes and the low-quality health infrastructure have hampered preparedness.

In addition, the availability of technology and equipment may affect the efficiency and effectiveness of disaster response. For example, post-disaster data collection may need to rely on quick, on-site surveys and surveillance tools. Importantly, data should be collected on both acute and immediate life-saving needs, as well as chronic medical conditions. Historically, information on chronic diseases is not identified as essential data to be collected during needs assessments. This practice essentially rules out resource allocation for chronic disease management service provision.

Health improvement and health promotion

Developing countries often fare poorly in their health promotion and improvement programmes as usually more immediate health needs are prioritised due to resource limitations. Most disaster risk reduction and community resilience building in these countries are usually fragmented.

What is "risk"?

Risk is the likelihood, or probability, of an event that may result in an adverse outcome. It is a function of the interactions between hazard, exposure and vulnerability (*risk factors*) and the manageability (*coping capacity*) of the affected individual or community. In the context of disaster, **risk** is defined as *"expected losses (of lives, persons injured, property damaged, and economic activity disrupted) due to a particular hazard for a given area and reference period"* (CRED, 2009). People who are *made **vulnerable*** from exposure to intense and frequent natural hazards are at higher risk. To reduce such risk, their coping and recovery capacity (also called "manageability" in the formula) from being exposed to the hazard should be increased.

The risk and impact of disaster at the individual and community levels must also be explored and assessed in order to guide effective disaster prevention and response protocol development. Various dimensions of risk and impact include: **what** (i.e. type and severity of consequences), **who** (i.e. socio-demographic characteristics of the people affected) and **when** (i.e. time and frequency of impact).

A well-managed disaster database could serve the following purposes: (1) assisting humanitarian actions at both national and international levels; (2) rationalising decision-making for disaster preparedness; and (3) providing an objective basis for vulnerability assessment and priority setting (Guha-Sapir, Below, & Hoyois, n.d.).

Disaster risk formula

The risk formula is a concept that helps us understand the risk of a disaster's impact. The risk formula shows the relationships between five components – namely: **risk, hazard**, **exposure**, **vulnerability** and **manageability**.

In the equation (Figure 2.9), risk is the product of four factors: hazard, exposure, vulnerability and manageability. Risk exists only if there is vulnerability and exposure to a hazard, and only if their product is greater than the manageability. Thus, the same triggering event that results in a disaster in one community may not become a disaster in another. The risk may be different depending on the factors in the equation and how they evolve within a community. This equation is important as it helps justify the need for disaster preparedness programmes and education.

Hazard is a dangerous phenomenon, substance, human activity or condition that may cause loss of life, injury or other health impacts, property damage, loss of livelihoods and services, social and economic disruption or environmental damage. **Exposure** describes people, property, systems or other elements present in hazard zones that are thereby subject to potential losses. **Vulnerability** is determined by

$$Risk = Hazard \times Exposure \times \frac{Vulnerability}{Manageability}$$

FIGURE 2.9 Risk formula

Source: Adapted from Rand (2008).

the characteristics and circumstances of a community, system or asset that make it susceptible to the damaging effects of a hazard. In the foregoing equation it refers to the degree of loss (from 0% to 100%) resulting from a potentially damaging phenomenon. **Manageability** refers to the organisational response to the hazard and the ability of the population to respond to it. **Risk** is the possibility of damage, loss, injury, death or other negative consequences as a result of the foregoing components (see Case Box 2.6).

This formula can be illustrated by the following example. Both the residents of concrete apartments and the residents of makeshift shelters in an earthquake-prone region are equally exposed to the natural hazard of tectonic movements. However, they are not at equal risk of suffering losses from an earthquake event because concrete buildings, if built according to stringent building codes, can absorb the shock of an earthquake without collapsing, allowing their inhabitants to survive. On the other hand, the makeshift shelters built of clay and tin may not survive an earthquake, causing injuries and loss of properties in an earthquake. In this case, *the type of shelter* and the building material of people's dwelling place are key *risk factors* that make people living in apartment buildings more *resilient* and slum dwellers more *vulnerable* to the *risk* of earthquake. In other words, the *potential impact* of an earthquake event on apartment dwellers is *different* from that on slum dwellers.

CASE BOX 2.6   GLACIAL LAKE OUTBURST FLOODS IN BHUTAN

By Rinzin Jamtsho

Background

The landlocked Kingdom of Bhutan is situated near the two Asia superpowers, China and India. Bhutan, which is still developing, nevertheless possesses a dynamic nature that makes itself felt in a variety of ways, ranging from its adoption in the 1970s of its own measure of prosperity, Gross National Happiness (GNH), to the unique type of natural disaster it is facing, glacial lake outburst flood (GLOF). A glimpse of Bhutan's landscape can be found in Figure 2.10.

GLOF is defined as a "flooding due to the outburst of a glacier lake". A glacier lake outburst flood occurs when a lake – dammed by a glacier or a terminal moraine – fails. The outburst can be triggered by erosion, a critical water pressure, a mass movement, an earthquake or cryoseism. A **jökulhlaup** is a special type of glacier lake outburst flood related to the outburst of an ice-dammed lake during a volcanic eruption (CRED, 2009). There are a total of 2,674 glacial lakes in Bhutan, of which 562 are associated with glaciers serving as a dam or primary water source at higher altitudes. Due to the effect of climate change, glaciers in the Himalayas are shrinking rapidly and the volume

FIGURE 2.10 Landscape of Bhutan

Source: Photo by CCOUC. All rights reserved.

of water carried by these lakes is increasing at a threatening rate. When the volume of water in the lake exceeds the holding capacity of the dam, whether it is overflowing or breaking down the dam altogether, GLOF occurs. The kingdom's Department of Geology and Mines has identified 24 glacial lakes as "potentially dangerous lakes" that could pose a GLOF threat to the livelihood of people living downstream in the river basins.

Vulnerability: The lack of construction regulations render physical infrastructures in both private and public domains susceptible to hazard. The lack of settlement regulation that prevents people from residing in hazard-prone districts and the dependency of people on agriculture and forestry products mean more and more people are becoming exposed. The destabilisation of slopes, primarily due to human activities, makes landslides or mudslides an additional hazard in a GLOF. The geographical location of Bhutan within the seismic zone means the chance of earthquake compounds the risk of the hazard. The lack of medical facilities and inaccessibility to communication networks and transportation systems further render the population vulnerable.

Hazard: The volume of water in glacial lakes is expanding quickly and some have been identified as "potentially dangerous lakes" which are at risk of releasing water.

Exposure: There are communities living downstream in the river basins of the lakes, as well as agriculture, industrial and other economic activities that take place along the way.

Manageability: The setting up of a designated Disaster Mitigation, Prevention and Preparedness Budget by the Royal Government of Bhutan, the establishment of a warning system with regular testing, and the education and training of officials, intervention teams and multidisciplinary teams across public and private sectors all build up the manageability against disasters.

Risk: GLOF took place in Bhutan in 1957, 1960 and most recently in 1994. The 1994 GLOF event damaged more than 1,700 acres of agricultural land and a dozen houses and washed away five water mills and 16 yaks. A total of 16 tonnes of foodgrain were destroyed by the incident (Royal Government of Bhutan Ministry of Home and Cultural Affairs, Department of Local Governance, Disaster Management Division, 2006; Royal Government of Bhutan National Environment Commission, 2006).

Disaster Risk Index (DRI)

Disaster Risk Index (DRI) is a calculation of the average risk of death per country in large- and medium-scale disasters associated with earthquakes, tropical cyclones, droughts and floods, based on data from 1980 to 2000. The components included in the DRI are hazard, physical exposure and vulnerability (United Nations Development Programme [UNDP], 2004). Physical exposure is the number of people in a country (in absolute terms) or the frequency of a hazard event per million people (in relative terms). Vulnerability refers to various social, economic, cultural, political and physical variables that make people more or less able to recover from the hazard event. In DRI, "risk" exclusively refers to the risk of death in disaster, and does not include the risk of damage to livelihoods and the economy, due to the limited data available from all countries. As emphasised in its definition, DRI measures only the medium- and large-scale disasters, defined as at least ten deaths, 100 affected people and/or a call for international assistance.

A sample of how the Disaster Risk Indices worldwide may be illustrated is shown in Figure 2.11. According to the DRI, Southeast and Southwest Asia face the highest and experience the most consistent disaster risk across regions, followed by Africa and Latin America. Northern America, Europe and Eastern Europe face the lowest risk.

In summary, a natural hazard will not become a disaster unless people are vulnerable and exposed to it. The degree of impact depends on people's vulnerability – that is the extent to which a community, structure, service or geographic area is likely to be damaged or disrupted by the impact of a particular hazard. This impact can also be mitigated by the manageability, or **coping capacity**, of the population, which often refers to the organisational response to the hazard and the ability of the population to respond. The foregoing equation indicates that in order to reduce risk, hazard, exposure and vulnerability must be reduced while manageability must be increased.

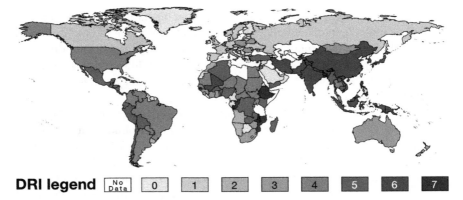

DRI legend [No Data] [0] [1] [2] [3] [4] [5] [6] [7]

FIGURE 2.11 Disaster Risk Index (DRI)

Source: Adapted from Peduzzi, Dao, Herold, and Mouton (2009).

KNOWLEDGE BOX 2.3 WORLD ATLAS OF NATURAL DISASTER RISK

Peijing Shi, co-chairman of the international disaster research group Integrated Risk Governance (IRG) Project, proposes the framework of Regional Disaster System Theory, which emphasises the spatial-temporal pattern of worldwide natural disasters. Employing this framework, his team published the work "World atlas of natural disaster risk" in 2015 to facilitate visualising the spatial pattern of natural disaster risks as associated with natural environment, exposure and disaster loss. The work covers earthquake, volcanic eruption, flood, storm surge, sand-dust storm, tropical cyclone, heatwave, cold wave and wild fire. This atlas assesses global natural disaster risks by taking into account factors like natural environment stability, hazard intensity and probability, the vulnerability of the exposure, concurrent coping capacity of reducing hazard severity and vulnerability, socioeconomic development level and global data incompleteness. It aims to support such disaster risk management endeavours like national and regional integrated disaster risk reduction planning, integrated risk governance strategic planning and sustainable development planning.

Source: Shi et al. (2015)

Risk and impact

Since the "impact" of previous disasters is observed and analysed to estimate "risk", the use of these terms can be confusing. In this book, "**risk**" refers to the *potential impact* of a disaster faced by humans; it involves a level of uncertainty about the occurrences of events in the future. "**Impact**" refers to the *actual damage or harm* as a result of a disaster (UNISDR, 2009) (see Case Box 2.7).

The economic and human impacts of disasters are illustrated in Figure 2.12, expressed in monetary loss (in US$) as well as the number of people affected and killed by disasters in the decade from 2005 to 2014 under the Hyogo Framework of Action, an international document on disaster risk reduction. These are the handful of common indicators for expressing the impact of disasters. They are useful for drawing comparisons and gross analysis at the macro level across countries, disaster types and population groups. But these indicators are not necessarily the most useful in guiding disaster response at the local level (see also Knowledge Box 2.3).

Emergency threshold

The concept of **emergency threshold** may be used to indicate if an accident or crisis may have reached a critical point that requires emergency response. Death rate or *mortality rate* is a typical measure to serve as such an indicator. Two types of mortality rates are most commonly used as the criteria for the emergency threshold:

- **Crude mortality rate (CMR)**: the mortality rate among people of all age groups due to all causes; and
- **Under-5 mortality rate (U5MR)**: the mortality rate of live born babies before reaching age five per 1,000 live births.

How big an increase does the mortality rate have to show to constitute an "emergency"?

In a non-disaster situation, the *crude mortality rate* (CMR) of every country is assumed to be 0.5/per 10,000 people per day, while the *under-5 mortality rate* (U5MR) is assumed to be 1/per 10,000 people per day. Toole and Waldman (1990) suggested the *doubling* of CMR, from 0.5 to 1/per 10,000 per day, or the doubling of U5MR from 1.0 to 2.0/per 10,000 people per day, as the emergency threshold. If the situation causes either one of the mortality rates to go beyond this threshold, it is declared as a "state of emergency", and certain international and humanitarian aid or relief mechanisms should be activated. Likewise, the emergency status is removed when either of the mortality rates falls below this threshold. Figure 2.13 shows the emergency threshold as doubling the baseline crude mortality (see also Knowledge Box 2.4).

Controversies over the "emergency threshold"

Although policy makers and responders generally agree to the idea that establishing an emergency threshold can facilitate a warning response, the major controversies are over how an emergency threshold should be calculated. Table 2.3 summarises the mortality thresholds commonly used to define emergency situations. Due to different demographic compositions, socio-economic development stages, epidemiological patterns and underlying health risks, the crude mortality rate (CMR) during non-disaster situations differs among countries. The regular CMR in certain countries during a non-disaster phase might have already exceeded the emergency threshold of other countries. For example, Darfur's non-disaster CMR of 1.1 per 10,000 people per day in 2003 (Guha-Sapir & Degomme, 2005) is already far beyond the

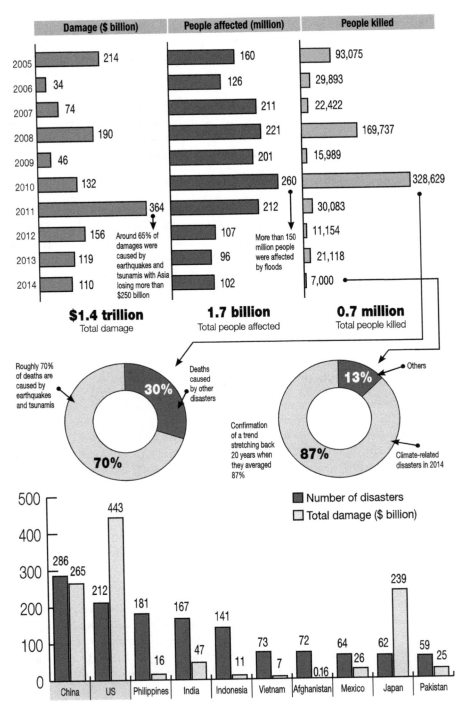

FIGURE 2.12 The economic and human impact of disasters 2005–2014

Source: Guha-Sapir et al. (2009).

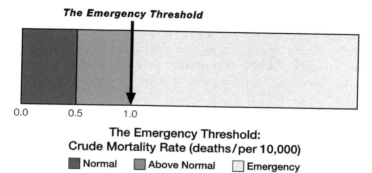

FIGURE 2.13 Emergency threshold

TABLE 2.3 Mortality thresholds commonly used to define emergency situations

Agency	Assumed baseline (per 10,000 per day)	Emergency threshold (per 10,000 per day)
Centers for Disease Control and Prevention, Médecins Sans Frontières Epicentre, Academia	Fixed at: CMR: 0.5 U5MR: 1	Emergency if: CMR: 1 or U5MR: 2
United Nations High Commissioner for Refugees (UNHCR)	Fixed at: CMR: 0.5 U5MR: 1	CMR > 1: "very serious" CMR > 2: "out of control" CMR > 5: "major catastrophe" (double for U5MR threshold)
The Sphere Project	Context-specific CMR/U5MR: Sub-Saharan Africa: 0.44/1.14 Latin America: 0.16/0.19 South Asia: 0.25/0.59 Eastern Europe, Former Soviet Union: 0.30/0.20 Note: If baseline is not known, the Sphere goal is CMR < 1.	Emergency if CMR/U5MR: Sub-Saharan Africa: 0.9/2.3 Latin America: 0.3/0.4 South Asia: 0.5/1.2 Eastern Europe, Former Soviet Union: 0.6/0.4

Source: Adapted from Checchi and Roberts (2005).

emergency threshold of countries such as Norway or Denmark. In response, some policy makers propose the adaptation of different thresholds according to different categorisations (income groups, regional foci, development stages). For example, categorised by region, CMRs in sub-Saharan Africa, Latin America, South Asia and Eastern Europe are different from each other, so their emergency thresholds would be different. However, this approach implies the ethically doubtful proposition that *what may be a disaster in some countries would be considered "normal" in others.* This might pose the ethical problem of valuing life and survival according to region.

In summary, major international organisations use **the emergency threshold** to determine whether a country is in an emergency situation. While the threshold may be set differently by different organisations, if an excessive increase in **crude mortality rate** and/or **under-5 mortality rate** is observed, it generally implies that a country/situation is in a state of emergency.

KNOWLEDGE BOX 2.4   WHAT CAN BE OTHER MEASURES FOR EMERGENCY THRESHOLD?

When trying to determine if a population is experiencing a public health emergency, the comparison of **mortality rate** of a population in crisis during the time of concern with their normal **baseline average mortality rate** (i.e. death rate of the population in the absence of the crisis) is often used. Comparatively, morbidity is a more complex and dynamic health outcome to track and measure. The following pyramid (Figure 2.14) illustrates the various health outcomes as experienced by a population. It suggests that a spectrum of health impacts exist, from more people experiencing milder forms of health impact, such as discomfort or non-specific symptoms, to those suffering from more severe forms of health impact that require more advanced interventions. This theoretical framework has significant implications for measuring the health impact of a disaster and the provision of care in post-disaster settings.

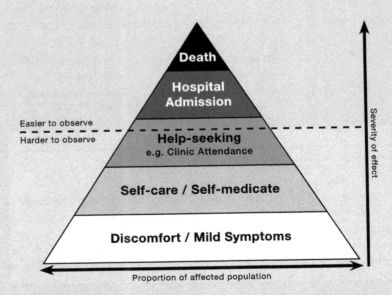

FIGURE 2.14   Measuring health impact

CASE BOX 2.7 THE HORROR OF THE GREAT KANTŌ EARTHQUAKE 1923 (PART 1): SECONDARY DISASTERS

On 1 September 1923, an earthquake of 7.9 magnitude struck the Kantō region. Seven prefectures were badly damaged by the quake: Tokyo, Kanagawa, Saitama, Chiba, Shizuoka, Yamanashi, and Ibaraki. The earthquake was followed by horrible fires that burned down many houses and buildings. In Tokyo and Yokohama, there were close to 300 major fires. Fires as secondary disasters occurred because people were preparing meals at the time of earthquake and many houses were made of wood. The death toll reached almost 140,000 people. Further discussion of this historical earthquake can be found in Chapter 5.

Conclusion

In a multidisciplinary subject like disaster and humanitarian assistance, proper classification of disasters may mitigate disaster risks and improve human well-being. Informed decisions could be made to identify priorities and reduce the health impact of disasters. In the context of disaster, risk is the likelihood or probability of an adverse outcome. Disaster risk is projected based on the impact of previous disasters, which is often associated with the demographic make-up and development status of a given country. The impact of a disaster is commonly reported as monetary loss, as well as the number of people affected, or killed, while an alternative is to measure it in relative terms. Globally, increasing number of disasters may be attributable to environmental degradation, climate change, poverty and rapid urbanisation. Asia and middle-income countries are among those most frequently struck by natural disasters and experience the highest burden of deaths as a result. The concept of risks, disaster risk indices, emergency thresholds are all important tools to support disaster preparedness and response. Hazard, exposure, vulnerability and manageability are four core components which help conceptualise human risk when a disaster is experienced. The risk formula helps policy makers, responders and researchers understand and take evidence-based and informed action to mitigate the impact of disasters.

References

Alexander, D. E. (2007). Misconception as a barrier to teaching about disasters. *Prehospital Disaster Medicine, 22*, 95–103.

Below, R., Wirtz, A., & Guha-Sapir, D. (2009). *Disaster category classification and peril terminology for operational purposes* (Working Paper No. 264). Brussels, Belgium: Centre for Research on the Epidemiology of Disasters (CRED); Germany: Munich Reinsurance (Munich RE). Retrieved from http://cred.be/sites/default/files/DisCatClass_264.pdf

Bennett, B., Repacholi, M., & Carr, Z. (2006). *Health effects of the Chernobyl accident and special health care programmes* (Report of the UN Chernobyl Forum Expert Group "Health"). Switzerland, Geneva: World Health Organization.

Centre for Research on the Epidemiology of Disasters (CRED), Université catholique de Louvain. (2009). *The EM-DAT glossary* [Internet]. Retrieved from EM-DAT The International Disaster Database of CRED website: http://www.emdat.be/glossary/9

Centre for Research on the Epidemiology of Disasters (CRED), Université catholique de Louvain. (2015). *The human cost of natural disasters 2015: A global perspective.* Brussels, Belgium: Author.

Chan, E.Y.Y., Hung, K.K.C., & Cai, Y. (2011). An epidemiological study of technological disasters in China: 1979–2005. *European Journal of Emergency Medicine, 18*(4), 234–237.

Chan, E.Y.Y., & Lee, P. Y. (2012). *CCOUC disaster technical case report series: Human health impact of Mindanao conflict in the Philippines since the 1970s.* Hong Kong, China: Collaborating Centre for Oxford University and CUHK for Disaster and Medical Humanitarian Response (CCOUC).

Chan, E.Y.Y., Wang, Z., Mark, C.K.M., and Liu, S. D. (2015). Industrial accidents in China: Risk reduction and response. *The Lancet, 386*(10002), 1421–1422.

Checchi, F., & Roberts, L. (2005). *Interpreting and using mortality data in humanitarian emergencies: A primer for non-epidemiologists.* (Network Paper No. 52) [Internet]. Retrieved from Humanitarian Practice Network at Overseas Development Institute website: http://odihpn.org/wp-content/uploads/2005/09/networkpaper052.pdf

Department for International Development (DFID). (2005a). *Natural disaster and disaster risk reduction measures: A desk review of costs and benefits* [Internet]. Retrieved from http://www.unisdr.org/files/1071_disasterriskreductionstudy.pdf

Department for International Development (DFID). (2005b). *Why we need to work more effectively in fragile states* [Internet]. Retrieved from https://www.jica.go.jp/cdstudy/library/pdf/20071101_11.pdf

Feng, C., & Wang, Y. (2008). Review of accidents and disasters in China in the year 2007. *Journal of Safety and Environment, 8*, 160–168.

Gray, P. (2002). *The human consequences of the Chernobyl nuclear accident: A strategy for recovery* [Internet]. United Nations Development Programme (UNDP) & United Nations Children's Fund (UNICEF). Retrieved from UNICEF website: http://www.unicef.org/newsline/chernobylreport.pdf

Guha-Sapir, D., Below, R., & Hoyois, P. (n.d.). *EM-DAT: The CRED/OFDA international disaster database* [Internet]. Brussels, Belgium: Centre for Research on the Epidemiology of Disasters (CRED), Université Catholique de Louvain. Retrieved from www.emdat.be

Guha-Sapir, D., & Degomme, O. (with Phelan, M.). (2005). *Darfur: Counting the deaths.* Retrieved from http://www.cred.be/sites/default/files/DarfurCountingtheDeaths.pdf

Guha-Sapir, D., & Hoyois, P. (2012). *Measuring the human and economic impact of disasters.* London, UK: Government Office of Science.

Guha-Sapir, D., Hoyois, P., & Below, R. (2015). *Annual disaster statistical review 2014: The numbers and trends.* Brussels, Belgium: CRED.

Nurhayati, D. (2007, August 16). Sidoarjo mudflow can be terminated: Petroleum expert. *The Jakarta Post* [Internet]. Retrieved from http://www.thejakartapost.com/news/2007/08/16/sidoarjo-mudflow-can-be-terminated-petroleum-expert.html

Office for the Coordination of Humanitarian Affairs (OCHA). (2003). *Glossary of humanitarian terms in relation to protection of civilians in armed conflict.* New York, NY: United Nations. Retrieved from https://www.humanitarianresponse.info/en/system/files/documents/files/ocha%20glossary.pdf

Pan American Health Organization (PAHO). (1982). *Epidemiological surveillance after natural disaster* (Scientific Publication 420). Washington, DC: Author.

Peduzzi, P., Dao, H., Herold, C., & Mouton, F. (2009). Assessing global exposure and vulnerability towards natural hazards: The Disaster Risk Index. *Natural Hazards and Earth System Sciences, 9*, 1149–1159.

People's Republic of China (PRC) Public Health Emergency Command Center, National Health and Family Planning Commission (NHFPC). (2015, August 15). *The fifth batch of medical experts from NHFPC arrives in Tianjin to continue the medical response for the 8.12*

Tianjin Port blast (in Chinese) [Internet]. Retrieved from the NHFPC website: http://www.nhfpc.gov.cn/yjb/s3586/201508/59c08dda337b414ea4e0c56e6698acd7.shtml

People's Republic of China (PRC) State Administration of Coal Mine Safety, State Administration of Work Safety. (2013). *Safety analysis* (in Chinese) [Internet]. Retrieved from http://www.chinasafety.gov.cn/anquanfenxi/anquanfenxi.htm

People's Republic of China (PRC) State Council. (2015, August 14). *The first official announcement on the emergency response of Tianjin incident* (in Chinese) [Internet]. Retrieved from http://www.gov.cn/xinwen/2015–08/14/content_2912733.htm

People's Republic of China (PRC) State Council. (2015, August 20). *Official announcement on types and quantity of chemical: 40 types with a quantity of 2,500 tons* (in Chinese) [Internet]. Retrieved from http://www.gov.cn/xinwen/2015–08/20/content_2915939.htm

People's Republic of China (PRC) State Council. (2015, August 31). *Tianjin blast death toll rises to 158* (in Chinese) [Internet]. Retrieved from http://www.gov.cn/xinwen/2015–08/31/content_2922569.htm

Piffaretti, N., Ralston, L., & Shaikh, K. (2014). *Information note: The World Bank's harmonized list of fragile situations* (World Bank Working Paper No. 89275) [Internet]. Retrieved from http://documents.worldbank.org/curated/en/692741468338471327/Information-note-the-World-Banks-harmonized-list-of-fragile-situations

Rand, E. C., (Ed.). (2008). *The Johns Hopkins and International Federation of Red Cross and Red Crescent Societies public health guide for emergencies* (2nd ed.). Geneva, Switzerland: Johns Hopkins Bloomberg School of Public Health and the International Federation of Red Cross and Red Crescent Societies.

Royal Government of Bhutan Ministry of Home and Cultural Affairs, Department of Local Governance, Disaster Management Division. (2006). *National disaster risk management framework: Reducing disaster risks for a safe and happy Bhutan* [Internet]. Retrieved from http://www.drrgateway.net/sites/default/files/bhutan_frameworK.pdf

Royal Government of Bhutan National Environment Commission. (2006). *Bhutan national adaptation programme of action* [Internet]. Retrieved from http://unfccc.int/resource/docs/napa/btn01.pdf

Satriastanti, F. E. (2008). Experts: Lapindo caused 2006 mudflow. *Jakarta Globe* [Internet]. Retrieved from http://jakartaglobe.beritasatu.com/archive/experts-lapindo-caused-2006-mudflow/

Shi, P., Wang, J., Xu, W., Ye, T., Yang, S., Liu, L. . .. Wang, M. (2015). World atlas of natural disaster risk: Understanding the spatial patterns of global natural disaster risk. In P. Shi & R. Kasperson (Eds.), *World atlas of natural disaster risk*. Heidelberg; New York; Dordrecht; London: Springer-Verlag Berlin Heidelberg and Beijing Normal University Press.

The Sphere Project. (2011). *Humanitarian charter and minimum standards in humanitarian response* (3rd ed.). Retrieved from http://www.spherehandbook.org/en/the-humanitarian-charter/

Stewart, F., & Brown, G. (2010). *An operational definition of 'fragile states'* (In Brief Issue No. 5) [Internet]. Oxford, England: Centre for Research on Inequality, Human Security and Ethnicity (CRISE), University of Oxford. Retrieved from http://r4d.dfid.gov.uk/PDF/Outputs/Inequality/CRISE-InBrief-05.pdf

Tampubolon, H. D. (2013, March 5). Mudflow erupting after 7 years. *The Jakarta Post* [Internet], p. 10. Retrieved from http://www.thejakartapost.com/news/2013/03/05/mudflow-erupting-after-7-years.html

Toole, M. J., & Waldman, R. J. (1990). Prevention of excess mortality in refugee and displaced populations in developing countries. *The Journal of the American Medical Association, 263*(24), 3296–3302. doi:10.1001/jama.263.24.3296

United Nations Development Programme (UNDP), Bureau for Crisis Prevention and Recovery. (2004). *A global report: Reducing disaster risk – A challenge for development*. New York: Author.

United Nations Office for the Coordination of Humanitarian Affairs (OCHA). (2012). *Humanitarian action plan for Philippines (Mindanao)*. New York, NY: Author.

United Nations Office for Disaster Risk Reduction (UNISDR). (2009). *2009 UNISDR terminology on disaster risk reduction* [Internet]. Geneva, Switzerland: Author. Retrieved from http://www.unisdr.org/files/7817_UNISDRTerminologyEnglish.pdf

United Nations Office for Disaster Risk Reduction (UNISDR). (2014). *Ten years on: The Indian Ocean Tsunami – From learning to action: Message from Khao Lak to Sendai* [Internet]. Khao Lak, Thailand: Author. Retrieved from http://www.wcdrr.org/wcdrr-data/uploads/870/The%20Indian%20Ocean%20Tsunami%2010%20Years%20On%20-%20%20Message%20from%20Khaolak%20to%20Sendai.pdf

United Nations Office for Disaster Risk Reduction (UNISDR). (2015a). *Lessons from megadisasters: Brief and concept note* [Internet]. Sendai, Japan: Author. Retrieved from http://www.wcdrr.org/wcdrr-data/uploads/870/Brief%20and%20Concept%20Note%20-%20Lessons%20from%20Mega%20Disasters.pdf

United Nations Office for Disaster Risk Reduction (UNISDR). (2015b). *Lessons from megadisasters: Summary report* [Internet]. Sendai, Japan: Author. Retrieved from http://www.wcdrr.org/wcdrr-data/uploads/870/Working%20Session%20Report%20-%20Lessons%20from%20Mega-Disasters.Final.pdf

United States Agency for International Development (USAID). (2005). *Fragile states strategy.* Washington, DC: Author.

United States Federal Emergency Management Agency (FEMA). (2008). *Producing emergency plans: A guide for all-hazard emergency operations planning for state, territorial, local, and tribal governments* (Interim Version 1.0) [Internet]. Retrieved from http://www.training.fema.gov/hiedu/docs/cgo/week%203%20-%20producing%20emergency%20plans.pdf

Wisner, B., & Adams, J. (Eds.). (2002). *Environmental health in emergencies and disasters: A practical guide.* Geneva, Switzerland: World Health Organization.

World Bank. (2005). *Fragile states – Good practice in country assistance strategies* [Internet]. Board Report 34790, 19 December. Retrieved from http://siteresources.worldbank.org/INTLICUS/Resources/388758–1094226297907/FS_Good_Practice_in_CAS.pdf

World Bank Global Facility for Disaster Reduction and Recovery (GFDRR). (2014). *Haiti earthquake 2010: Recovery from a mega disaster* (Recovery Framework Case Study) [Internet]. Retrieved from http://www.wcdrr.org/wcdrr-data/uploads/870/Haiti%20Earthquake%202010%20-%20Recovery%20from%20a%20mega%20disaster.pdf

World Bank Global Facility for Disaster Reduction and Recovery (GFDRR). (2015). *The Great East Japan earthquake: Learning from megadisasters* [Internet]. Retrieved from http://www.wcdrr.org/wcdrr-data/uploads/870/Learning%20from%20Megadisasters.pdf

World Health Organization, Emergency and Humanitarian Action (WHO/EHA). (2002). *Disasters & emergencies: Definitions* (Training Package) [Internet]. Addis Ababa, Ethiopia: Panafrican Emergency Training Centre, WHO/EHA. Retrieved from http://apps.who.int/disasters/repo/7656.pdf

World Health Organization (WHO), United Kingdom Health Protection Agency (HPA), & partners. (2011a). *Chemical safety* (Disaster Risk Management for Health Fact Sheets) [Internet]. Retrieved from http://www.who.int/hac/events/drm_fact_sheet_chemical_safety.pdf

World Health Organization (WHO), United Kingdom Health Protection Agency (HPA), & partners. (2011b). *Mass fatalities/dead bodies* (Disaster Risk Management for Health Fact Sheets) [Internet]. Retrieved from http://www.who.int/hac/events/drm_fact_sheet_mass_fatalities.pdf

World Health Organization (WHO), United Kingdom Health Protection Agency (HPA), & partners. (2011c). *Radiation emergencies* (Disaster Risk Management for Health Fact Sheets) [Internet]. Retrieved from http://www.who.int/hac/events/drm_fact_sheet_radiation_emergencies.pdf

3

GENERAL PUBLIC HEALTH IMPACTS OF NATURAL DISASTERS

Unlike clinical medicine, where physicians and allied health professionals focus on treating diseases and managing the health of individuals, **public health** professionals focus on managing the *health and well-being of populations*. This chapter discusses the general public health implications of natural disasters.

After most natural disasters, there are five general public health consequences that might affect the community. Disasters may (1) overwhelm local response capacity with unexpected mortality and morbidity, (2) destroy health infrastructure and disrupt the provision of services, (3) bring adverse effects on the environment and population, (4) affect psychological and social behaviour, and (5) result in undesirable long-term consequences to the affected community.

Overwhelming of local response capacity with unexpected mortality and morbidity

Unexpected mortality and morbidity often overwhelm the local emergency and relief response system. Excess negative health impacts may be caused by either direct or indirect result of the crisis. *Mortality refers to a measure of deaths in a given population, location or other measures of interest; **crude mortality rate** and **under-5 mortality rate** are two common mortality indicators in use. **Morbidity** is a measure of disease incidence or prevalence in a given population; it refers to physical or psychological states resulting from disease, illness, injury or sickness.* Morbidity may present in different ways, but the number of people with a specific disease and the duration of illnesses are common measures of morbidity. In disasters, factors affecting these health outcomes might include the magnitude and causes of unexpected mortality and morbidity, which vary according to the type of disaster as well as the demographic and epidemiologic profile of the population.

Type, duration and severity of disaster – Each **type** of natural disaster will incur specific human health impacts and will present the related health and medical needs accordingly (see Chapters 5 and 6). The **duration** of the disaster also affects medical and health care utilisation. For instance, natural disasters may lead to a dramatic surge of accumulated deaths and injuries within the first 72 hours, while for crises resulted from chronic violence and conflict, mortality and morbidities may span a longer period of time. The **severity** of the disaster also affect human health. In general, the more severe a disaster is, the higher the unexpected mortality and morbidity will be.

Demographic characteristics of the affected population – The underlying age, sex, race, fertility rate, immigration and emigration patterns and dynamics of the affected population will influence the health outcome patterns. **Demographic transition** (Kirk, 1996) also plays an important part in the community health needs. In low- or middle-income countries where death rates are low but birth rates remain high (Stage 2), the affected community is more likely to be younger and thus the underlying disease burden and post-disaster medical needs might be different, whereas high-income developed countries are likely to see unexpected mortality and morbidity among the older population.

Epidemiologic characteristics of the population – Underlying disease patterns of a population are associated with disease prevention and health protection efforts during disaster responses. General underlying health status and risks (e.g. infectious disease risk), vaccination coverage, lifestyles and health service arrangements are all important factors which might influence health needs, patterns and services that might be provided after emergencies. Table 3.1 shows the common health indicators to quantify health impacts after a disaster.

Impact on disaster survivors and bystanders

In addition to excess deaths and health problems associated with a disaster, adverse health outcomes may also affect "bystanders". For instance, disruption and the surge of medical and health needs may overwhelm local capacity to manage regular services. The circumstances associated with a disaster may also increase health and disease risks (e.g. overcrowding, inadequate shelter, insufficient nutrient intake, insufficient vaccination coverage, unclean water, poor sanitation, unhygienic conditions and high exposure to the proliferation of disease vectors) for a population. However, many of these indirect health impacts are preventable and their effects can be minimised by proactive planning and responses (e.g. continuous and careful situational assessment and monitoring to ensure detection).

Destruction of health infrastructure and the provision of health services

While severely injured people might require tertiary, technical and technology-intensive specialist medical management, the majority of the health care needs post

TABLE 3.1 Common health indicators for quantifying health impacts of disasters

Severity of effect	Health indicator	Application
Death	• Number of deaths/ population of disaster area	• Rough assessment of disaster severity
	• Number of impact-related deaths/population of a given age	• Identification of vulnerable groups for further health protection planning
	• Number of deaths/number of houses destroyed	• Assessment of building structure adequacy
	• Number of impact-related deaths per unit of time after the disaster/population of disaster area	• Evaluation of pre-disaster community rescue training
		• Evaluation of self-reliance of community
Hospital admission	• Number of casualties/ population of disaster area	• Evaluation of pre-disaster and mitigation measures
	• Distribution of types of complaints	• Evaluation of warning adequacy
	• Hospital bed occupancy and duration of stay in hospital	• Estimation of emergency care available and relief needs
	• Geographical origin of hospitalised patient	• Identification of critical services to be maintained in emergency phase
		• Monitoring of health facilities and medical care evaluation
		• Needs assessment for relief supplies, including field hospitals
Health-seeking behaviour	• Number of consultations/ surviving population	• Estimation of the type and volume of medical relief and resources needed
	• Time distribution of consultations	• Scheduling of medical relief

Source: Lechat (1979).

CASE BOX 3.1   2008 CYCLONE NARGIS IN MYANMAR

Eyewitness account of the logistical challenge facing Médecins Sans Frontières (MSF) teams in the most devastated region of Myanmar

"I'm in the capital of Irrawaddy division, the worst-hit part of Myanmar. Between 95% and 100% of the houses have been destroyed. One location is in the extreme south western part of Myanmar, where there are a lot of very small islands and small villages on the islands. Many small villages have been completely deserted; there are probably no survivors. Those villages are no longer inhabitable.

In some villages there are only five to 10 survivors, who have been transferred to other villages because they can no longer live in their own village. Many people are still unaccounted for. All the boats locally were stranded or destroyed by the cyclone so it is very difficult for us to move from the place where we arrived to the other islands.

So far we have been managing with the supplies we had inside the country. We had operations already running so we could mobilise materials, medicines and food from the existing programme very quickly. So far we are procuring locally, but I guess this will very soon no longer be possible. We have authorization to land a charter from abroad so this will solve a little bit our problem of availability of goods.

Most of the water sources have been contaminated. We are working on decontaminating the existing wells, but our capacity is very limited because we have not been able to send any materials like big water bladders with modern decontamination technology.

It's a catastrophe that there were no preventive measures taken. The casualties and the damage are very, very high. It's a big catastrophe. What's needed is a quick mobilization in terms of water supply and other sanitation work. In terms of food and shelter, we're going to scale up our distributions in the coming days."

Source: Dr Asis Min's eyewitness account of the logistical challenge facing MSF teams in the most devastated region of Myanmar (Médecins Sans Frontières [MSF] Canada, n.d.).

---

disaster can be addressed through basic primary and community care. Figure 3.1 demonstrates the four tiers of post–disaster health care services.

Destruction of medical facilities might affect health care access and lead to undesirable health outcomes (Kruse, 2012; Shi, 2012) (see Case Box 3.1). In **primary health care** settings, care providers often serve as the contact point between the community and the health care system. **Community health clinics** and maternal and child health centres are primary care facilities that can be easily found in a community and provide services like general management of common diseases, family planning, immunisation, health education and medical referral. **Secondary health care** services are usually provided in hospital settings where medical conditions that cannot be handled with basic equipment and medications at the primary care level. **Tertiary health care** services or care usually take place in an advanced hospital setting (e.g. a burn unit, a transplant unit or an intensive care unit with specialised health care personnel may be needed). These patients require a high level of care with specific resources/expertise requirements. Of note, in the absence of a functional health care centre, most care or emergency response are provided at the **informal care** level (at home, by family, friends, neighbours and bystanders) (see Case Box 3.2).

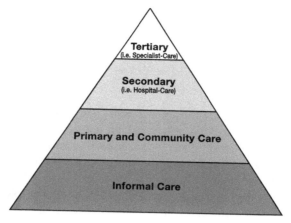

FIGURE 3.1 Four tiers of health care

CASE BOX 3.2   THE 2010 HAITI EARTHQUAKE

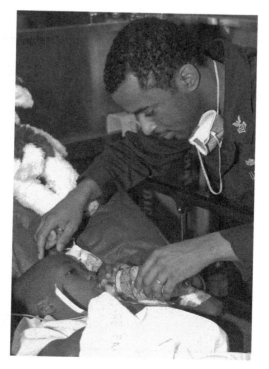

FIGURE 3.2 Medical humanitarian response after 2010 Haiti earthquake

Source: Photo by Timothy Wilson/Public Domain (https://en.wikipedia.org/wiki/File:Usns_comfort_patient_haiti_jan22.jpg).

On Tuesday 12 January, 2010, at 16:53 local time, a 7.0 Richter scale earthquake hit Léoĝane, about 25 km from Port-au-Prince, the capital of Haiti. The earthquake resulted in 220,000 deaths that amounted to 1/50 of the country's population and destroyed 60% of Haiti's health infrastructure. In more detail:

- The earthquake greatly affected secondary and tertiary health care facilities, with over 60% of the facilities at least severely damaged.
- Within the affected districts, 30 out of 49 hospitals were damaged or destroyed, capacity to respond was greatly reduced and service delivery became disorganised.
- The Ministry of Health was unable to fulfil its leadership role due to the complete destruction of the main administrative building.
- In contrast, over 90% of primary health care centres remained intact or suffered only light damage. (Table 3.2 summarises the infrastructure damage in this earthquake.)
- The earthquake destroyed the buildings that housed the National Center for Transfusions and the National Blood Safety Program. For the first eight

TABLE 3.2 Infrastructure damage in the 2010 Haiti earthquake

Level of damage by type of structure	No damage or very little damage	Light damage	Severe damage	Completely destroyed	Total
Health centres and clinics	215	38	12	9	274
Secondary and tertiary hospitals	14	5	22	8	49
Ministry of Health and other administrative buildings	4	8	1	10	23
University and training institutes	23	2	3	19	47
Total	256	53	38	46	393
Total as a percentage (%)	65	14	10	12	100

Source: de Ville de Goyet, Sarmiento, and Grünewald (2011).

days after the earthquake, there was no Haitian blood available for transfusion services.

- The sole hospital for patients with chronic mental diseases was severely damaged in the earthquake. Most of the 76 patients slept on the hospital grounds without protection for a sustained period of time.
- In contrast, over 90% of primary health care centres remained intact or suffered only light damage.
- Out of 5,879 health workers at the Ministry of Health institutions within the affected districts: 61 of them were killed (medical or nursing students not included); 67% of them were made homeless, which explains their absences from duty; and 2.2% of them lost a member of their immediate family.

The earthquake in Haiti resulted in mass casualties, demonstrating how the number, severity, and diversity of injuries can rapidly overwhelm the ability of local medical resources. In an emergency, mass casualty management is the health sectors' immediate priority. On-site and hospital medical responses are therefore important (See Figure 3.2). Search, rescue and triage are life-saving acts. Well-managed systems and procedures are required to bridge the on-site operations with fixed health facilities (World Health Organization [WHO], United Kingdom Health Protection Agency [HPA], & partners, 2011).

Adverse impact on environment

Disasters, whether natural or man-made, have major environmental implications. Take the Indian Ocean tsunami in 2004 as an example; the coastal areas, coral reefs, mangroves, agricultural areas and forests were heavily damaged. Moreover, the depletion or contamination of natural resources may reduce the availability of supplies for basic needs for health and pose other hazards that increase the vulnerability of the population. Figure 3.3 is an illustration of the possible environmental causes and consequences of disasters.

The environmental impacts of disasters can be devastating, pose serious health risks to a community and can be classified into three types. (1) **Acute risk from release of hazardous materials**. Disasters can induce the release of toxic substances that may cause environmental emergencies. The earthquake and tsunami in Japan, as mentioned in Chapter 2, triggered the explosion of a nuclear power plant that released radioactive materials into the air, posing health risks to the neighbouring communities. It is worth noting that these toxic materials and pollutants might also leave deposits on the ground and soil and have a long-lasting impact on health, agriculture and the ecology of the affected locations. (2) **Debris**

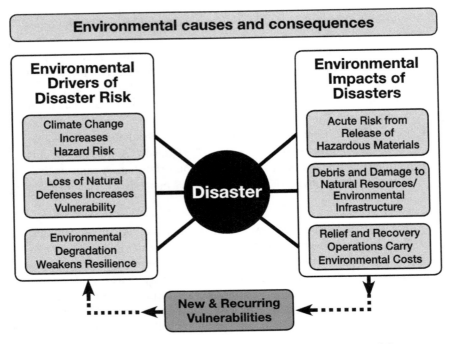

FIGURE 3.3 The correlation of environmental causes and consequences of disasters

Source: Adapted from United Nations Environment Programme (UNEP) and United Nations International Strategy for Disaster Reduction (UNISDR) Working Group on Environment and Disaster (2007).

and damage to natural resources/environmental infrastructure. Direct and indirect damage caused by disasters to the environment may result in environmental degradation (e.g. landslides) that can create new vulnerabilities and/or exacerbate the population's existing ones. (3) **Relief and recovery operations carry environmental costs**. Improper management of health care waste, expired medicines, chemicals required for health protection (e.g. chemicals used for water treatment), debris, human cadavers and animal carcasses might bring long-term health risks to communities. Table 3.3 provides some examples of some potential environmental impact of disaster.

During the relief period of a disaster, the priority of relief work is usually given to the provision of basic needs for health, such as water supplies and sanitation, food aid, temporary shelters and health services. It is important to point out that environmental issues are often not considered as a top priority during this phase even if they have similar importance and have long-term implications (see Case Box 3.3).

TABLE 3.3 Some potential environmental impact of disaster on population

Environmental impact on population	Concerned areas	Population and humanitarian activities' impact on environment
Contamination of water sources by chemicals, hazardous waste; Damage of infrastructures (i.e. drainage pipes) leading to cross contamination; Presence of debris and carcasses	 **FIGURE 3.4** Water and sanitation 	Over-pumping of groundwater; Improper rehabilitation and decommissioning of wells; Water contamination from sewage disposal; Use of energy-intensive water, sanitation and hygiene systems (e.g. desalination plants)
Contamination of land by chemicals, hazardous waste and weapons; Environmental hazards (e.g. landslides, aftershocks); Loss of forests leading to reduced access to fuel for cooking/ warmth and building materials	 **FIGURE 3.5** Shelter 	Unsustainable supply of shelter construction materials; Inappropriate design for needs or culture, which may lead to non–use or misuse; Deforestation and soil erosion; Inadequate disposal of construction and packaging waste
Loss of infrastructure, electricity, and manpower; Release of asbestos from collapsed buildings	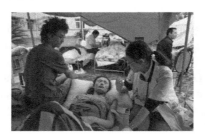 **FIGURE 3.6** Health services 	Improper management of health care equipment and the use of expired medicines; Improper management of chemicals, waste, debris and carcasses

(Continued)

TABLE 3.3 (Continued)

Environmental impact on population	Concerned areas	Population and humanitarian activities' impact on environment
Damage of roads, terminals and airports; Environmental hazards (e.g. floods, volcanoes)	 **FIGURE 3.7** Logistics Photo by CCOUC. All rights reserved.	Improper management and disposal of fuel, waste oil and tires; Excess chemicals and waste from logistics base operations; Procurement of goods produced through unsustainable practices

Source: World Wide Fund and American National Red Cross (2010).

CASE BOX 3.3   CHALLENGES OF CONSECUTIVE FLOODS AND DROUGHTS IN THE DEMOCRATIC PEOPLE'S REPUBLIC OF KOREA (DPRK)

By Mayling Chan

Democratic People's Republic of Korea (DPRK) is prone to consecutive droughts and floods which have a significant impact on food security and public health. The most serious flood in the recent history of the DPRK in 1995–96 resulted in a drastic drop of food availability in domestic production. The total domestic cereal production decreased by more than three times compared to 1993.

According to the officials in the Academy of Agricultural Science, DPRK is not accustomed to droughts but floods. However, this trend is changing. An extended period of abnormally dry spells, the worst in 100 years according to the government, started in early summer 2014 and continued into 2015, resulting in a drought that set back agricultural production and water availability. The combined impact has led to a deterioration in nutrition, health and sanitary conditions, with increasing cases of water-borne and other diseases detected in local clinics according to WHO. In total, it is reported that at least 70% of the country's population are vulnerable to fluctuations in crop production (United Nations Office for the Coordination of Humanitarian Affairs [OCHA], 2015, July 1).

Building up resilience in the DPRK to food insecurity is challenging in the face of consecutive floods and droughts. The country also has natural constraints, such as the fact that sunlight is only available for six months annually, and arable land only amounts to 0.07 hectare per capita.

At the national level, the government has researched drought-resistant seeds, which could adapt to the changing climate, in order to mitigate the impact of extreme dry weather on crop growth. They have a dual strategy of engaging the Academy of Agricultural Science (a research-based national organisation) in an advisory role and quickly disseminating information and applying new systems through the Ministry of Agriculture. Applications could take place in extended fields and are spread through a hierarchical dissemination system from national to provincial to county level. For instance, new seeds have passed the experimental test and been certified for use in the past few years for the purpose of mitigating the negative consequences of droughts. In some areas, farm leaders are advised to grow more maize than rice as the latter is more sensitive to water shortage. Adaptation can be effective in this manner.

Having these measures at the national level for mitigation is a positive step. However, farmers are organised in a work teams' and sub-work teams' management system of collective farming to carry out centralised plans. In these large farms, some of them spanning more than 1,000 hectares of land, there is little scope for adapting necessary strategies at an individual level to cope with the consequences of floods and droughts. It is not easy to switch to other crops in a short period of time when farm inputs are centrally distributed rather than available in free markets as in other countries. Nevertheless, in recent years, the household kitchen garden has become tremendously important for food diversification in the DPRK. In times of natural disaster, this could be an effective means for farmers to remain resilient, as observed by Oxfam in its project sites in South and North Pyongan provinces. Oxfam has supported more sustainable farm practices as a strategy to overcome difficulties posed by natural disasters. By avoiding "putting all the eggs in one basket", and diversifying into a number of grain and vegetable crops, farmers can adapt better in periods of difficulty.

Source: Oxfam Hong Kong (n.d.).

Adverse psychological and social behaviour

The health and well-being of an individual are affected by not only physical risk factors but also the mental and social factors which surround him/her. Psychosocial health refers to psychological and social factors that influence our health. It consists of: spiritual health (being), emotional health (feeling), mental health (thinking)

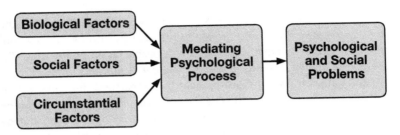

FIGURE 3.8 Biopsychosocial model of mental disorder

Source: Adapted from Kinderman (2005).

and social health (relating). As described by the biopsychosocial model of mental disorder (Kinderman, 2005; See Figure 3.8), psychological and social problems may be the result of a combination of biological factors, social factors and circumstantial factors through mediating psychological processes.

After a disaster, survivors may suffer from adverse mental health after witnessing or going through traumatising events. Apart from direct physical injuries, people may experience drastic changes in their socio-environmental determinants (Carballo, Heal, & Horbaty, 2006), such as the loss of loved ones, housing and property.

Factors which affect mental health outcomes include: physiological and mental statuses before disaster; increased stress as well as feelings of powerlessness due to bereavement; loss of property and loss of livelihood; mental health problems, such as post-traumatic stress disorder, depression and anxiety disorder; the scarcity of basic provisions and disruptions to the economy; destruction of social networks; the breakdown of law enforcement; and the cessation of violence prevention and other social support programmes.

Violence is not associated with *all* types of disaster. The risk of violence increases with physiological traumas (e.g. brain damage), behaviours (e.g. drug and alcohol addiction), distress responses (e.g. fear and a sense of helplessness) and breakdown of social networks and legal system (WHO, 2002). There are a few types of violence that have been shown to increase after some disasters, including abuse and neglect, intimate partner violence, sexual violence, exploitation and trafficking (in areas where trafficking is already prominent). These acts of violence may also induce other health and social-related consequences. For example, sexual violence may lead to unwanted pregnancy, transmission of HIV/AIDS and suicide (WHO, 2005). Meanwhile, the prevailing myth of excessive post-disaster violence and cities becoming "a burglar's paradise" has not been supported by any empirical evidence. In her article "The Myth of Disaster Looting", Katy Welter (2012), a law and policy analyst for the Chicago Appleseed Fund for Justice, discusses the exaggeration of media reports on looting in disaster-affected communities (see Chapter 6 for further discussion on mental health).

Long-term consequences

Few published studies have examined the long-term impact and recovery challenges in disaster-affected communities. Most published studies focus on the reporting and documentation of excess deaths and morbidities in the early phase of disasters and only few published studies have examined the long-term impact and recovery challenges in disaster-affected communities. Much like the short-term impact of disasters, the long-term health effects vary according to the type of disaster, its duration and the affected area. Disasters may change the social-demographic make-up of a community. For example, a disproportionally high number of orphans and widows has significant implications on long-term population planning and welfare spending.

Long-term consequences of disasters not only affect individuals but also can be felt at the community and country level. Excess cases of cancers, infertility, adverse pregnancy outcomes and birth defects were also observed after the atomic bombings of Hiroshima and Nagasaki of Japan and the Chernobyl accident in the former U.S.S.R. Within the internally displaced communities in Bosnia, common medical problems included chronic and psychological illnesses. The long-term consequences on the country's economy will be discussed in the next section.

In summary, the impact of disasters can be understood through the three main dimensions in health – physical, mental and social well-being. As health is a result of a combination of modifiable and non-modifiable determinants that exist across the intrapersonal, interpersonal, community/institutional and macro public-policy realms, multi-dimensional risk factors and their potential consequences should be considered.

Economic consequences of disasters

The public health impact and needs after natural disasters vary according to disaster type, magnitude of the event, as well as the sociodemographic and epidemiological risk factors associated with the affected communities.

Regardless of the type of disaster event, any disaster can leave economic consequences that may linger for years. Disaster losses manifest themselves in numerous ways and it is immensely difficult to measure them with great accuracy. **Direct losses** are those resulting from building, lifeline and infrastructure damages, while **indirect losses** are those lost as a result of the physical damage, such as reduced tourism, disrupted service provision and decreased productivity (Hallegatte & Przyluski, 2010). In contrast, **costs** refer to resources required to undertake replacement, repairs and reinforcement of the tangible assets that are destroyed.

Recent trends of economic impact from disasters

Evidence suggests that disasters can affect the economy at the national level by hampering the gross domestic product (GDP) for a short period. A study of 35 disaster events in in Latin America and the Caribbean from 1980 to 1996 identified a decline of GDP in 28 cases in the year of the disaster's occurrence and a sharp increase two years after the disaster (Charvériat, 2000).

How natural hazards affect the country's economic condition

The vulnerability of a country's economy to natural hazards depends on many factors. Although detailed discussion of this important topic is beyond the scope of this book, five factors which are related to health systems and their resilience to the impact of disasters need to be highlighted: (1) **Type of natural hazards**. For example, hydro-meteorological hazards can affect agricultural performance, particularly in countries which rely heavily on agriculture. (2) **Economic structure**. It may affect a system's productivity, the diversity and competition between sectors, and the nature of productive capital, which in turn can affect the community's ability to bounce back after a disaster. For instance, the Dominican Republic, which traditionally based its economy on its banana plantation industry, would have suffered enormous setbacks due to the increased frequency and intensity of disasters affecting its agricultural industry. But, in recent years, the country developed a diversified economic setup with industries that are less dependent on the climate, which means it has a stronger capability to recover. (3) **Geographic size of a country and its hazard distributions**. For very small countries, the hazards may be countrywide, whereas for larger countries, the hazards may affect only certain parts of the country. (4) **A country's socio-economic development**. Although absolute economic loss in developing countries may be small when compared with developed countries, disasters may disrupt the whole economy of the country. (5) **The prevailing socio-economic conditions**. For example, the economic policy, price fluctuation and market regulation may have an important role in lessening or exacerbating the impact of a disaster (see Case Box 3.4).

In summary, the economic impact of a disaster may imply additional expenditure or reallocation of financial resources to repair or rebuild public infrastructure. This may lead to the abandonment of ongoing or planned projects and reduce the provision of public services. On the positive side, acknowledging the possible economic impact would help the country to prepare special budgets allocated for disaster mitigation, preparedness and rehabilitation, reducing the potential consequences.

CASE BOX 3.4   ECONOMIC IMPACT OF DISASTERS IN HIGH- AND LOW-INCOME COUNTRIES

While the economic impact of disasters is dependent on the type of hazards, economic structure, geographic size, income level, stages of development, and the socio-economic conditions, the impact of disaster experienced by each country is different because of the difference in the severity of the disaster, the level of resiliency and the level of development. The economic impact and mortality resulting from disasters among high-income, middle-income and low-income countries differ widely: high-income countries seem to suffer more economically but less in death toll. However, comparing these three groups in terms of the economic impact of disasters relative to the countries' GDPs and their mortality rates tells a different story.

Economic impact of disasters from high- to low-income countries

Figure 3.9A shows that the amount of money lost as a result of disasters is positively related to the income level of the countries' economy status; high-income countries suffer the highest monetary loss in absolute terms, followed by middle-income countries and low-income countries. However, the mortality figure is lowest in high-income countries and highest in middle-income countries. The two patterns are more consistent if the comparison is made in relative terms (Figure 3.9B): high-income countries suffer less in terms of

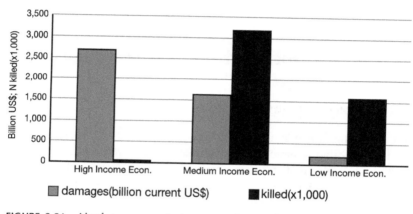

FIGURE 3.9A Absolute economic impact and mortality rate of disasters from high- to low-income countries

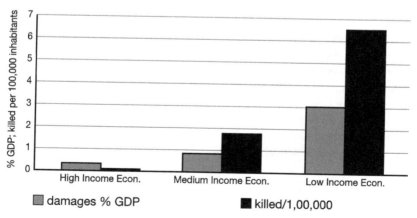

FIGURE 3.9B Relative economic impact and mortality rate of disasters from high- to low-income countries

Source: Adapted from Guha-Sapir and Hoyois (2012).

economic loss as a proportion to GDP and mortality rate, while low-income countries fare worst in both economic and human losses. For example, the Great East Japan earthquake in 2011 alone resulted in a loss of about US$309 billion (5.7% of GDP), but the Pacific Islands lost a higher percentage of their GDP from disasters in the same year. Countries with less income usually have higher number of deaths in both absolute and relative terms. For instance, the Great East Japan earthquake in 2011 resulted in more than 20,000 deaths, while the Haiti earthquake in 2010 killed over 220,000 people in a country of smaller population, despite a smaller economic loss of US$8.3 billion.

CASE BOX 3.5 THE GREAT EAST JAPAN EARTHQUAKE IN 2011

By Carman Mark and Makiko Kato MacDermot

The devastating Great East Japan earthquake combined with a tsunami and nuclear explosion resulted in great mortality, massive destruction of health facilities, and release of radioactive material. Figure 3.10 shows the destruction caused. It can be understood by identifying the five general public health consequences and the economic impact.

Background

A magnitude 9.0 earthquake occurred at 14:46 JST on 11 March 2011 off the north-east coast of Japan. It was an earthquake with the highest magnitude in the history of Japan and the fifth largest in the history of the world. The earthquake induced a 15-meter high tsunami that struck the land and caused widespread flooding and electricity failure about 40 minutes after the initial quake. The tsunami also triggered partial nuclear meltdowns and explosions at the Fukushima Daiichi Nuclear Power Plant located 150 km north-east of the epicentre. Radioactive material was released into the air, water and food, and a 20-kilometre evacuation zone was established where tens of thousands of people had to be evacuated. More than 24,000 people were killed or went missing in the catastrophe.

Unexpected mortality and morbidity

Most deaths were due to drowning, and the highest mortality was among the elderly. Hypertension, deep-vein thrombosis and respiratory problems were the most common reported illnesses among the victims. In addition, outbreaks of influenza and infectious gastroenteritis were identified in evacuation centres.

FIGURE 3.10 The aftermath of the Great East Japan earthquake

Source: Photo by Dylan McCord / Public Domain (https://en.wikipedia.org/wiki/
Aftermath_of_the_2011_T%C5%8Dhoku_earthquake_and_tsunami#/media/
File:2011TsunamiFireVehicles.jpg).

Destruction of health infrastructure

Health infrastructure and services were heavily disrupted. Unofficial sources
reported that health facilities were damaged in 11 municipalities and at least
30 nursing facilities for the elderly were destroyed. After two weeks, the health
facilities were still incapable of performing. In Iwate, Fukushima and Miyagi,
52% of health facilities were unable to accept new patients. Fourteen per cent
of them were lacking health workers. In addition, electricity failure and lack of
water supply disturbed the facilities' operation.

Adverse effects on the environment and population

The tsunami washed away many of the coastal and river bank areas. The
coastal ecosystems may have been destroyed, and reconstruction operations

could cause environmental pollution. If seawater penetrates far inland, it may also affect the groundwater quality. The damage to the water supply and sewage networks could contaminate the water, leading to the risk of water-borne diseases.

Influence on social behaviour and psychological health

Many people lost their loved ones, their homes and possessions. Unemployment was prominent immediately after the disaster. Six months later, post-traumatic stress disorder cases were reported.

Undesirable long-term consequences

The accident was regarded as a "severe accident" or level 7 (the highest level) on the International Nuclear and Radiological Event Scale. WHO Report on the Health Risk Assessment from the nuclear accident indicated the increased lifetime risks for the development of leukaemia, breast cancer, thyroid cancer and all solid cancers. The emergency workers were also at a high risk of developing cancer and non-cancer risks related to radiation. Five days after the accident, Japan's Nuclear Safety Commission recommended local authorities to instruct their citizens to ingest single-dose iodine as a precaution, and close to 2,000 workers were given stable iodine in the emergency response. The long-term consequences due to the released radioactive material are still unknown, requiring further monitoring.

Economic impact

The total loss and damage was estimated at US$309 billion (5.7% of GDP). The damage was the sum calculation from triple disasters: earthquake, tsunami and nuclear explosion. Most severely affected areas were dependent on agriculture, fishing and manufacturing. These industries were heavily damaged. In addition, internationally, the United States Food and Drug Administration banned imports of spinach and kakina leafy vegetables from the affected region. All milk and dairy products manufactured in the affected prefectures were not allowed to enter the US market unless proved free from radioactive contamination (Asian Disaster Reduction Center [ADRC], 2011; Nohara, 2011; United Nations Environment Programme [UNEP], 2011; WHO Regional Office for the Western Pacific, 2011).

Conclusion

Five general public health consequences of disasters are usually observed after natural disasters (see Case Box 3.5). These include unexpected mortality and morbidity, destruction of health infrastructures and service provision, adverse impact on the environment and population, adverse impact on the psychological and social well-being of the population, and other effects with long-term consequences, such as development setbacks in low-income countries resulting from the frequent economic losses related to disasters.

References

Asian Disaster Reduction Center (ADRC). (2011). *Great East Japan earthquake: Update on damage and recovery* (2nd report). Retrieved from http://www.adrc.asia/documents/disaster_info/Great_East_Tokyo_Earthquake_ver.2.pdf

Carballo, M., Heal, B., & Horbaty, G. (2006). Impact of the tsunami on psychosocial health and well-being. *International Review of Psychiatry, 3*(18), 217–223.

Charvériat, C. (2000). *Natural disasters in Latin America and the Caribbean: An overview of risk* (Research Department Working Paper Series No. 434) [Internet]. Retrieved from Inter-American Development Bank website: http://www.iadb.org/res/publications/pubfiles/pubWP-434.pdf

de Ville de Goyet, C., Sarmiento, J. P., & Grünewald, F. (2011). *Health response to the earthquake in Haiti January 2010: Lessons to be learned for the next massive sudden-onset disaster* [Internet]. Washington, DC: Pan American Health Organization (PAHO). Retrieved from http://reliefweb.int/sites/reliefweb.int/files/resources/Full_Report_3342.pdf

Guha-Sapir, D., & Hoyois, P. (2012). *Measuring the human and economic impact of disasters* [Internet]. Retrieved from United Kingdom Government Office for Science website: https://www.gov.uk/government/uploads/system/uploads/attachment_data/file/286966/12-1295-measuring-human-economic-impact-disasters.pdf

Hallegatte, S., & Przyluski, V. (2010). *The economics of natural disasters: Concepts and methods* (Policy Research Working Paper No. 5507) [Internet]. Washington, DC: Office of the Chief Economist, Sustainable Development Network, World Bank. Retrieved from World Bank Open Knowledge Repository website: https://openknowledge.worldbank.org/bitstream/handle/10986/3991/WPS5507.pdf?sequence=1

Kinderman, P. (2005). A psychological model of mental disorder. *Harvard Review of Psychiatry, 13*(4), 206–217. doi:10.1080/10673220500243349

Kirk, D. (1996). Demographic transition theory. *Population Studies: A Journal of Demography, 50*(3), 361–387.

Kruse, J. (2012). The organization of health care: The contrasting role of primary care and consulting specialties. *Family Medicine, 44*(7), 516–518.

Lechat, M. F. (1979). Disaster and public health. *Bulletin of the World Health Organization, 57*(1), 11–17.

Médecins Sans Frontières (MSF) Canada. (n.d.). *Cyclone Nargis in Myanmar* [Internet]. Retrieved from http://www.msf.ca/en/cyclone-nargis-myanmar

Nohara, M. (2011). Impact of the Great East Japan earthquake and tsunami on health, medical care and public health systems in Iwate Prefecture, Japan, 2011 [Internet]. *Western Pacific Surveillance and Response Journal, 2*(4), 24–30. doi:10.5365/wpsar.year.2011.2.4.002

Oxfam Hong Kong. (n.d.). *DPR Korea (North Korea)* [Internet]. Retrieved from http://www.oxfam.org.hk/en/dprkbak_2010.aspx

Shi, L. (2012). The impact of primary care: A focused review. *Scientifica, 2012,* 432892. doi:10.6064/2012/432892

United Nations Environment Programme (UNEP). (2011). *Great East Japan earthquake and tsunami* [Internet]. Retrieved from http://www.unep.org/tsunami/

United Nations Environment Programme (UNEP), & United Nations International Strategy for Disaster Reduction (UNISDR) Working Group on Environment and Disaster. (2007). *Environmental and disaster risk: Emerging perspectives*. Geneva, Switzerland: Author.

United Nations Office for the Coordination of Humanitarian Affairs (OCHA). (2015, July 1). *Democratic People's Republic of Korea: Drought* [Internet]. Retrieved from ReliefWeb website: http://reliefweb.int/sites/reliefweb.int/files/resources/PRK_drought_150701.v3.pdf

Welter, K. (2012). *The myth of disaster looting* [Internet]. Retrieved from Next City website: http://nextcity.org/daily/entry/the-myth-of-disaster-looting

World Health Organization (WHO). (2002). *World report on violence and death*. Geneva, Switzerland: Author.

World Health Organization (WHO). (2005). *Violence and disasters* [Internet]. Retrieved from http://www.who.int/entity/violence_injury_prevention/publications/violence/violence_disasters.pdf?ua=1

World Health Organization (WHO), United Kingdom Health Protection Agency (HPA), & partners. (2011). *Mass casualty management* (Disaster Risk Management for Health Fact Sheets) [Internet]. Retrieved from http://www.who.int/hac/events/drm_fact_sheet_mass_casualty_management.pdf

World Health Organization (WHO) Regional Office for the Western Pacific. (2011). *The Great East Japan earthquake: A story of a devastating natural disaster, a tale of human compassion* [Internet]. Retrieved from http://www.wpro.who.int/publications/docs/japan_earthquake.pdf?ua=1

World Wide Fund, & American National Red Cross. (2010). *Environmental impact assessment tools and techniques* (Green Recovery & Reconstruction: Training toolkit for humanitarian aid Module 3) [Internet]. Retrieved from http://green-recovery.org/wordpress/wp-content/uploads/2010/11/Module-3-Content-Paper.pdf

4

THE SPECIFIC HUMAN HEALTH IMPACTS OF NATURAL DISASTERS

The human health impact of natural disasters varies according to the risk factors associated with the specific hazards, exposure and community vulnerabilities. Health impact caused by earthquakes, tsunamis, volcanic eruptions, floods, extreme temperature events, cyclones, droughts and famines will be discussed in this chapter.

Geophysical hazards: earthquake and tsunami

An **earthquake** is a geophysical event caused by seismic waves which lead to the shaking and displacement of the ground. It is the result of a sudden release of energy stored in the earth's crust. During an earthquake, individuals located in places near the epicentre can feel the shaking or displacement of the ground (Centre for Research on the Epidemiology of Disasters [CRED], 2009). After-shocks are also caused by seismic waves after the major earthquake and might be of similar and lesser intensity. **Tsunamis** are a specific by-product of earthquakes, which originate beneath the ocean floor. A tsunami may produce high waves, which approach the shoreline. The health impact of a tsunami is similar to that of a flash flood, which will be discussed in a later section.

How is it reported?

The **Richter scale** is the most commonly used scale to report the strength or the amount of energy released by an earthquake. It is calculated from the amplitude of the largest seismic wave recorded for a given earthquake and reported on a logarithmic scale. For each whole number increment of the Richter scale score, the strength of the earthquake increases ten times. A level-8 earthquake on the Richter scale is ten times stronger than a level-7 earthquake. However, the Richter

KNOWLEDGE BOX 4.1   THE MODIFIED MERCALLI SCALE AND RICHTER SCALE

Table 4.1 draws an approximate parallel between the modified Mercalli scale and the Richter scale based on the records of past earthquakes. If an earthquake with the same seismic wave's amplitude was to hit the United States, a high-income country, and Haiti, a low-income country, would the report of its strength or impact based on (1) the Richter scale, or (2) the Mercalli scale be different? How so? The value reported based on the **Richter** scale would be the same in both countries. The reported value based on the **Mercalli** scale would be **lower** in the United States than in Haiti. This is because the actual effect of an earthquake on livelihoods is dependent on the vulnerability and manageability of each country. Since the Mercalli scale is not a mathematical calculation of the actual damages caused by the earthquake but merely founded on observations, the reported value it is based upon would be lower in a rich country that is assumed to be much more resilient to absorbing the shocks of an earthquake, as compared with a poor country which is more vulnerable to the same earthquake, resulting in higher damages and destruction.

TABLE 4.1 The modified Mercalli scale versus the Richter scale

Category	Effect	Richter scale (approximate)
I. Instrumental	Not felt	1–2
II. Just perceptible	Felt by very few people, mostly those on upper floors of tall buildings	3
III. Slight	Felt by people lying down, seated on a hard surface or on upper floors of tall buildings	3.5
IV. Perceptible	Felt by many indoors, but by only a few outside; dishes and windows rattle	4
V. Rather strong	Generally felt by everyone; sleeping people may be awakened	4.5
VI. Strong	Trees sway, chandeliers swing, bells ring; some damage from falling objects	5
VII. Very strong	General alarm; walls and plaster crack	5.5

Category	Effect	Richter scale (approximate)
VIII. Destructive	Felt in moving vehicles; chimneys collapse; poorly constructed buildings seriously damaged	6
IX. Ruinous	Some houses collapse; pipes break	6.5
X. Disastrous	Obvious ground cracks; railroad tracks bent; some landslides on steep hillsides	7
XI. Very disastrous	Few buildings survive; bridges damaged or destroyed; all services (electricity, water, sewage, railroad) interrupted; severe landslides	7.5
XII. Catastrophic	Total destruction; objects thrown into the air; river course and topography altered	8

Source: Adapted from USGS (2013).

scale itself does not reflect the severity of the impact upon human populations. The other common scale used for earthquakes is the **Mercalli scale**, which indicates the amount of damage and destruction from an earthquake. The scale has no mathematical basis and is composed of 12 levels of increasing intensity that range from imperceptible shaking to catastrophic destruction (United States Geological Survey [USGS], 2013) (see Knowledge Box 4.1).

What are the known risk factors associated with adverse health outcomes?

The main factors associated with the adverse health outcomes of an earthquake include: the level of seismic hazard, population density and the concentration of buildings. In general, settlements located in earthquake-prone regions, or seismic belts, are at a higher risk of earthquakes. The higher the population and building density, the greater the damage may be. Figure 4.1 illustrates where several tectonic plates meet and the resulting high seismic activity. The timing of an earthquake may also be related to the magnitude of damage it brings to the community. More casualties are expected if an earthquake occurs at midnight since people are not able to react immediately while sleeping (Chou et al., 2004). Figure 4.1 is a map showing the distribution of earthquake-prone regions around the globe, also known as seismic belts, where there is a higher risk of earthquakes.

GLOBAL SEISMIC HAZARD MAP

Produced by the Global Seismic Hazard Assessment Program (GSHAP),
a demonstration project of the UN/International Decade of Natural Disaster Reduction, conducted by the International Lithosphere Program.

Global map assembled by D. Giardini, G. Grünthal, K. Shedlock, and P. Zhang
1999

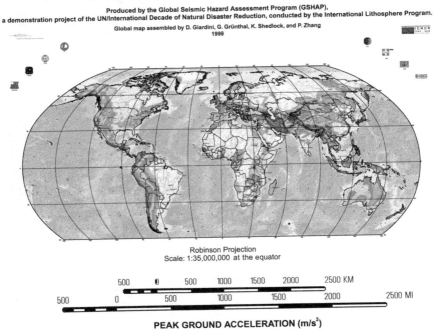

Robinson Projection
Scale: 1:35,000,000 at the equator

| 500 | 0 | 500 | 1000 | 1500 | 2000 | 2500 KM |

| 500 | 0 | 500 | 1000 | 1500 | 2000 | 2500 MI |

PEAK GROUND ACCELERATION (m/s^2)

10% PROBABILITY OF EXCEEDANCE IN 50 YEARS, 475-year return period

| 0 | 0.2 | 0.4 | 0.8 | 1.6 | 2.4 | 3.2 | 4.0 | 4.8 |

| LOW | MODERATE | HIGH | VERY HIGH |
| HAZARD | HAZARD | HAZARD | HAZARD |

FIGURE 4.1   Global seismic hazard map

Source: Global Seismic Hazard Assessment Program (http://www.seismo.ethz.ch/static/GSHAP/global/).

What are the direct health impacts of an earthquake?

The majority of the health impacts of an earthquake stem from the collapse of buildings and infrastructure. Falling debris and entrapment may directly cause trauma, crush injuries and fractures to victims. Cuts and bruises are expected for most of the patients admitted to the hospital during the first week. Other associated health risks of entrapment include: hypoxia (lack of oxygen), hypothermia (especially during winter) and electrocution. Debris from collapsed infrastructure may also cause dust inhalation, which in turn may trigger acute respiratory distress.

What are the response needs?

Search and rescue are fundamental to the immediate earthquake response. The most successful rescues are carried out by the immediate action of nearby survivors during the first phase of the disaster, when the chance of survival is the highest (see Case Box 4.1). Medical services are also needed to manage the casualties caused by the earthquake. A high volume of injuries and fractures is expected in the first weeks after an earthquake. Entrapped individuals face the risks of oxygen deficit, hypothermia, gas leak, smoke, water penetration and electrocution. Orthopaedic surgeons, anaesthesiologists, nephrologists or physicians specialising in renal care are all important specialisations required at the initial phase of disaster relief as patients with crush injuries may develop acute kidney failure (see Knowledge Box 4.2). Since earthquakes bring huge destruction and damage to buildings, management of the homeless population is also crucial (Portilla et al., 2010).

CASE BOX 4.1   THE 1976 TANGSHAN EARTHQUAKE: TIMELINESS OF EXTRICATION AND SURVIVAL

In earthquakes, timeliness of extrication determines survival. Figure 4.2 shows the inverse relationship between the time point of rescue operation and the survival rate (%) of those extricated in the Tangshan earthquake in 1976. A total of 89.6% of the survivors were extricated within 24 hours of the earthquake.

Time of Rescue	Extricated		Surviving		Cumulative rate(%)
	Number	rate(%)	Number	rate(%)	
0.5 hour	2277	21.3	2261	99.3	29.9
1 day	5572	52.1	4513	81.0	89.6
2 days	1638	15.3	552	33.7	96.9
3 days	348	3.3	128	36.7	98.6
4 days	399	2.7	75	19.0	99.6
5 days	459	4.3	34	7.4	100.0

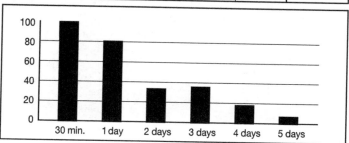

FIGURE 4.2   Survival rates (%) of extricated people by rescue time after Tangshan earthquake in 1976

Source: Yuan (2001).

KNOWLEDGE BOX 4.2 CRUSH INJURY AND CRUSH SYNDROME

What are they?

Crush injury refers to trauma occurring when body parts are subjected to high and long-lasting continuous pressure. The pressure causes extensive necrosis to the affected muscles. It is commonly associated with earthquakes due to prolonged compression of muscles and compromised local circulation under collapsed buildings and debris. Figure 4.3 shows an earthquake victim extricated by a rescue team, who may suffer from crush injury. **Crush syndrome** is defined as a crush injury with systemic complications and is strongly associated with mortality. It may lead to sepsis, acute renal failure, hyperkalaemia and hypovolemic shock, all of which could be lethal.

The incidence of crush syndrome after a major earthquake ranges from 2% to 15%. Typically, it affects the lower extremities (74%), upper extremities (10%) and trunk (9%). Fifty per cent of the patients with crush syndrome develop acute renal failure and over 50% need **fasciotomy**. Among those with renal failure, 50% need dialysis (Briggs, 2006).

FIGURE 4.3 A victim of crush injury

Source: Photo by Israel Defence Forces/CC BY-SA 2.0 (https://en.wikipedia.org/wiki/Home_Front_Command#/media/File:Flickr_-_Israel_Defense_Forces_-_Rescue_of_a_Haitian_Man_from_Government_Building.jpg; http://creativecommons.org/licenses/by-sa/2.0/).

Management of crush injury

Prior to the release of crushed body parts, early fluid administration with isotonic saline followed by hypotonic saline-alkaline solution is vital in a pre-hospital setting. In a hospital setting, fluid intake and urinary output must be closely monitored. Any electrolyte abnormalities should be corrected and supportive care, such as haemodialysis, should be provided as needed. One of the urgent complications of crush injury is **compartment syndrome**, which is "produced when the tissue pressure within a confined space rises to the point where the circulation and the function of the tissues within that space are compromised" (Boyce, Saravanan, & Wolfson, 2016, p. 115). Patients with crush injuries should also be monitored for compartment syndrome using the "6Ps" (British Medical Journal [BMJ], 2013).

Pain: Pain that seems out of proportion to the injury
Paresthesia: "Pins and needles" sensation
Pallor: Unhealthy pale appearance
Paralysis: Inability to move the limbs
Pulselessness: Diminished or absence of pulse
Pressure: Presence of tightness in the compartment

What are the public health needs after an earthquake?

Earthquakes will incur large amounts of injuries and destroy transportation and communication systems to place a huge burden on the lifeline infrastructure (e.g. water and sanitation, food supply, electricity and health care system). However, unlike flooding, disease outbreak is not a major concern. Water resources are usually not contaminated and there is no evidence that the unburied dead would inevitably cause the spread of infectious diseases. Despite this low risk of the spreading of disease, the burying of the dead may be beneficial to the mental well-being of their family members (see also Knowledge Box 4.3).

KNOWLEDGE BOX 4.3   TSUNAMI

Tsunamis are the result of earthquakes or volcanic eruptions under the sea; volcanic tsunamis are usually greater in magnitude and impact than the seismic ones. Most deaths are due to drowning, while damage to infrastructure is caused through the initial impact and drag. People living close to the sea line and lowland areas are the most endangered. Literature indicates that the amount of death may outnumber the injured in tsunamis.

Geophysical hazard: volcanic eruption

A volcanic eruption is the process which transports magma and/or gases from the central core of the earth to the surface. It can be accompanied by tremors on the ground and interactions of magma and water (e.g. groundwater, crater lakes) below the earth's surface. Depending on the composition of the magma, eruptions can be either explosive or effusive, and result in variations of rock fall, ash fall, lava streams, pyroclastic flows, emission of gases and so forth (CRED, 2009). Volcanic eruptions can also affect populations that live hundreds of kilometres away due to the airborne dispersion of gases and ash. Since the eighteenth century, there have been more than 270,000 volcano-related fatalities, with two to four fatal eruptions per year. Globally, many volcanic areas are densely populated. In 1990, nearly 10% of the global population lived within 100 kilometres of an active volcano (see Knowledge Box 4.4) (Ciotonne et al., 2006; Hansell, Horwell, & Oppenheimer, 2006).

KNOWLEDGE BOX 4.4   THE RING OF FIRE

The Ring of Fire, also called the **Circum-Pacific Belt** or **Pacific Ring of Fire,** is a horseshoe-shaped seismically active belt of earthquake epicentres, volcanoes and tectonic plate boundaries that fringe the Pacific basin (see Figure 4.4).

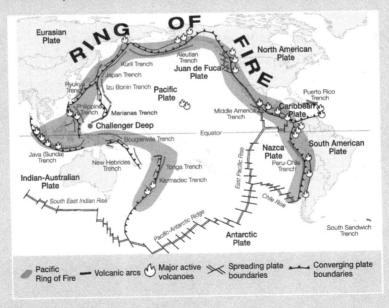

FIGURE 4.4   The Ring of Fire

Source: Adapted from Encyclopaedia Britannica (http://media-1.web.britannica.com/eb-media/57/5457-050-84F0FBED.jpg).

Volcanoes are associated with the movements of tectonic plates along this belt; thus, the belt is called the "Ring of Fire". An overwhelming majority of the world's strongest earthquakes and approximately 75% of the world's volcanic activities occur within the Ring of Fire. Ecuador, Papua New Guinea and the Philippines are examples of countries that are located in the active volcano regions. Volcanoes along the Ring of Fire are not equally distributed. Indonesia is the country with the highest number of active volcanoes in the world, followed by Japan, the United States and Chile. The Ring of Fire has been the setting for several of the largest earthquakes in recorded history, including the Chile earthquake of 1960, the Alaska earthquake of 1964, the Chile earthquake of 2010, the Japan earthquake of 2011 and the earthquake that generated the devastating Indian Ocean tsunami of 2004.

Other than the Ring of Fire, areas prone to volcanic eruptions include "hot spots" in the ocean where the earth's crust is weak and island chains that are formed by the erupted magma, like the one across the North and South Atlantic Oceans.

Sources: USGS (2015), Ring of Fire (n.d.).

What are the known risk factors associated with adverse health outcomes?

The activity level of a volcano, such as the frequency of emissions of harmful gases and volcanic mudflows between eruptions, is a key factor that indicates the future behaviour of the volcano and the current impact it has on neighbouring communities. While there are currently no standardised tools to estimate the population risk from being exposed to volcanic activities, the Smithsonian Global Volcanism Program (GVP) is a method of assessing the volcanic hazard risk by scoring eruption characteristics, such as type of lava flow, maximum output capacity, eruption history and volume of surrounding glaciers and snowcaps. It is worth noting that most of the active volcanoes in the twenty-first century are in highly dense urban areas, such as Tokyo, Mexico City, Jakarta and Manila. For a location with a high population density, a good early warning system and evacuation plans are vital to mitigating the impact of volcanic eruptions. Countries typically classify volcanoes into "high", "medium" and "low" risk based on the volcanoes' eruption history, number of people affected and potential economic losses.

What are the health impacts of volcanic eruption?

Volcanic eruptions result in the highest mortality rates when compared with other types of natural disasters. This high level of mortality is due to the risks of **pyroclastic flows**, which can result in high levels of deaths, fatal injuries and severe burns. Pyroclastic flow is a mass of hot volcanic ash, lava fragments and gases that erupt from a volcano and move rapidly down its slope. It can travel more than 300 kilometres per hour and may reach temperature as high as 600°C to 900°C (Jay, 2006; Hogan & Bearden, 2007). The fragmentary material emitted from a pyroclastic flow is called **tephra** (Hansell et al., 2006). **Ashes** are tephra fragments that are less than 2 mm in size. Ashfall that follows an eruption, particularly wet ash, can damage buildings and contaminate water sources. Heavy ashfall can cloud the sky, leaving people living in complete darkness during the day. The free silica and high iron content of ash irritates the upper and lower respiratory airways, eyes and skin. High levels of airborne ash (daily average total suspended particles (TSP) of 3,000–33,000 µg/m3) can result in a two- to threefold increase in hospital admissions and a three- to fivefold increase in emergency room visits for respiratory-related illnesses (Baxter, Ing, Falk, & Plikaytis, 1983). **Lapilli** are tephra fragments between 2 and 64 mm in size, while **lava bombs or blocks** are those larger than 64 mm (Jay, 2006). The ejection of lava bombs can cause severe head injuries, burns and **blunt trauma**. **Volcanic gases**, such as sulphur dioxide, carbon dioxide and hydrogen fluoride, also impose significant health hazards. Sulphur dioxide can be irritating to respiratory airways, eyes and skin. Hydrogen fluoride can also generate the same effect, but when it is ingested by animals, it will produce fluorosis and cause death. Breathing carbon dioxide with a concentration greater than 20% can also cause unconsciousness and **asphyxiation** in humans (Baxter, 1990).

What are the responses needed?

Volcanic events are relatively uncommon compared to other natural disasters. The important health problems to consider when responding to the health needs after volcanic eruptions are the provision of health care for burns, injuries, inhalation and respiratory trauma from exposure to ash and toxic gases. Securing all the lifeline infrastructure and managing post-impact health risks are also crucial.

Health risks include mucosal (eye) irritations and skin and respiratory tract burn injury from volcanic ashfall, pyroclastic flows, mudflows, tsunamis and volcanic earthquakes. Toxic gases may also cause suffocation and respiratory diseases. Volcanic eruptions cause loss of infrastructure, agricultural land and property and economic loss. Indirect health impacts from relocation and the loss of homes are more likely to cause greater adverse outcomes than direct injuries from falling rocks and burns. Surveillance systems to detect volcanic movements and early warning systems are regarded as the most effective ways to prevent the adverse impacts of this type of disaster.

In summary, volcanic activities are common in places located along the Ring of Fire. Volcanic eruptions with pyroclastic flows of ash and lava bombs result in a high mortality rate and respiratory problems. Volcanic ash can affect people miles away from the volcano. These events are likely to affect neighbouring communities by emitting hazardous gases and particles.

Meteorological hazard: tropical cyclone/hurricane/typhoon

While **storms** refer to a wider variety of disturbances in the atmosphere and are often accompanied by strong wind, rain, snow, thunder and lightning, hail, flying sand or dust, **tropical cyclones** are meteorological hazards which are characterised by low atmospheric pressure, spiral rain bands and strong winds of 64 knots or more. Depending on the location, these hazards are named differently. Tropical cyclones occurring in the Indian Ocean and South Pacific are called **cyclones**, those originating in the Western Atlantic and Eastern Pacific are called **hurricanes** and those happening in the Western Pacific are called **typhoons** (CRED, 2009). Tropical cyclones may bring heavy rain, strong winds or even large storm surges. Secondary disasters, such as mudslides and landslides, may occur near mountainous areas. Landed tropical cyclones can also generate tornadoes that may bring further health and socio-economic risks to the community.

How is it reported?

A number of measuring scales are used regionally to describe the intensity and impact of tropical cyclones. The World Meteorological Organization (WMO) recommends the relevant scale according to the geographic location of the oceanic basin and the maximum speed of sustained winds (see Table 4.2).

TABLE 4.2 Scales for measuring the intensity of cyclones in various oceanic basins

Region	Scale
Atlantic and Eastern Pacific Oceans	Saffir-Simpson Hurricane Scale
Western Pacific Ocean	RSMC Tokyo's Tropical Cyclone Intensity Scale
North Indian Ocean	India Meteorological Department Tropical Cyclone Intensity Scale
Southwestern Indian Ocean	Southwest Indian Ocean Tropical Cyclone Intensity Scale

Source: WMO (n.d.).

What are the known risk factors associated with adverse health outcomes?

Vulnerability to a tropical cyclone depends on location and infrastructure. Populations residing in low-lying coastal areas face the highest risk of an adverse impact from tropical cyclones. These coastal areas are particularly vulnerable to storm surges and heavy rain, which may cause coastal flooding or temporary displacement. People residing near rivers are also at risk of flash floods. Infrastructure factors that increase vulnerability include poor building design, lack of or ineffective early warning systems, insufficient evacuation time and inaccurate perceptions of risks and safety. Vulnerability to cyclones is further increased by population growth, urbanisation, increasing coastal settlement and global warming (Doocy, Daniels, Murray, & Kirsch, 2013). Since the twentieth century, populations in Southeast Asia, the Western Pacific and the Americas have faced increasing risks posed by cyclones, typhoons and hurricanes.

What are the direct health impacts of a cyclone?

A tropical cyclone could cause events such as flooding, storm surges, landslides and infectious disease outbreaks. As information and records in less-developed countries are often inaccurate or inaccessible, the true health impacts of a cyclone are hard to measure and only partially documented (see also Case Box 4.2). Clinically, the most common health conditions observed after a cyclone are minor injuries, including lacerations, blunt trauma and puncture wounds

---

CASE BOX 4.2   TYPHOON HAIYAN IN THE PHILIPPINES

Typhoon Haiyan hit the Philippines on 8 November 2013. It affected nine regions, 44 provinces and nearly 600 municipalities. Its economic impact is estimated to be about $700 million in damage to agriculture and infrastructure alone.

Key figures

- 14.1 million affected people
- 4.1 million displaced
- 6,190 deaths
- 1,785 people missing

Shelters

- More than 1.1 million houses damaged, half of which were completely destroyed
- Lack of relocation sites
  - Only 2% of displaced population housed at 381 temporary evacuation sites
  - 3,993,753 displaced people living outside evacuation centres

Food security

- 30% of the affected population facing food insecurities and dependent on food assistance for survival
- Food security and agriculture cluster targeting 3 million people in need of food assistance

Water

- The majority of the affected population have limited access to safe drinking water
- Water supply damage and contamination: Many water systems destroyed, and over half of the surface resources and half the groundwater contaminated by polluted waters from industry activities, agricultural chemicals, and domestic waste and septic systems, increasing the threat of disease outbreaks

Source: Joint UNEP/OCHA Environment Unit (2014).

The 2013 Super Typhoon Haiyan in Asia was the third Category 5 typhoon to strike the Philippines since 2010, and tore through Tacloban in the province of Leyte, affecting about 13 million people. Figure 4.5 shows a devastated Tacloban after Typhoon Haiyan. Merely four weeks earlier, the Super Typhoon Usagi landed in southern China and affected more than 2.7 million people. With an increasing number of extreme weather events due to climate change (from 99 in 1980 to 269 in 2011), Asia is likely to be hit by stronger typhoons more frequently in the coming decades. The 2013 World Disaster Report identified access to information and technology as one of the major challenges to a community's disaster preparedness, survival, and recovery.

FIGURE 4.5   The aftermath of Typhoon Haiyan in the Philippines

Source: Photo by Trocaire/CC BY 2.0 (https://commons.wikimedia.org/wiki/File:Tacloban_Typhoon_Haiyan_2013-11-14.jpg; https://creativecommons.org/licenses/by/2.0/deed.en).

caused by collapsed buildings and falling debris. Eighty per cent of cyclone-related injuries are found in the lower limbs (Shultz, Russell, & Espinel, 2005). Asphyxiation, trauma and electrocution are commonly observed in a tropical cyclone disaster. Post-traumatic stress disorder and depression have also been observed after large-scale tropical cyclones. However, the true human impact is hard to measure. A tropical cyclone can cause secondary disasters, like flooding, storm surges and landslides, leading to additional deaths and injuries. Unless cyclones are related to floods or sea surges, they usually cause relatively few deaths and injuries.

Of note, although outbreaks of infectious disease rarely occur after major hurricanes and associated floods, waterborne and food-borne diseases can result from contamination of water and food crops. Displacement of people to crowded shelters can lead to transmission of infectious respiratory disorders. Standing water can promote mosquito breeding and in turn lead to vector-borne diseases. Damaged wires can also cause electrocutions and fires.

What are the response needs?

Cyclones are characterised by strong winds and precipitation. They could result in high numbers of injuries and massive destruction of infrastructure. Injuries are the most common direct health effect of a tropical cyclone. Victims need wound management, antibiotic treatment and tetanus prophylaxis. Health care facilities located in at-risk areas should take precautions by ensuring building safety, preparing a contingency electricity supply and practising evacuation protocols.

What are the public health needs after cyclones/typhoons/ hurricanes?

Effective response after storm disasters requires that responders address (1) the basic survival needs of affected people, including food, safe water, sanitation, shelter, health care and access to necessary information, and (2) disaster-related injuries with sound management: antibiotic treatment, where indicated; tetanus prophylaxis and measures against other health risks. Specifically, environmental health risks should be anticipated and minimised through measures such as ensuring adequate supplies of safe food and water and controlling disease vectors. Health care facilities should have contingency electricity and water supplies. Regularly updated evacuation protocols and emergency drills are essential to ensure the relevancy of the emergency plans and familiarity of community residents with these important procedures. Last but not least, access to information is critical for preparedness, survival and recovery after community disasters (see also Knowledge Box 4.5 and Case Box 4.3).

Although media coverage of cyclones and their aftermath often focuses on the immediate ravages, injuries, deaths and economic loss, typhoons and hurricanes also bring less visible long-term consequences for health. Well-organised longitudinal data and comprehensive surveillance information are often limited in low-income settings, and, as a result, information about the long-term physical and mental health consequences of cyclones and the ensuing floods for the population is not available to guide evidence-based disaster emergency preparedness and response planning. Research agendas at the community level should identify predictors of and barriers to the ability of households and communities to respond to disaster warnings, and also assess the effectiveness with which information about health responses after a disaster is delivered. Research also needs to explore the best way to organise surveillance data and systems to reduce post-disaster health risks. How to mobilise community volunteers to engage in evidence-based, post-disaster health action remains a major operational challenge for governments, frontline workers and academics, and gaps in technical knowledge must be tackled.

Tropical cyclones are likely to adversely affect populations in low-lying coastal areas. For disaster mitigation, solution should target modifiable risk factors, such as poor building design, lack of early warning systems, inadequate disaster preparedness, insufficient time for evaluation and inaccurate perception of risks and safety. Improved weather forecasting systems with community-wide, early warning systems and continuous public education may mitigate the adverse health impact by heightening community risk perception and people's responsiveness to warnings.

KNOWLEDGE BOX 4.5   LANDSLIDES

Landslides may result from heavy rain and destabilised soil and rocks, particularly in deforested areas. They may come after a tsunami, earthquake, heavy rains or flooding. Crush injury and entrapments are common morbidities resulting from these events.

In Hong Kong, with hilly terrain covering 60% of its land area, many urban developments located near man-made slopes and hillside and intense and prolonged rainfall in spring and summer brought about by monsoons and tropical cyclones, there is a high risk of landslide. While the Geotechnical Engineering Office of the government has improved more than 11,000 higher risk slopes since its establishment in the late 1970s, another 17,000 slopes close to roads remains to be fixed. More slopes on private land are supposed to be taken care of by the private landowners.

Source: Hong Kong Special Administrative Region (2015, September).

CASE BOX 4.3 FLOODS AND LANDSLIDES IN BRUNEI IN THE PAST DECADE

By Chi Shing Wong

In recent years, partly attributable to global climate change, the population of Brunei Darussalam, a small Southeast Asian country on northwest Borneo Island, has experienced, almost annually, the twin disasters of floods and landslides, causing extensive damage to property, infrastructure and the natural environment, as well as evacuations and other socio-economic disruptions. Floods and landslides are particularly severe in the monsoon season of January and caused huge chaos in 2009, 2011 and 2014 due to unpredictable episodic deluges and flash floods. This presents a severe challenge to the meteorologically-induced disaster preparedness and management of the country, which has emphasised disaster response rather than preparedness and mitigation.

Although the National Disaster Management Centre (NDMC), chaired by the Crown Prince, was established in August 2006 to handle disaster operations and hold disaster exercises and workshops, it is made up mostly of Fire and Rescue Services officials who are responsible for the coordination of any rescue and other work caused by natural disasters. In addition, as of 2011, there had been no specific allocation in the national budget for disaster risk reduction in the country (Rahman, 2011; Brunei Darussalam Prime Minister's Office, 2013).

The weakness in the infrastructure (the generally shallow urban stormwater drains, canalisation of streams and rivers in the city centre and inadequate attention to slope stability and soil water retention characteristics prior to construction) adds to the country's vulnerability to hydro-meteorological disasters (Ndah, Kumar, & Becek, 2015). In 2014, the government allocated 68 million Brunei dollars (US$55.4 million) specifically for flood mitigation projects in addition to a budget of 35 million Brunei dollars (US$28 million) for repair work on public infrastructure and government assets damaged by floods and landslides (Brunei Darussalam Prime Minister's Office, 2014).

Despite improvements in drainage and infrastructure in some flood-prone areas, such as drainage works at Kedayan River in Kg Menglait and Kg Kumbang Pasang, and the installation of hard drains to alleviate flood issues in Jalan Sg Tampoi, Jalan Mulaut and Kg Bebatik, there are still areas around the country like Tutong district that continue to be affected by the ongoing floods. Similar problem exists in many countries where exposure of people and assets has increased faster than vulnerability has decreased (Mohamed, 2014).

Sources: Gupta (2010), Rahman (2011), Brunei Darussalam Prime Minister's Office (2013, 2014), Mohamed (2014) and Ndah et al. (2015).

Hydrological hazard: flood

Globally, floods are the most common type of natural disaster. They account for 40% of natural disasters worldwide and flooding is an annual event in many places. It is the leading cause of natural disaster mortality, leading to 6.8 million deaths in the twentieth century (Doocy et al., 2013). Almost half of the flood-related fatalities in the last quarter of the twentieth century occurred in Asia. In many places, floods are an annual event.

The Center for Research on the Epidemiology of Disasters (CRED) defines a flood as a significant rise of water level in a stream, lake, reservoir or coastal region. Generally, floods can be classified into three types: general flood, flash flood and storm surge/costal flood (CRED, 2009).**General flood** describes the accumulation of water on the surface due to long-lasting rainfall (water logging) and the rise of the groundwater table above the surface. It can be induced by the melting of snow and ice, backwater effects or special causes, such as the outburst of a glacial lake or the breaching of a dam. **Flash flood** is a sudden flooding episode which occurs within a short duration. It is typically associated with thunderstorms and can virtually occur in any place. **Storm surge/coastal floods** are the rise of the water level in the sea, an estuary or lake as a result of strong wind driving seawater towards the coast. The areas threatened by storm surges are coastal lowlands.

Although a tsunami is not a flood but a series of waves generated by an (underwater) earthquake on the sea floor, as discussed in an earlier section, the sudden flooding of coastal areas and the potential damage on infrastructure may cause health impacts largely similar to those of floods. (Please also refer to Knowledge Box 4.3 on tsunami.)

What are the known risk factors associated with adverse health outcomes?

Flood types are associated with different impacts. For example, as flash floods occur quickly and leave people with little lead time to respond, they may result in higher mortality rates as compared to general floods. On the other hand, general floods, despite the slower onset, affect larger populations and a wider area. In addition, floods with higher water depth and greater flow velocity result in greater damage.

Rainfall is a main cause of floods. Other factors contributing to this hazard include: **human factors** (lack of structural flood control measures, such as embankments, obstruction of river water flow due to debris and waste, and lack of drainage basins in urban areas), **meteorological factors** (solidified ground surface after a drought reducing the ability of soil to quickly absorb excessive rainwater, and excessive precipitation over a prolonged period oversaturating the soil and increasing overland run-off), and **topographical factors** (landscape around a river influencing how quickly rainwater reaches the channel – e.g. a river channel surrounded by steep slopes and lacking in vegetation or woodland could easily lead to the river bank bursting and the overflow of water onto the floodplain since there is a lack of trees and plants to intercept precipitation) (Associated Programme on Flood Management [APFM], 2013) (see Case Box 4.4).

What are the health impacts of floods?

The health impact of floods is complex and difficult to generalise across contexts. High mortality is rare in floods. During the past few decades, only 58 events resulted in more than 1,000 deaths. Settlements in **floodplains** are more prone to floods than houses on higher ground. The size of floodplains can be varied. For example, Vietnam's Mekong River delta floodplain covers an area of over 12,000 square kilometres. People living in a flood-prone area can mitigate the impact of floods by adopting **flood-resistant designs** in their houses, such as reinforcing walls with waterproof coatings and equipping homes with backup generators. In urban settings, flood damage is often more intense due to the higher population density and the high proportion of **impervious surfaces** and a lack of **green infrastructure** to absorb excess precipitation. With the increasing intensity and frequency of cyclones due to climate change, urban areas are also becoming more susceptible to flash floods.

Floods may be caused by fresh water or salt water. Freshwater floods may leave mud and soil when the waters recede, saltwater can affect the salinity of ground water, making water undrinkable and harming the aquatic animals (Smith, 2009). Floods may cause water contamination by bacteria and viruses. For example, floods in Mozambique in 2000 caused a rising number of diarrhoea cases, floods in Mauritius in 1980 triggered an outbreak of typhoid fever, and floods in West Bengal in 1998 created a cholera epidemic (WHO, 2005). Cholera is an infectious diarrhoeal disease, caused by *Vibrio cholerae*. It is estimated that there are 1.4 to 4.3 million cases of cholera annually, causing 28,000 to 142,000 annual deaths (World Health Organization [WHO], 2015a). Studies have shown that *V. cholerae* is native to coastal ecosystems, particularly in the tropics and subtropics (Colwell, Kaper, & Joseph, 1977; Lipp, Huq, & Colwell, 2002). Therefore, coastal flooding increases the risk of cholera infections. Furthermore, stagnant water, remaining for days or weeks after the initial flood, increases the risk of vector-borne illnesses by providing new breeding sites for vectors. Floodwater also destroys power lines and submerges electrical equipment, causing **electrical shocks** and increasing the risk of fires. Table 4.3 summarises the health impact of flooding.

Flood-related mortality. Drowning and traumatic injuries are common causes of death during floods as fast-flowing floodwater carries vehicles, trees or building materials, causing orthopaedic injuries, trauma and lacerations. A study of 13 floods in Europe and the United States found approximately two-thirds of the 247 deaths occurred through drowning, and males were highly vulnerable to dying in floods, partially due to unnecessary risk-taking behaviour (Jonkman & Kelman, 2005). Another review of relevant literature found mortality by drowning in the home occurred largely among the elderly. The

TABLE 4.3 Direct and indirect health impact of flooding

Type of effect	Health impact
Direct impacts —e.g. direct exposure to floodwater	• Drowning and injuries from walking or driving through floodwater, contact with debris in floodwater, falling into hidden manholes, injuries from submerged objects, injuries while trying to move possessions during floods
	• Building collapse and damage (injuries)
	• Electrocution
	• Diarrhoeal, vector- and rodent-borne diseases
	• Respiratory, skin and eye infections
	• Chemical contamination, particularly carbon monoxide poisoning from generators used for pumping and dehumidifying
	• Water shortages and contamination due to loss of water treatment works and sewage treatment plants
	• Stress, short- and long-term mental health issues, including the impact of displacement
Indirect impacts —e.g. impacts on other health determinants	• Loss of access to health care
	• Damage to health care infrastructure and other vital community facilities
	• Damage to water and sanitation infrastructure
	• Damage to crops, disruption of food supplies
	• Disruption of livelihoods and income
	• Population displacement
	• Mental and social health problems due to length of flood recovery and fear of recurrence

Source: Adapted from Ahern, Kovats, Wilkinson, Few, and Matthies (2005).

primary risk factors for immediate flood-related deaths depend on the characteristics of the flood: speed, depth and the extent of water. For example, flash floods are more hazardous due to their speed when compared with general floods (Ahern et al., 2005). In addition to drowning and injuries, victims are prone to **hypothermia**, especially in cooler weather, and animal bites if the floodwaters originate from rivers and other water bodies with snakes or other dangerous animals.

Flood-related morbidity. Floods cause various morbidities directly or indirectly. Injuries, communicable diseases, and mental health problems are found to be associated with floods. **Injuries**: Flood-related injuries, such as contusions and lacerations, may occur as individuals attempt to remove themselves and their family from danger. Secondary injuries are also commonly associated with post-flood, clean-up operations – for example those related to unstable buildings. **Communicable diseases**: The risk of outbreaks after flooding is small in industrialised countries due to established water, sewage and public health infrastructure. In developing countries, these infectious disease risks are increased. *Waterborne disease*: Flooding presents a community with an increased risk of waterborne diseases (e.g. cholera, leptospirosis and hepatitis A) that are transmitted through the faecal-oral route since the drinking water source may be contaminated with pathogens. Heavy rainfall can damage the water and sanitation infrastructure, triggering sewage overflows into drinking water. *Vector-borne disease*: Although floodwater initially washes away mosquito breeding sites, standing water may be a perfect breeding site for mosquitoes, thus increasing the risk of vector-borne diseases, such as dengue and malaria. For example, the flooding in Costa Rica in 1991 and in the Dominican Republic in 2004 led to malaria outbreaks. **Mental health problems**: There can be an increase in the incidence of mental health problems, which results directly from the experience of living in the flooded areas and indirectly from geographic displacement, damage to houses and assets, and stress in the restoration process.

Uncertainties in assessing health impacts of flood

The true health impact of flooding is difficult to estimate as it is difficult to quantify health impacts as the adverse human health consequences of flooding are complex. Understanding the vulnerability of population subgroups may help guide appropriate solutions to reduce the impact of flooding. The elderly, the disabled, children, women, ethnic minorities and those with low incomes are particularly at risk (Hajat et al., 2005). Additionally, displaced populations often experience compromised access to clean water and sanitation.

In short, floods are characterised by the accumulation of water on the surface. There are three types of floods: general floods, flash floods and storm surges. Drowning, hypothermia, animal bites, injuries, electrical shocks and waterborne and vector-borne illnesses are the common health impacts resulting from floods.

What are the responses needed?

In general, floods and high winds do not result in high levels of mortality. Search and rescue, and evacuation of the affected population are the primary responses needed in a flood disaster. Specific attention needs to be directed towards reducing the risk of exposure to waterborne and vector-borne diseases. Sewage and other pollutants might contaminate water supplies, potentially leading to the transmission of waterborne diseases. Damage to crops, housing and infrastructure may affect food production and can lead to economic loss. Clean-up activities, maintenance of **clean water** and **food security** are key public health response needs for the affected population.

CASE BOX 4.4 FLOODS IN PERU AND CHILE, MARCH 2015

By Chi Shing Wong

Heavy unseasonal rains caused flash floods and mudslides in many regions in Peru and Chile, including the Atacama Desert, one of the driest regions of the world. Half day of rainfall on 26 March brought seven times greater precipitation than the desert normally gets in a full year. The Chilean city of Antofagasta received 14 times its annual rainfall in two days. Rivers burst their banks and destroyed thousands of homes, roads and railway bridges.

At least 28 people died, nearly 30,000 lost their homes and more than 160,000 were affected in Chile. Residents in Antofagasta, Atacama and Coquimbo were stranded by 17 mudslides. A state of emergency was declared for the Atacama Region and Antofagasta in Chile, while a sanitary alert by the Health Ministry of Chile was in effect in Copiapó, Tierra Amarilla, Diego de Almagro and Alto del Carmen. Critical needs of the affected population included mud removal, water and sanitation, health, shelter and education.

In the Loreto region in southern Peru, more than 115,000 people were affected. Eight people died and 25 were injured in a mudslide in Chosica on 23 March. The Peru government declared a 60-day state of emergency on 9 April in 22 districts of four provinces. The needs of the affected population included health, livelihoods, shelter management, water and sanitation and education.

Sources: Adonai (2015), Sim (2015), United Nations Office for the Coordination of Humanitarian Affairs [OCHA] (2015 April 15, 2015 April 20).

Climatological hazards: drought and famine

Droughts and famines are disasters with impact that may last for prolonged periods. Droughts are climatological events that can last from a couple of weeks to several years and famines are a subtype of disaster that slowly affects a large population over months and years. Both of these calamities have a devastating impact on the health and livelihood of people as well as the ecosystems of the affected communities. Drought is usually a preceding factor of famine but not every drought results in a famine. These two disasters will be discussed together in this section because they often go hand in hand.

What is a drought?

A **drought** is a climatological natural disaster defined as a deficiency in a region's water supply for an extended period of time as a result of persisting below–average

TABLE 4.4 Types of drought

Drought type	Used by	Description	Potential impact
Meteorological	General public	Prolonged below-average precipitation period	Water shortage
Agricultural	Farmers	Low soil moisture to support crop production	Reduced crop production
Hydrological	Urban planners for managing water supplies	When water reserves in reservoirs fall below average	Water shortage

Source: Adapted from Stanke, Kerac, Prudhomme, Medlock, and Murray (2013).

precipitation. Table 4.4 shows how a drought may be conceptualised differently. A drought can affect inland navigation and hydropower plants, lead to a lack of drinking water and cause famine as a result of losses in agriculture (CRED, 2009). Climate change is affecting the global trends of drought and the Intergovernmental Panel on Climate Change (IPCC) identified some regions (southern Europe and West Africa) may experience longer and more intense droughts while other regions (central North America and Northwestern Australia) may have less frequent and less intense droughts.

What is a famine?

A **famine** is an extreme form of **food crisis** or **food insecurity**. A food crisis is "[a] combination of drought, rising food prices, poverty, natural disasters, conflicts, global food prices, disease, and complex emergencies. A food crisis develops when families experience these stresses for several years and run out of ways to cope, and governments and aid agencies fail to intervene" (World Vision Hong Kong, n.d.). When food crises continue and reach certain measures of mortality, malnutrition and hunger, they can develop into a famine. A famine is, according to the United Nations definition, when "at least 20% of households in an area face extreme food shortages with a limited ability to cope; acute malnutrition rates exceed 30%, and the death rate exceeds two persons per day per 10,000 persons" (United Nations [UN], 2011). It is described as a regional failure of food production or supply, sufficient to cause a marked increase in disease and mortality due to a severe lack of nutrition, and necessitating emergency intervention, usually at an international level (Cox, 1981). Famines are often accompanied by an economic and social collapse of the community. Famines can be a result of a natural disaster, but because much of their underlying causes are related to food distribution, management of food prices and regulation of other economic activities, nowadays they are considered to be a man-made disaster.

What are the risk factors for drought?

Due to the lack of reliable data and the relationship complexity between rainfall and actual water access, there is insufficient evidence to pinpoint the global trends in drought from the 1950s onward. The IPCC projects that an increased risk of drought is likely in currently dry regions, such as the Mediterranean, Southwest United States and southern Africa, due to decreases in soil moisture by 2100. When a period of unusual dryness and rainfall deficit occurs before the harvest season, it can have a more devastating health impact than if it happens after the harvest season. The failure to harvest leads to a reduction of food availability. Poor irrigation systems and water supply infrastructure also play an important role in increasing the health impact (see Case Box 4.5).

The lack of clean water and ensuing diarrhoeal diseases cause more than 760,000 under-five deaths annually, while malnutrition kills 3.1 million people globally (WHO, 2015b). The increased frequency of droughts in the future may intensify this disease risk. There are many risk factors that influence drought vulnerability, including: demographic pressure on the environment, inappropriate land use, food insecurity, the socio-economic status of the population, economic systems strictly dependent on agriculture, poor infrastructure (e.g. inadequate irrigation, water supply and sanitation), the poor health status of the population prior to the disaster, the season/timing of drought occurrences (with the most critical period being before the harvest), the absence of warning systems, population displacement and other concurrent situations (e.g. economic crisis, political instability and armed conflict). However, it is important to point out that a rainfall-related drought is usually predictable; therefore it is important to develop and disseminate an early warning, so people can prepare for and store food before the drought happens.

CASE BOX 4.5   EASTERN HORN OF AFRICA DROUGHT CRISIS 2010–2011

Despite early warnings in September 2010 by meteorological services of the extended period of reduced rainfall, proactive action was not taken by governments and community stakeholders to alleviate the predicted water stress situation. As a result, drought-related famine and acute malnutrition crises were subsequently declared in many parts of Somalia, Kenya, Ethiopia, and Djibouti. As of 2012, 13.3 million people in the region were in need of humanitarian assistance. Furthermore, the drought situation in Somalia further aggravated the ongoing conflict in the country, leading to a large exodus of refugees into neighbouring states.

Sources: WHO (2011) and OCHA (2012).

What are the risk factors for famine?

Famine is traditionally believed to be associated with the decline of food supplies. As Brown and Eckholm (1974, p. 25) had described, "a sudden, sharp reduction in food supply in any particular geographic locale has usually resulted in widespread hunger and famine." The decline in food supply may be resulted from one or more of the following: climate events, **pestilence** (i.e. an infectious epidemic disease that is virulent and devastating), war, overpopulation and economic mismanagement. However, a new theory regarding the cause of famines was proposed by Amartya Sen (1981) and focuses on each person's entitlement to commodity bundles, including food, and views starvation as a failure to be entitled to a bundle with enough food. Therefore, famine is not simply a product of climate events or natural disasters but also related socioeconomically to the decline in both income and employment opportunities. The lack of financial access to commodities, and limitations in social, political and human rights are also important contributors to modern famine. In the past, food crises affected rural food producers first but now the rise in food prices, a key feature of modern times, places the urban poor more at risk (World Vision Hong Kong, n.d.) (see also Case Box 4.6).

Another important concept related to famine is the decrease in **food security**, which consists of three components: **food availability, food access and food use**. As food security continues to decrease, action taken to sustain survival becomes less reversible. As people start to sell household possessions and productive tools,

---

CASE BOX 4.6   INDIAN FAMINE CODE

A severe drought occurred in Bengal of British East India Company in 1769. While rural distress had been reported, the reports were ignored by the Company. Starvation started in early 1770 and reached its height in mid-1770. Subsequent infectious diseases further increased the death toll. The famine and diseases ultimately claimed 10 million lives, one third of the total population. As a result, large areas were depopulated and may cultivated lands were abandoned. The Great Bengal famine of 1770 was the first and most severe one among a series of famines in British India that killed tens of millions of Indians.

To address the issue of famine in colonial India, the British created the Indian Famine commission to formulate the Indian famine code in 1880. The code classified food insecurity on a three-level scale of intensity with corresponding steps the government were required to take to mitigate famine risk: near-scarcity, scarcity (three successive years of crop failure, crop yields dropping to one-third to one-half of the normal level and large number of people in distress) and famine (an increase in food prices by 40% or more, the movement of people searching for food and widespread mortality). This code is one of the earliest famine scales and became the basis of famine prevention until the 1970s.

Source: Brennan (1984).

they lose their capacity to generate income (endowments) for further exchange of food and other necessities (entitlements) in the future. This generates a vicious cycle that continues to worsen the food insecurity.

What are the health impacts of droughts and famines?

The impact of a drought is dependent on the context and underlying population vulnerability (such as the underlying water-use practices, infrastructure and socio-economic environment) (Stanke et al., 2013). With drought and its subsequent decrease in the quantity and/or quality of the food available, acquiring sufficient nutritional intake is the greatest challenge for affected communities.

Health impacts of drought

Drought may have health impacts via a variety of pathways. The complex and slowly evolving effects of drought make it difficult to categorise the true impact; however, various risk factors may determine the degree of drought's impact on the health of the affected communities.

Disrupted food production/distribution caused by drought can lead to reduced food intake, **malnutrition** and various nutrient deficiencies. Specifically, people who reduce their food consumption may encounter **protein–energy malnutrition** and morbidities related to **micronutrient deficiencies** (such as iron-deficiency **anaemia, scurvy** due to vitamin C and vitamin A deficiency that increases the risk of developing **measles**). **Undernutrition** is a major cause of morbidity and mortality, particularly among children and pregnant women. Inadequate maternal nutrition may result in **intrauterine growth retardation, low birth weight** or various gestational problems. A study investigating 7,874 adults born between 1954 and 1964 during the famine in China revealed that exposure to famine during the foetal stage was associated with a higher risk of developing **metabolic syndrome** during adult life. In addition, undernutrition during the developmental stage can cause impairment in physical and cognitive abilities (Li et al., 2011) (see also Knowledge Box 4.6).

Communicable diseases: lack of clean drinking water and sanitation, compounded by the effects of malnutrition and displacement, can contribute to a higher population vulnerability to infectious diseases, such as cholera, typhoid fever, diarrhoea, acute respiratory infections and measles. Water stress also changes the dynamics of **vector-borne diseases**. Unprotected stagnant water sources might promote the breeding of vectors like mosquitoes and flies.

Psychosocial stress and mental health disorders: although more studies are needed to evaluate the impact of drought on mental health, it may create a broad range of stressors and weaken an individual's ability to avoid mental health problems.

Reduced health service delivery: the disruption of local health services due to the lack of water supplies or out-migration of health care workers can compromise the access to health care of a community. Loss of buying power and lack of health facilities limit people's access to health services and increase overall morbidity and mortality (Stanke et al., 2013).

Socio-economic and environmental impacts of drought

Economic impacts: the reduction of crop production decreases farmers' incomes. Furthermore, reduced food availability causes an increase in food market prices.

Environmental impacts: droughts might trigger insect infestations, increasing plant diseases, worsening air quality and aggravating soil erosion and landscape degradation. While the natural ecosystems can usually rebound after short-term droughts, the impact of long-term droughts requires a lengthy recovery period.

Social impacts: water utilisation rights may be disputed and cause conflict among users. Additionally, migrants from a drought-stricken area may increase the demand for water and threatens water security in host communities, possibly leading to complex emergencies, such as conflicts and civil wars.

What are the responses needed?

Young children, women, older population and people with chronic diseases are the most at-risk groups in drought and famine situations. In addition, famine relief organisations must consider not only people's dietary needs and food preferences but also both the physical and economic access to food. Relief organisations must also pay attention to micronutrient deficiency in long-term feeding camps and food aid.

In summary, droughts are slow-onset disasters characterised by an extended period of unusual dryness, while famine is an extreme form of failure in food production or supply. The impacts of droughts and famines result in various health presentations, such as vector-borne diseases, communicable diseases, malnutrition, vitamin and micronutrient deficiency, metabolic syndrome, gestational problems and impairment in physical and cognitive abilities.

Climatological hazards: extreme temperatures – heatwaves and cold waves

What is a cold wave?

A **cold wave** can be a prolonged period of excessively cold weather or a sudden invasion of very cold air over a large geographic area. If accompanied by frost, it can cause damage to agriculture, infrastructure and property (CRED, 2009).

What is a heatwave?

Since the average temperature differs across countries, there is no standard operational definition of a heatwave. A **heatwave** may be defined as a length of five or more

KNOWLEDGE BOX 4.6   GLOBAL HUNGER INDEX

The Global Hunger Index (GHI) is designed to comprehensively measure and track hunger globally, by country and by region. Calculated each year by the International Food Policy Research Institute (IFPRI), the GHI highlights successes and failures in hunger reduction, and provides insights into the drivers of hunger. Figure 4.6 shows the GHI by region in 1990, 1995, 2000, 2005 and 2014. South Asia and sub-Saharan Africa had the highest GHI, which is a reflection of the regions' high prevalence of underweight children, the proportion of undernourishment in their populations and the under-five mortality rate.

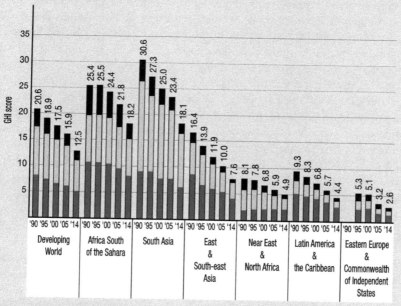

■ Under-five mortality rate
☐ Prevalence of underweight in children
■ Proportion of undernourished

FIGURE 4.6   Contribution of components to 1990, 1995, 2000, 2005 and 2014 Global Hunger Index Scores, by region

Source: Adapted from International Food Policy Research Institute (http://www.ifpri.org/sites/default/files/ghi14fig21lg.jpg).

Source: von Grebmer et al. (2014).

consecutive days of heat exceeding the average maximum temperature of a particular area by 5°C (CRED, 2009). In general, it is a prolonged period of excessively hot weather, usually accompanied by high humidity. Heatwaves usually happen during the summertime in a high atmospheric pressure area with little or no rain.

What are the known risk factors associated with adverse health outcomes?

Climate change increases the frequency and intensity of extreme temperature events, such as heatwaves and cold waves. Heatwaves with stronger intensity and longer-lasting have been recorded more frequently in the last decade (Meehl & Tebaldi, 2004). Extreme temperatures are more likely to affect the very young (infants and preschool children), very old, chronically ill populations (whose metabolisms fail to adjust to these extreme temperatures) and socially disadvantaged subgroups in a community. In some countries, women and certain ethnic groups are also at a higher risk of death and adverse health outcomes. People who have a low socio-economic status, work outdoors or have poor access to air conditioning and other temperature-regulating machines (e.g. fans and heaters) are also at a higher risk (Chan, Goggins, Kim, & Griffiths, 2012). Hence, there is a high association between the demographic and disease profile of a country and the population's vulnerability to temperature-related health impacts. In cold waves, people who live in poverty are more prone to suffer and experience an impact on their health because their house-hold may not have enough resources to produce heat. This condition is known as fuel poverty, which "occurs when a family are unable to afford adequate warmth" (Boardman, 1991, p. 205), and "adequate heating is affordable if it can be obtained for 6 per cent of [a household's] income" (Boardman, 1991, p. 201).

Extreme heat and cold do not affect the health of populations equally. Populations' susceptibility and vulnerability to temperature-related events are determined by many local factors, such as host factors, geography and adaptation capacity.

Host factors: The demography of the exposed population, such as age, socio-economic level and health status, determines vulnerability to heat-related illness – for example the inability to access air conditioning results in higher health burdens from heat.

Geographical factors: Location of habitats may exacerbate the effects of an extreme weather event. For example, people living in urban areas may be at greater health risk from a prolonged heatwave due to the *urban heat island* effect, which causes temperatures in urban environments to be a few degrees warmer than rural areas.

Adaptive capacity: Local adaptive capacity to cope and respond to the extreme temperatures determines population vulnerability.

What is the direct health impact?

Both heatwaves and cold waves are associated with increased mortality. When the body fails to self-regulate the core body temperature and allows it to go consider-ably above or below its normal temperature (37°C), the vital organs are at risk.

Heatwaves commonly cause **heat strokes**, heat exhaustion and heat cramps. **Heat stroke** is defined as an extreme hyperthermia of core body temperature which reaches 40°C or above. It happens when the body fails to regulate its own temperature. Symptoms include weakness, nausea and vomiting, headache, dizziness, muscle cramps and pain. Cold waves commonly lead to **hypothermia** and frostbite. **Hypothermia** refers to a core body temperature below 35°C. It occurs when the body loses heat faster than it can generate heat. The heart, nervous system and other vital organs are at risk of shutting down. Both conditions can be fatal if untreated, and are best treated with supportive care in hospital settings. Extreme temperatures can also trigger the deterioration of respiratory diseases and increase the onset of cardiovascular episodes (Chan, Goggins, Yue, & Lee, 2013), such as myocardial infarction, stroke and heart failure. In extremes, it might lead to excessive deaths. A study in Hong Kong found that an average 1°C increase in daily mean temperature above 28.2°C was associated with an estimated 1.8% increase in mortality (Chan et al., 2012).

What are the responses needed?

The physiological acclimatisation to extreme temperatures can occur over a few days, but behavioural adaptation and technological advancement may take several years or even decades (see Case Box 4.7). To mitigate the effects of extreme weather, health promotion and preparation are very important (Huang et al., 2013). Some of these actions include: reduction of exposure to hot/cool temperatures, increased awareness and education about responding to temperature warnings, increased access to temperature-regulating mechanisms, alleviation of fuel poverty, surveillance and mapping of at-risk populations, well-insulated and well-ventilated building designs, and mindful urban planning to reduce heat island effect. Research also plays important roles in protecting communities (see Case Box 4.8).

CASE BOX 4.7   COLD WAVES IN A SUBTROPICAL CITY, HONG KONG 2008

Between 1998 and 2008, an estimated decrease of 1°C in mean temperatures below 24°C (threshold) was associated with a 3% increase in natural deaths, including delayed effects. A study on the relationship between mortality and extreme temperatures from 1998 to 2008 found that the 2008 Cold Wave led to 882 excess deaths from natural causes. This was 19% higher than seasonal norms after confounders, such as trend, flu and pollutants, were adjusted for (12 per 100,000 people) (Goggins, Chan, Yang, & Chong, 2013; Goggins, Ren, Ng, Yang, & Chan, 2013). This is a substantial rise when compared with other headlining health threats such as the 2003 SARS epidemic (299 total deaths in Hong Kong) and the 2003 French heatwave (15,000 total deaths, or 23 per 100,000 people).

CASE BOX 4.8 TEMPERATURE-MORTALITY VERSUS TEMPERATURE-MORBIDITY THRESHOLD IN AN URBAN ASIAN CITY

Current studies indicate that temperatures above a locally specific threshold result in higher mortality rates. For every 1°C above a temperature-mortality threshold level, deaths increase by 2–5%. Specifically, the relative risk of mortality due to respiratory infection for every 1°C above the threshold is 1.129 (p > 0.05). Thus, when the temperature is 3°C above the threshold, the respiratory infection mortality rate is increased by approximately 13%.

The relationship between morbidity and temperature was also studied through a retrospective ecological study of data on outdoor temperature, pollution levels, and routine hospital admissions in Hong Kong (1998–2009). During the hot season, a 1°C increase above 29.0°C is associated with a 4.5% increase in hospital admissions. For every increase of 1°C above 29°C, admissions for unintentional injuries increased by 1.9%. During the cold season, a 1°C decrease below 26.9°C is associated with a 1.4% increase in hospital admission. For every decrease of 1°C within the 8.2–26.9°C range, admissions for cardiovascular diseases and intentional injuries rose by 2.1% and 2.4%, respectively. Hospital admissions for respiratory and infectious diseases increased during both extreme heat and cold events, but cardiovascular disease hospital admissions increased only during cold temperatures.

Sources: Chan et al. (2012, 2013) and Goggins, Chan, Yang, and Chong (2013).

In brief, due to the effects of climate change, the intensity and frequency of extreme temperature events are increasing. While these temperature events may not have an agreed universal definitions, both are associated with excess mortality among the elderly and people with chronic illnesses.

Biological hazard: epidemic

An **outbreak of infectious disease** can be defined as a sudden increase in the number of cases of a disease, which is above what is normally expected in the specific population and area. An **epidemic** occurs when an outbreak spreads through a larger geographical area with a higher proportion of infected people. Epidemics are classified as a biological natural hazard (International Federation of Red Cross and Red Crescent Societies [IFRC], n.d.) and are considered to be disasters, as they affect a large number of people and result in public health emergencies.

How is it reported?

Disease outbreaks are generally classified by the level of disease intensity, and placed into one of the following four categories (Centers for Disease Control and Prevention [CDC], 2012): **sporadic** refers to a disease that occurs infrequently and irregularly; **endemic** describes a disease within the expected prevalence and localised in a geographical region and community (e.g. malaria in Africa); **epidemic** refers to a disease whose incidence increases unusually and which spreads through a larger geographical area (e.g. SARS in 2003); **pandemic** describes a widespread epidemic that affects a sizeable portion of people in a region or a continent or across the world (e.g. pandemic influenza).

What are the known risk factors associated with adverse health outcomes?

While epidemics of different diseases have specific risk factors, the risk of an epidemic generally increases when the interaction between host, disease agent and environment becomes abnormal. Poverty is a main socioeconomic risk factor for epidemics. It can lead to impaired immunity as a result of malnutrition and low vaccination uptake. Moreover, it inhibits access to health care facilities and resources for disease control when an outbreak occurs. The risk of an epidemic also increases after the occurrence of natural disasters. Altered environments can favour the proliferation of pathogens and decrease the immunity of the host population. In particular, disasters with large-scale population displacement, resulting in overcrowding of temporary settlements and lack of water supplies and sanitation, render people vulnerable to waterborne and other infectious diseases (Watson, Gayer, & Connolly, 2006; Spiegel, Le, Ververs, & Salama, 2007). Climate change is another risk factor since it alters the breeding environment of disease-transmitting vectors. Epidemics may also happen due to the introduction of new pathogens in a setting that previously did not have them and the related diseases. People in the region might not have immunity to the new pathogens, a situation which favours the spread of the diseases by these pathogens.

What is the health impact of epidemics?

Depending on the disaster characteristics, the immediate health impact of epidemics may range from minor ailments to death. Pandemic influenza, cholera, dengue fever, malaria and measles are major diseases with high epidemic potential. The economic losses and sociopolitical disruptions from the epidemic can lead to psychological and social impact of the affected community.

Epidemics that affect animals and vegetation can lead to a major reduction in food production. In poorer countries, the shortage of food may eventually lead to economic disaster and malnutrition. In addition, some epidemics can also be transmitted across species. Animal epidemics should not be ignored as 61% of human infectious pathogens are zoonotic (Taylor, Latham, & Woolhouse, 2001). For example, swine influenza, which normally circulates only among swine species, caused a human pandemic in 2009.

What are the responses needed?

The choice of epidemic control measures depends on the route of transmission of the disease agent and the context. Principles for epidemic response include enhancing disease surveillance, controlling or eliminating agents at the source of transmission, improving environmental conditions and increasing the host's defences. Common

---

CASE BOX 4.9 CONTROLLING THE EMERGENCE OF NEW INFECTIOUS DISEASES: SEVERE ACUTE RESPIRATORY SYNDROME (SARS) 2002–2003

In November 2002, there were reports of an outbreak of unknown infectious disease in Guangzhou, the capital city of Guangdong Province in mainland China. Although as a geographic neighbour of Hong Kong, there was limited documentation of relevant exchanges between health authorities of the two communities. In February 2003, a visitor from Guangzhou, who had contracted the infection before travelling, visited Hong Kong. This visitor became the primary source of spreading the infection, later named severe acute respiratory syndrome (SARS), first in Hong Kong, and later to other cities around the world. During the subsequent months, the outbreak of SARS in Hong Kong had infected 1,755 people, among whom 299 eventually died (WHO, 2004, April 21). About 20% of the infected were health care personnel working in hospital wards where the SARS patients were treated and six of them died. The outbreak of SARS not only impacted the health of the population, but also had a great socio-economic impact on the city.

Consequences

New public health measures were established after the SARS incident to protect this urban community from future infectious disease risk. To name a few:

- Expansion and strengthening of public health services against infectious diseases;
- Establishment of Schools of Public Health in local universities to advance knowledge in infectious disease public health emergency response capacity building;
- Development of closer collaboration between Hong Kong, mainland China counterparts and the World Health Organization (WHO) in infectious disease surveillance and communication; and
- New contingency plans and infectious disease control protocols and public risk communication approaches had been developed.

Source: Lee (2014).

---

public health responses include ensuring a safe water supply to prevent waterborne diseases spreading, rigorous hygiene practices to protect humans from contaminated sources, vaccination campaigns to boost body immunity, and isolation and quarantine to prevent further contact with infected people (see Case Box 4.9).

The concept of one health is important to ensure health of other species (e.g. birds and poultries as to avian flu) should also be maintained and continuous surveillance efforts should be invested by the at-risk community.

In summary, infectious disease outbreaks are characterised by an unexpected, sudden and severe disease occurrence in a geographical location. Such outbreaks may occur when the interaction of host, disease agent and environment become unbalanced. Health impacts vary among different epidemic agents, but often some consequence might be severe and fatal. Continual surveillance and appropriate infection control measures targeting specific epidemic agents and settings help reduce the further spread of disease and alleviate the health impact.

Conclusion

This chapter examines the characteristics, health impacts and risk factors of several types of natural disasters, including earthquakes and tsunamis, volcanic eruptions, floods, cyclones, droughts and famines, heatwaves and cold waves, and epidemics. In general, each natural hazard poses unique health threats to at-risk populations. Disaster medical relief efforts should address both specific health threats associated with the disaster subtype as well as to cater for the general health needs of the underlying population.

References

Adonai. (2015, March 28). *Atacama desert flooded after 7 years of rain fell in just 12 hours* [Internet]. Retrieved from The Watchers website: http://www.thewatchers.adorraeli. com/2015/03/28/atacama-desert-flooded-after-7-years-of-rain-fell-in-just-12-hours/

Ahern, M., Kovats, R. S., Wilkinson, P., Few, R., & Matthies, F. (2005). Global health impacts of floods: Epidemiologic evidence. *Epidemiologic Reviews*, 27(1), 36–46. doi:10.1093/epirev/mxi004

Associated Programme on Flood Management (APFM). (2013). *Flood forecasting and early warning* (Integrated Flood Management Tools Series No. 19) [Internet]. Geneva, Switzerland: World Meteorological Organization. Retrieved from http://www.apfm.info/publications/tools/APFM_Tool_19.pdf

Baxter, P. J. (1990). Medical effects of volcanic eruptions. *Bulletin of Volcanology*, 52(7), 532–544.

Baxter, P. J., Ing, R., Falk, H., & Plikaytis, B. (1983). Mount St. Helens eruptions: The acute respiratory effects of volcanic ash in a North American community. *Archives of Environmental Health*, 38(3), 138–143.

Boardman, B. (1991). *Fuel poverty: From cold homes to affordable warmth*. London, UK: Belhaven Press.

Boyce, W. H. III, Saravanan, S. A., & Wolfson, N. (2016). Traumatic injuries during earthquakes. In N. Wolfson, A. Lerner, & L. Roshal (Eds.), *Orthopedics in disasters: Orthopedic injuries in natural disasters and mass casualty events* (pp. 109–121). Springer-Verlag Berlin Heidelberg.

Brennan, L. (1984). The development of the India Famine Codes: personalities, policies and politics. In B. Currey & G. Hugo (Eds.), *Famine as a geographical phenomenon* (GeoJournal Library Vol. 1; pp. 91–110). Dordrecht, Holland: D. Reidel Publishing Company.

Briggs, S. M. (2006). Earthquakes. *Surgical Clinics of North America, 86*(3), 537–544. doi:10.1016/j.suc.2006.02.003

British Medical Journal (BMJ). (2013). *Compartment syndrome of extremities: Step-by-step diagnostic approach* [Internet]. Retrieved from BMJ Best Practice website: http://bestpractice.bmj.com/best-practice/monograph/502/diagnosis/step-by-step.html

Brown, L. R., & Eckholm, E. P. (1974). *By bread alone.* New York, NY: Overseas Development Council.

Brunei Darussalam Prime Minister's Office. (2013). *NDMC to bolster disaster preparedness.* Retrieved from http://www.pmo.gov.bn/Lists/PMO%20News/NewDispForm.aspx?ID=118

Brunei Darussalam Prime Minister's Office. (2014). *Opening ceremony of the First Meeting of 10th Legislative Council Session* [Internet]. Retrieved from http://www.pmo.gov.bn/Lists/News/ItemDisplayForm.aspx?ID=121

Centers for Disease Control and Prevention (CDC). (2012). Section 11: Epidemic disease occurrence (Lesson 1: Introduction to epidemiology). In *Principles of epidemiology in public health practice: An introduction to applied epidemiology and biostatistics* (3rd ed.) (pp. 1-72–1-79) [Internet]. Retrieved from http://www.cdc.gov/ophss/csels/dsepd/ss1978/ss1978.pdf

Centre for Research on the Epidemiology of Disasters (CRED), Université catholique de Louvain. (2009). *The EM-DAT glossary* [Internet]. Retrieved from EM-DAT The International Disaster Database of CRED website: http://www.emdat.be/glossary/9

Chan, E.Y.Y., Goggins, W. B., Kim, J. J., & Griffiths, S. M. (2012). A study of intracity variation of temperature-related mortality and socioeconomic status among the Chinese population in Hong Kong. *Journal of Epidemiology and Community Health, 66*(4), 322–327.

Chan, E.Y.Y., Goggins, W. B., Yue, J. S. K., & Lee, P. (2013). Hospital admissions as a function of temperature, other weather phenomena and pollution levels in an urban setting in China. *Bulletin of the World Health Organization, 91*(8), 576–584. doi:10.2471/BLT.12.113035

Chou, Y. J., Huang, N., Lee, C. H., Tsai, S. L., Chen, L. S., & Chang, H. J. (2004). Who is at risk of death in an earthquake? *American Journal of Epidemiology, 160*(7), 688–695. doi:10.1093/aje/kwh270

Ciotonne, G. R., Anderson, P. D., Auf Der Heide, E., Darling, R. G., Jacoby, I., Noji, E., & Suner, S. (2006). *Disaster medicine* (3rd ed.). Philadelphia, PA: Mosby Elsevier.

Colwell, R. R., Kaper, J., & Joseph, S. W. (1977). *Vibrio cholerae, Vibrio parahaemolyticus,* and other vibrios: Occurrence and distribution in Chesapeake Bay. *Science, 198*(4315), 394–396.

Cox, G. W. (1981). The ecology of famine: An overview. In J. R. K. Robson (Ed.), *Famine: Its causes, effects and management* (pp. 5–18). New York, NY: Gordon and Breach.

Doocy, S., Daniels, A., Murray, S., & Kirsch, T. D. (2013). The human impact of floods: A historical review of events 1980–2009 and systematic literature review (Version 1). *PLoS Currents Disasters, 5*(April 16), 1–34. doi:10.1371/currents.dis.f4deb457904936b07c09daa98ee8171a

Goggins, W. B., Chan, E.Y.Y., Yang, C., & Chong, M. (2013). Associations between mortality and meteorological and pollutant variables during the cool season in two Asian cities with sub-tropical climates: Hong Kong and Taipei [Internet]. *Environmental Health, 12*(59), 1–10. doi:10.1186/1476–069X-12–59

Goggins, W. B., Ren, C., Ng, E., Yang, C., & Chan, E.Y.Y. (2013). Effect modification of the association between meteorological variables and mortality by urban climatic conditions in the tropical city of Kaohsiung, Taiwan. *Geospatial Health, 8*(1), 37–44.

Gupta, S. (2010). *Synthesis report on ten ASEAN countries disaster risks assessment: ASEAN disaster risk management initiative* [Internet]. Retrieved from United Nations Office for Disaster Risk Reduction (UNISDR) website: http://www.unisdr.org/files/18872_asean.pdf

Hajat, S., Ebi, K. L., Kovats, R. S., Menne, B., Edwards, S., & Haines, A. (2005). The human health consequences of flooding in Europe: A review. In W. Kirch, B. Menne, & R. Bertollini (Eds.), *Extreme weather events and public health responses* (pp. 185–196). Berlin, Germany: Springer.

Hansell, A. L., Horwell, C. J., & Oppenheimer, C. (2006). The health hazards of volcanoes and geothermal areas. *Occupational and Environmental Medicine, 63*(2), 149–156. doi:10.1136/oem/2005.022459

Hogan, D. E., & Bearden, J. (2007). Volcanic eruptions. In D. E. Hogan & J. L. Burstein (Eds.), *Disaster medicine* (2nd ed., pp. 266–276). Philadelphia, PA: Lippincott Williams & Wilkins.

Hong Kong Special Administrative Region, Environment Bureau. (2015, September). *Hong Kong climate change report 2015*. Retrieved from http://www.enb.gov.hk/sites/default/files/pdf/ClimateChangeEng.pdf

Huang, C., Barnett, A. G., Xu, Z., Chu, C., Wang, X., Turner, L. R., & Tong, S. (2013). Managing the health effects of temperature in response to climate change: Challenges ahead. *Environmental Health Perspectives, 121*(4), 415–419.

International Federation of Red Cross and Red Crescent Societies (IFRC). (n.d.). *Biological hazards: Epidemics* [Internet]. Retrieved from http://www.ifrc.org/en/what-we-do/disaster-management/about-disasters/definition-of-hazard/biological-hazards-epidemics/

Jay, G. (2006). Volcanic eruption. In G. R. Ciottone, P. D. Anderson, E.A.D. Heide, R. G. Darling, I. Jacoby, E. Noji, & S. Suner (Eds.), *Disaster medicine* (3rd ed., pp. 502–505). Philadelphia, PA: Mosby Elsevier.

Joint UNEP/OCHA Environment Unit. (2014). *Typhoon Haiyan (Yolanda) Philippines: Environmental situational overview* [Internet]. Retrieved from ReliefWeb website: http://reliefweb.int/sites/reliefweb.int/files/resources/Philippines%20Haiyan%20Environmental%20Situational%20Overview%2014–1–14.pdf

Jonkman, S., & Kelman, I. (2005). An analysis of causes and circumstances of flood disaster deaths. *Disasters, 29*(1), 75–97. doi:10.1111/j.0361–3666.2005.00275.x

Lee, S. H. (2014). Historical perspectives in public health: Experiences from Hong Kong. In S. M. Griffiths, J. L. Tang, & E. K. Yeoh (Eds.), *Routledge handbook of global public health in Asia* (pp. 5–20). Oxford, UK: Routledge.

Li, Y., Jaddoe, V. W., Qi, L., He, Y., Wang, D., Lai, J., . . . Hu, F. B. (2011). Exposure to the Chinese Famine in early life and the risk of metabolic syndrome in adulthood. *Diabetes Care, 34*, 1014–1018. doi:10.2337/dc-10–2039

Lipp, E. K., Huq, A., & Colwell, R. R. (2002). Effects of global climate on infectious disease: The cholera model. *Clinical Microbiology Reviews, 15*(4), 757–770. doi:10.1128/CMR.15.4.757

Meehl, G. A., & Tebaldi, C. (2004). More intense, more frequent, and longer lasting heat waves in the 21st century. *Science, 305*(5686), 994–997. doi:10.1126/science.1098704

Mohamed, N. (2014). *Ten-year review on progress towards and contributions made by the Pacific region to the Hyogo Framework for Action (HFA) from 2005–2015* [Internet]. Retrieved from

Pacific Disaster Net website: http://www.pacificdisaster.net/pdnadmin/data/original/UNISDR_2014_10YR_Review_PacificRegion_HFA_progress.pdf

Ndah, A. B., Kumar, L. D., & Becek K. (2015). *Revisiting the recurrent floods and landslide disasters in Brunei Darussalam: A satellite remote sensing perspective* (Working Paper 2) [Internet]. Retrieved from Academia website: http://www.academia.edu/9855128/REVISITING_THE_RECURRENT_FLOODS_AND_LANDSLIDE_DISASTERS_IN_BRUNEI_DARUSSALAM_A_SATELLITE_REMOTE_SENSING_PERSPECTIVE

Portilla, D., Shaffer, R. N., Okusa, M. D., Mehrotra, R., Molitoris, B. A., Bunchman, T. E., & Ibrahim, T. (2010). Lessons from Haiti on disaster relief. *Clinical Journal of the American Society of Nephrology, 5*(11), 2122–2129. doi:10.2215/CJN.03960510

Rahman, Y.H.A. (2011). *Brunei Darussalam: National progress report on the implementation of the Hyogo Framework for Action (2009–2011)* [Internet]. Retrieved from PreventionWeb website: http://www.preventionweb.net/files/18630_brn_NationalHFAprogress_2009–11.pdf

Ring of Fire. (n.d.). *Encyclopaedia Britannica* [Internet]. Retrieved from http://www.britannica.com/EBchecked/topic/118426/Ring-of-Fire

Sen, A. (1981). *Poverty and famines: An essay on entitlement and deprivation.* Oxford: Clarendon Press.

Shultz, J. M., Russell, J., & Espinel, Z. (2005). Epidemiology of tropical cyclones: The dynamics of disaster, disease and development. *Epidemiologic Reviews, 27*(1), 21–35. doi:10.1093/epirev/mxi011

Sim, D. (2015, March 27). Floods in Chile and landslides in Peru after heaviest rain in 80 years. *International Business Times* [Internet]. Retrieved from http://www.ibtimes.co.uk/floods-chile-landslides-peru-after-heaviest-rain-80-years-1493792

Smith, M. (2009). *Lessons learned in WASH response during urban flood emergencies* (The Global WASH Learning Project). New York, NY: Global WASH Cluster. Retrieved from http://www.bvsde.paho.org/texcom/desastres/washurbfl.pdf

Spiegel, P. B., Le, P., Ververs, M.-T., & Salama, P. (2007). Occurrence and overlap of natural disasters, complex emergencies and epidemics during the past decade (1995–2004) [Internet]. *Conflict and Health, 1*(2), 1–9. doi:10.1186/1752–1505–1–2 .

Stanke, C., Kerac, M., Prudhomme, C., Medlock, J., & Murray, V. (2013). The health effects of drought: A systematic review of the evidence (Version 1). *PLoS Currents Disasters, 5*(January 5), 1–44. doi:10.1371/currents.dis.7a2cee9e980f91ad7697b570bcc4b004

Taylor, L. H., Latham, S. M., Woolhouse, M. E. (2001). Risk factors for human disease emergence. *Philosophical Transaction of the Royal Society of London, Series B, 356*(1411), 983–989. doi:10.1098/rstb.2001.0888

United Nations (UN). (2011). *When a food security crisis becomes a famine* [Internet]. Retrieved from UN News Centre website: http://www.un.org/apps/news/story.asp?NewsID=39113&Cr=somalia&Cr1=#.VjxrVU3lqUk

United Nations Office for the Coordination of Humanitarian Affairs (OCHA). (2012). *Horn of Africa: Humanitarian snapshot* [Internet]. Retrieved from ReliefWeb website: http://reliefweb.int/sites/reliefweb.int/files/resources/map_2664.pdf

United Nations Office for the Coordination of Humanitarian Affairs (OCHA). (2015, April 12). *Chile: Floods and mudslides* (Informative note) [Internet]. Retrieved from ReliefWeb website: http://reliefweb.int/sites/reliefweb.int/files/resources/CL-Information_Note-Floods_Nothern_Region-20150415.pdf

United Nations Office for the Coordination of Humanitarian Affairs (OCHA). (2015, April 20). *Heavy rain and floods* (Redlac: Latin America and the Caribbean Weekly Note on Emergencies, Volume 400) [Internet]. Retrieved from ReliefWeb website: http://reliefweb.int/sites/reliefweb.int/files/resources/LAC-Report-Weekly_Note_On_Emergencies-ROLAC-ENG-20150420-MR-16323.pdf

United States Geological Survey (USGS). (2013). *The severity of an earthquake* [Internet]. Retrieved from http://pubs.usgs.gov/gip/earthq4/severitygip.html

United States Geological Survey (USGS). (2015). *Volcano hazards program* [Internet]. Retrieved from http://volcanoes.usgs.gov/

von Grebmer, K., Saltzman, A., Birol, E., Wiesmann, D., Prasai, N., Yin, S., . . . Sonntag, A. (2014). *2014 Global hunger index: The challenge of hidden hunger.* Bonn, Germany, Washington, DC, and Dublin, Ireland: Welthungerhilfe, International Food Policy Research Institute, and Concern Worldwide. doi:10.2499/9780896299580

Watson, J., Gayer, M., & Connolly, M. A. (2006). Epidemic risk after disasters. *Emerging Infectious Diseases, 12*(9), 1468–1469.

World Health Organization (WHO). (2004, April 21). *Emergencies preparedness, response: Summary of probable SARS cases with onset of illness from 1 November 2002 to 31 July 2003* [Internet]. Retrieved from http://www.who.int/csr/sars/country/table2004_04_21/en/

World Health Organization (WHO). (2005). Flooding and communicable diseases fact sheet: Risk assessment and preventive measures [Internet]. Retrieved from http://www.who.int/hac/techguidance/ems/en/FloodingandCommunicableDiseasesfactsheet.pdf

World Health Organization (WHO). (2011). *Horn of Africa crisis: August 2011 update* [Internet]. Retrieved from http://www.who.int/hac/events/hoa_crisis_update_1sep11.pdf?ua=1

World Health Organization (WHO). (2015a). *Cholera* [Internet]. Retrieved from http://www.who.int/mediacentre/factsheets/fs107/en/

World Health Organization (WHO). (2015b). *Climate change and health* [Internet]. Retrieved from http://www.who.int/mediacentre/factsheets/fs266/en/

World Meteorological Organization (WMO). (n.d.). *Tropical cyclones: Questions and answers* [Internet]. Retrieved from https://www.wmo.int/pages/mediacentre/factsheet/tropical cyclones.html

World Vision Hong Kong. (n.d.). Learn about hunger [Internet]. Retrieved from https://www.worldvision.org.hk/en/news/ireports/hunger-related-issues

Yuan, Y. F. (2001). Assessing countermeasures to emergency response in earthquakes. In B. F. Spencer, Jr., & Y. X. Hu (Eds.), *Earthquake engineering frontiers in the new millennium: Proceedings of the China-US Millennium Symposium on Earthquake Engineering, Beijing, 8–11 November 2000* (pp. 143–148). Lisse; Exton, PA: A.A. Balkema.

5

WHEN PUBLIC HEALTH AND DISASTER COLLIDE

Responding to health needs in natural disasters

Disasters cannot be prevented but their human health impact can be mitigated. Public health focuses on prevention and protection and adopts a population-based, life-course approach. Disaster response is a core competency in public health practice and public health approaches to disasters and crises are of a proactive, preventive and multidisciplinary nature. It includes risk management with a focus on disaster preparedness and risk reduction to help reduce the vulnerabilities of communities and increase their coping capacity. This chapter will highlight *humanitarian principles, public health responses in disasters and the basic requirements for heath.*

Humanitarian principles

Despite the end of the Cold War in the 1990s globally, protracted conflict and the need for humanitarian assistance has increased dramatically during the past three decades.

Humanitarian principles are the guiding rules and fundamental principles of humanitarian action. There are four key humanitarian principles endorsed by the UN General Assembly. **Humanity**: human suffering must be addressed wherever it is found. The purpose of humanitarian action is to protect life and health and ensure respect for human beings. **Neutrality**: humanitarian actors must not take sides in hostilities or engage in controversies of political, racial, religious or ideological nature. **Impartiality**: humanitarian action must be carried out on the basis of need alone, giving priority to the most urgent cases of distress and making no distinctions on the basis of nationality, race, gender, religion, belief, class or political opinion. **Operational independence**: humanitarian action must be autonomous from the political, economic, military or other objectives that any actor may hold with regard to areas where humanitarian action is being implemented (Leader, 2000; Mackintosh, 2000; UN, 2003; OCHA, 2010).

These humanitarian principles reflect important principles of non-discrimination, of how every human person should be considered as a human being and not be judged by his/her identity. Moreover, when it comes to how the assistance is being provided, it should be delivered according to the principle of proportionality – that is without any **subjective distinction** – and should not carry imbalanced advantages to conflicted parties. The International Red Cross and Red Crescent Movement supplemented these four basic principles with three more, as enshrined in the Red Cross Code of Conduct (1994) and Statute of the Movement (1986). **Voluntary service**: the movement is a voluntary relief movement and not be prompted in any manner by desire for gain. **Unity**: there can be only one Red Cross or Red Crescent society in any one country. It must be open to all. It must carry on its humanitarian work throughout its territory. **Universality**: all societies have equal status and share equal responsibilities and duties in helping each other worldwide. These seven "fundamental principles" were unanimously adopted in 1965 by the 20th International Conference of the Red Cross held in Vienna (International Federation of Red Cross and Red Crescent Societies [IFRC], n.d.a).

Although most humanitarian organisations are highly experienced in working on the front line, they still encounter numerous challenges. Firstly, even though humanitarian organisations must at all times adhere to humanitarian principles of impartiality, independence and neutrality, and ensure respect for people, they also need to maintain good relations with local authorities and communities in order to be permitted by them to work on disaster sites. Organisations need to gain trust from all parties in the conflict and volatile environment to stay absolutely impartial in political matters. Secondly, funding of many humanitarian groups comes from private donations or government subsidies, which are often unstable and insufficient. Humanitarian organisations must also respect and conform to the religious and cultural customs of disaster sites. Organisations with religious backgrounds may encounter greater difficulties when entering regions with a different religious belief. Amid the chaos of wars and disasters, the personal safety of rescuers may be seriously threatened. For instance, five members of Médecins Sans Frontières (MSF) died in an ambush in Afghanistan on 2 June 2004 and 50 staff members of IFRC were killed in just four years since the conflict broke out in Syria in March 2011. These unfortunate incidents have brought a tinge of sadness to humanitarian work. Besides, humanitarian workers may not be able to work effectively on disaster sites due to a lack of training, preparation and coordination. An example is the Sichuan earthquake in 2008, where a large number of NGOs and volunteers came forward to help on site. Despite their passion, the lack of experience, professional knowledge and backup support rendered their attempt to help in the rescue futile. Some of them even had to live on government aid, increasing the pressure on limited resources.

The general public health response in disasters

Effective care in disaster settings cannot be taken for granted. There are three principles in the general public health response to any disaster or crisis. These include: (1) securing the basic resources that human beings require to maintain health; (2) determining the current and likely health threats to the affected community, given the local environment and community's resources and knowledge, and enabling health-maintaining behaviours; and (3) finding and providing the resources required to address principles 1 and 2. Many public health concepts and epidemiology methods can be applied to support assessment, planning implementation, monitoring and evaluation of relief response and programmes in a disaster context.

The Sphere Project

The Sphere Project is a voluntary initiative covering various humanitarian actors, such as international and national NGOs, the IFRC, UN agencies, host governments and local affected communities. Its aim is "to help improve the quality of assistance to people affected by disaster or conflict, as well as the accountability of humanitarian agencies and states towards their constituents, donors and affected populations" (The Sphere Project, 2012, September). Its guiding values are based on two components: international humanitarian initiatives, human rights and refugee law; and the Code of Conduct for The International Red Cross and Red Crescent Movement and NGOs in Disaster Relief (IFRC & International Committee of Red Cross [ICRC], n.d.) (see Knowledge Box 5.1).

In terms of the standards for disaster and humanitarian action, the Sphere Project provides a set of minimum standards for humanitarian actors to plan, manage or implement interventions within the key sectors for survival. The Sphere Project was initiated in 1997 by a group of humanitarian NGOs and the International Red Cross and Red Crescent Movement. It was launched following the 1994 Rwanda crisis, which highlighted the need to establish certain standards in the humanitarian

KNOWLEDGE BOX 5.1   THE SPHERE PROJECT

As a voluntary initiative bringing together various humanitarian actors, the Sphere Project advocates that the basic requirements of health include clean water and sanitation, food and nutrition, shelter and clothing, health services and information. According to the Sphere guidelines, and in line with the organisation's aim of improving the quality of humanitarian assistance to people affected by disaster or conflict and the accountability of humanitarian agencies and states to their constituents, donors and the affected populations, securing these resources is the number one priority immediately following a disaster (The Sphere Project, 2012, September).

field. Minimum standards were identified in four key sectors: water supply and sanitation, nutrition and food aid, shelter and clothing, and health services. This led to the publication of the first Sphere handbook in 2000.

Since the first edition's publication, the Sphere handbook has gone through revisions and updates (The Sphere Project, 2004, 2011). These revisions attempted extensive clarification of concepts and modification of outcome indicators. The Humanitarian Charter, in particular, was revised in the third edition to give a clearer focus on the moral and legal bases for the Sphere standards and to reflect four major recent developments: the role of the crisis-affected state, the role of crisis-affected communities themselves as humanitarian actors, the engagement of humanitarian agencies in the protection of civilians in conflict-related crises, and the growing body of norms and practices around internally displaced persons (IDPs) and continuing concern with refugee protection (The Sphere Project, 2012). Knowledge Box 5.2 and Figure 5.1 summarise some minimum standards for how much is needed in different sectors as suggested by the Sphere Project.

KNOWLEDGE BOX 5.2 SOME KEY STANDARDS FOR SUPPORTING BASIC REQUIREMENTS OF HEALTH POST-DISASTER

1. **Water supply, sanitation and hygiene promotion (WASH)**

	Key indicators
Water quantity	2.5 to 3 litres per person per day for drinking and food;
	2 to 6 litres per person per day for basic hygiene practices;
	3 to 6 litres per person per day for basic cooking needs;
	7.5 to 15 litres per person per day for total basic water needs.
Water access	A maximum distance of 500 metres from any household to the nearest water point;
	Queuing time at a water source no more than 30 minutes.
Water quality	No faecal coliforms per 100 ml at the point of delivery and use;
	A chlorine residual of 0.5 mg per litre and turbidity below 5 nephelometric turbidity units (NTUs) at the tap at times of risk of diarrhoea epidemic;
	No negative health effects due to short-term contamination from chemical or radiological sources;
	No outbreak of waterborne or water-related diseases.

	Key indicators
Water facilities	At least two clean water collecting containers of 10–20 litres per household, one for storage and one for transportation;
	At least one washing basin per 100 people.
Excreta disposal	All excreta containment measures – i.e. trench latrines, pit latrines and soak-away pits, at least 30 metres away from any groundwater sources;
	One family toilet for a maximum of 20 people; possible to start with one for 50 people when there are no existing toilets;
	Separate, internally lockable toilets for women and men available in public places;
	Toilets no more than 50 metres from dwellings.
Waste management	Access to refuse containers for all households, which are emptied twice a week at minimum and are no more than 100 metres from a communal refuse pit;
	All wastes generated by populations living in settlements removed on a daily basis, and from the settlement environment a minimum of twice a week;
	At least one 100-litre refuse container available for ten households;
	All medical waste isolated and disposed of separately in a correctly designed pit.
Personal hygiene	Access to 250 g of bathing soap per person per month;
	Access to 200 g of laundry soap per person per month;
	Sanitary materials for menstruation for women and girls;
	Twelve washable nappies or diapers which are typically used for infants and children up to two years old;
	At least two hygiene promoters per 1,000 affected people in a camp scenario.

2. Food security and nutrition

	Key indicators
Nutrition	The average minimum population requirement of energy for population groups incorporating the requirements of all age groups and both sexes is 2,100 kcal per person per day.

3.   Shelter and clothing

	Key indicators
Covered living space	An initial minimum covered floor area of 3.5 square metres per person;
	All shelter solutions and materials meet agreed technical and performance standards and are culturally acceptable.
Construction	All construction in accordance with agreed safe building practices and standards;
	The involvement of the affected population and the maximising of local livelihood opportunities in construction activities.
Clothing	At least two full sets of clothing per person in correct size and appropriate for season, culture and climate.

4.   Health services

	Key indicators
Health facilities	One basic health unit per 10,000 population;
	One health centre per 50,000 people;
	One district or rural hospital per 250,000 people;
	At least ten inpatient and maternity beds per 10,000 people.
Health workers	At least one medical doctor per 50,000 population;
	At least one qualified nurse per 10,000 population;
	At least one midwife per 10,000 population;
	At least one community health worker per 1,000 population;
	At least 22 qualified health workers (including medical doctors, nurses, midwives, community health workers, etc.) per 10,000 population.
Essential health services	Control of communicable diseases;
	Child health;
	Sexual and reproductive health;
	Injury;
	Mental health;
	Non-communicable diseases.

Source: The Sphere Project (2011).

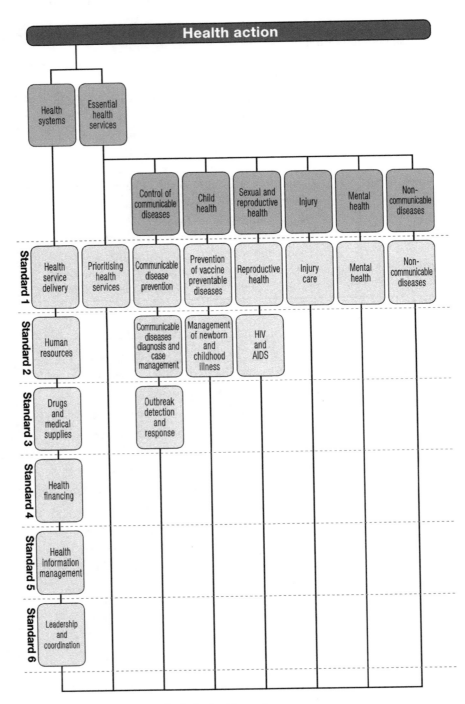

FIGURE 5.1   Minimum standards for health services

Source: Adapted from The Sphere Project (2011).

Securing basic requirements for health

Bolton (2006) suggests five basic requirements for health: (1) clean water and sanitation, (2) food and nutrition, (3) shelter and clothing, (4) health services and (5) information. Each of these key areas has its own technical challenges, standards and key respondents and stakeholders.

Water supply, sanitation and hygiene promotion (WASH)

Water is essential for human life and everyone has a right to have access to safe water and sanitation, as declared by the United Nations (n.d.). The lack of an adequate quantity or acceptable quality can pose health threats to humans (see also Knowledge Box 5.3).

"WASH" stands for water, sanitation and hygiene and is one of the major determinants of health outcomes. Increasing equitable access to safe water and basic sanitation services and improving hygiene practices are proven to reduce child mortality and improve health outcomes (United Nations Children's Fund [UNICEF], 2005). WASH programmes are important not only during emergency situations but also for health maintenance in the normal routine of life.

The World Health Organization (WHO) recognised these needs and emphasised the WASH programmes to reduce faecal-oral transmission of disease and exposure to disease-bearing vectors (WHO, Health Protection Agency, & partners, 2011b). WHO estimated that diarrhoeal diseases caused the deaths of more than 13,500 children under 14 years in the Eastern European and Central Asian countries of the WHO European region in 2011, due to poor drinking-water quality and inadequate sewage and sanitation systems (Valent et al., 2004). However, in disasters, people are often challenged with substandard sanitation, inadequate water supplies and poor hygiene that make affected people more vulnerable to **water- and sanitation-related illnesses**, such as diarrhoeal diseases, measles, cholera and

---

KNOWLEDGE BOX 5.3 FACTS AND TRENDS OF HEALTH PROBLEMS RELATED TO WATER AND SANITATION

- More than 11 million people have died due to drought since 1900.
- Between 2001 and 2006, there were 2,163 water-related disasters, which have killed more than 290,000 people, affected more than 1.5 billion and inflicted more than US$422 billion of damage.
- The WASH programme could help curb the nearly 300 million school days being missed each year due to diarrhoea.

(CARE et al., 2010; United Nations Office for Disaster Risk Reduction [UNISDR], 2011; United Nations Water [UN-Water], 2013)

malaria. Water supply facilities might be damaged seriously during natural disasters like earthquakes, or contaminated in man-made disasters such as chemical spill accidents when the public water system can no longer support the distribution of water to the affected population or supply a sufficient amount of water for daily use.

Investigating situations in the late 1990s and early 2000s, Connolly et al. (2004) found more than 40% of deaths in emergency camp situations were due to preventable diarrhoeal diseases, of which more than 80% happened in children under two years of age. Factors related to the spread of these infectious diseases are contaminated water, lack of water, unwashed hands and flies. **Vector-related diseases**, such as malaria, dengue fever, filariasis and skin irritation, can also occur in emergency settlements with poor water access and management (e.g. uncovered water sources) (World Health Organization [WHO], United Kingdom Health Protection Agency [HPA], & partners, 2011b).

Who is the key player in this sector?

The United Nations Children's Fund (**UNICEF**) is one of the most important global actors in ensuring provision of water, sanitation and hygiene in emergency situations. UNICEF was established in December 1946 by the United Nations to meet the emergency needs of children in post-war Europe and China. The UN agency gained their water and sanitation expertise after serving in a prolonged drought affecting a community in northern India in 1966 (see also Case Box 5.1).

CASE BOX 5.1   IMPLICATIONS OF THE DAMAGE TO WATER SUPPLIES IN THE 1995 GREAT HANSHIN-AWAJI EARTHQUAKE

On 17 January 1995, the Great Hanshin-Awaji earthquake struck the southern part of the Hyogo prefecture in Japan. With a magnitude of 7.0 measured by the Richter scale, it injured more than 6,300 people, brought down more than 237,000 houses and interrupted water supplies in 10 cities and seven towns, affecting 1,265,730 households. The economic cost resulting from the water supply facilities destruction was estimated to be ¥55,800 million. Service pipes in 180,000 households (13% of the total population) in the affected areas were damaged. The reservoirs at both the Niteko Dam and Kitayama Dam almost collapsed; the water intake facilities in Ashiya River were buried by landslides; and there were many water leakages from pipes in the disaster-struck area. A lack of clean drinking water can lead to dehydration and the development of water-related illnesses, such as diarrhoea, typhoid fever, cholera and leptospirosis. Insufficient amounts of clean water may drive people to search for polluted water resources in order to survive. In addition, the lack of clean water may limit the safe practice of health workers (Magara & Yano, 2005).

In disaster, the role of UNICEF includes ensuring there is a water supply during the first 72 hours of a disaster, promoting hygiene practices, such as proper hand washing, excreta disposal and safe household water treatment and storage, and implementing the WASH programme in schools. UNICEF works in partnership with local communities, national authorities and other international organisations (UNICEF, 2012b). UNICEF is responsible for coordinating the overall emergency WASH response under the United Nations Inter-Agency Standing Committee (IASC) Cluster Approach, which will be discussed further in Chapter 7.

How can these needs be addressed?

Clean water is the immediate need in the early phase of an emergency. **Water tankering** or water trucking is one of the rapid means of transporting water to the affected areas (Reed, 2011a). Normally during disasters, the water resources are contaminated or the water pipe system is disrupted. There are different ways of treating water before it can be properly consumed by humans. **Water treatment**, such as filtration, boiling, chlorination and solar disinfection, and proper **water storage** are some of the simple methods that can be done at the household level. Figure 5.2

FIGURE 5.2   Water treatment using chlorine tablet

Source: Adapted from Sustainable Sanitation and Water Management (SSWM) Toolbox (http://www.sswm.info/sites/default/files/toolbox/IFRC%202008%20How%20to%20 treat%20water%20with%20chlorine%20tablets.jpg).

shows the disinfection method using chlorine tablets. Besides the water quality, it is actually the quantity that should be prioritised. Children and women may need to find water during water shortages and have no time to go to school and work (WHO, HPA, & partners, 2011b).

During emergency phase, sanitation facilities are also essential to avoid health risks associated with improper management of excreta or waste (Reed, 2011b). A **simple pit latrine structure** (see Figure 5.3) is the easiest and quickest type of latrine that can be built. However, building permanent structures is better, and many agencies thus prefer the use of ready-made sanitation solutions while waiting for the installation of communal toilets. If water is available, the wet system is preferable, such as **trench latrines**. The basic principle when building these latrines is to design and place the latrines at least 15–30 metres away from the groundwater sources and ensure the bottom of the latrine is at least 1.5 metres above the water table (The Sphere Project, 2011, p. 105). As soon as the community is likely to stay in a new place, a **communal latrine** should be constructed. Special attention needs to be considered in building latrines for **vulnerable populations**, such as the elderly and disabled people. Some modifications, such as providing a chair, a handrail and a rope tied onto the handrail and fed through a pulley to the door for closing, should be considered to enable these

FIGURE 5.3 A typical simple pit latrine design in a school in Kenya

Source: Photo by Sustainable Sanitation Alliance (SuSanA) Secretariat/CC BY 2.0 (https://www.flickr.com/photos/gtzecosan/5324341452/; https://creativecommons.org/licenses/by/2.0/deed.en).

people to go to the toilet independently (Oxfam, 2007). Another important concern is women's susceptibility to violence and sexual assault when they walk to the toilet at night. Therefore, facilities for men and women should be well separated, and **lighting** should be provided (IASC, 2005) (see also Case Box 5.2).

CASE BOX 5.2   SCHOOL-LED TOTAL SANITATION (SLTS) IN NEPAL

After a decade of violence and conflicts that caused 14,000 deaths, Nepal was still struggling with political instability in 2006, which kept the country's provision of basic services, such as sanitation facilities, to the minimum. Around 43% of the children under five were stunted, while about 50% of the population defecated in open areas and over 10 million cases of diarrhoeal disease were reported annually.

Introduced by UNICEF, the term Community Approaches to Total Sanitation (CATS) covers a wide range of community-based activities aiming at eliminating open defecation, inducing changes in behaviour, and promoting local innovations. This approach tried to achieve the Millennium Development Goals (MDGs) of halving, "by 2015, the proportion of population without sustainable access to safe drinking water and basic sanitation."

Under CATS, UNICEF worked with the Nepal government and local communities in 2005 to pilot School-led Total Sanitation (SLTS), a community-based

FIGURE 5.4   School children in Nepal

Source: Photo by Dmitry A. Mottl/CC BY-SA 3.0 (https://en.wikipedia.org/wiki/Education_in_Nepal#/media/File:Nepalese_school.jpg; http://creativecommons.org/licenses/by-sa/3.0/).

initiative that begins at schools and extends to the surrounding communities. Figure 5.4 shows some Nepalese school children with their teacher on the road in Pokhara. SLTS works with children's clubs along with the sanitation subcommittee comprised of the school headmaster, chairperson of one of the children's clubs, as well as representatives of the school management committee, the parent-teacher association, the Mother's Club, and the Water Users and Sanitation Committee. Together they lead the campaign to educate parents and neighbours on the importance of keeping the environment clean.

Interventions

By June 2006, the programme had reached nearly 500,000 people across 15 districts. The project aimed at achieving an open-defecation-free community; enhancing personal, household, and environmental hygiene behaviour; engaging children in development activities; increasing the ownership of sanitation and increasing hygiene activities by schools and communities; and enabling a strong school-community partnership. Project teams also assessed the sanitation and hygiene situations of schools' catchment areas by calculating the volume of faeces collected in the areas, and created maps to identify households with and without access to latrines. "One toilet, one household" was the slogan adopted by the project and was introduced to the communities using a participatory approach.

Conclusion

SLTS had reached nearly 90,000 households through 300 schools and over 1,000 settlements in 250 school catchment areas had been declared open-defecation-free (ODF) by June 2009. Fewer cases of diarrhoeal and communicable diseases were reported after the campaign.

Sources: Adhikari and Shrestha (2008, 2008), November, Adhikari, Shrestha, Malla, and Shrestha (2008), UNICEF (2009a, 2009b) and Shrestha (n.d.).

The promotion of good hygiene practices, the provision of safe drinking water and the reduction of environmental health risks are the highest priority interventions in emergency situations (WHO, & HPA, 2011b). The first step is to generate **rapid needs assessment** in order to have an overview of the existing WASH problems, the services availability and the coverage. **Gender analysis** and **cultural sensitivity** should also be incorporated to counter unequal access to aid supplies for women and to consider the different types of latrines used in different cultures. Effective **hygiene promotion** is believed to be one of the tools for reducing the incidence of water-related diseases. Hygiene promotion covers a wide range of activities that aim to reduce disease transmission through good hygiene practices, such as hand washing and proper latrine use.

Food and nutrition

What is malnutrition, undernutrition, wasting and stunting?

Food and nutrition are the cornerstones of survival. The right to adequate food, enshrined as a human right in Article 25(1) of the Universal Declaration of Human Right (UN, 1948), needs to be ensured in all circumstances (see Knowledge Box 5.4). Food shortages are associated with some emergencies. **Malnutrition** is a broad term that commonly refers to undernutrition and overnutrition. **Undernutrition** is a condition of malnutrition that occurs when intake and absorption of energy, protein or micronutrients are insufficient. Acute undernutrition can result in **wasting**, which is characterised by a rapid deterioration in nutritional status over a short period of time defined as having a weight-to-height ratio that is two standard deviations below the median of a reference population. Chronic undernutrition due to poor maternal nutrition status, poor infant and young child feeding practices or repeated infections can lead to **stunting**, which is characterised by achieving a height two standard deviations below the median height of people of the same age (UNICEF, 2012a). On the other hand, **overnutrition** is a condition of malnutrition that occurs when an excessive amount of nutrients is absorbed as a result of overconsumption of food; overweight and obesity are forms of overnutrition. Undernutrition is the usual form of malnutrition in emergency situations.

Severe acute malnutrition is especially of concern in low-income countries afflicted by droughts, famines, wars and conflicts. Both short- and long-term health impacts may result from malnutrition, such as growth retardation and lowered immunity from **protein–energy malnutrition**; anaemia, material and foetal mortality and intra-uterine growth retardation from **iron deficiency**; and night blindness from **vitamin A deficiency**. In emergency settings, it is important to ensure the affected population's access to adequate and safe food (The Sphere Project, 2011). Disaster recovery is hampered by the morbidity and mortality associated with food shortages (WHO, 2000).

On the other hand, **overnutrition** is a condition of malnutrition that occurs when an excessive amount of nutrients is absorbed as a result of overconsumption of food; overweight and obesity are forms of overnutrition. Overall, undernutrition is the usual form of malnutrition in emergency situations.

Who are the key players?

The World Food Programme (WFP) and Food and Agriculture Organization of the United Nations (FAO) are the two international agencies which are mainly responsible for agriculture and food assistance and the United States Children's Fund (UNICEF) is responsible for nutrition in emergencies and leads the Global Nutrition Cluster (GNC).

Established in 1961, **WFP** is part of the United Nations system and is voluntarily funded. WFP's vision is to ensure every man, woman and child has access at all times to the food needed for an active and healthy life. It coordinates food supply during an emergency, including natural disasters, wars and civil conflicts. After

KNOWLEDGE BOX 5.4   FACTS AND TRENDS OF NUTRITION

- Malnutrition is a major contributor to diseases and premature deaths among mothers and children.
- Malnutrition is the underlying cause of about one-third of all child deaths under five years old. About 52 million children were suffering from acute malnutrition in 2011.
- In 2011, stunting affected about 165 million children under five years old globally; 42% of children in Eastern Africa were stunted, which was the highest rate globally.
- Wasting contributed to about 1.5 million child deaths annually. It results from acute food shortages and is compounded by illnesses.
- Maternal and child undernutrition accounted for more than 10% of the global burden of diseases in 2011 (WHO, 2012).

FIGURE 5.5   Food aid distribution

Source: Photo by Kate Holt/AusAID/CC BY 2.0 (https://www.flickr.com/photos/dfataus tralianaid/10665202905/; https://creativecommons.org/licenses/by/2.0/deed.en).

the emergency phase, it helps communities rebuild their lives with food. WFP is also responsible for coordinating logistics. WFP augments logistics infrastructure, provides common logistics services and provides logistic information, such as the

United Nations Humanitarian Air Service (UNHAS) flight schedule and detailed lists of available local transport for humanitarian workers during an emergency response (WFP, n.d.a, n.d.b). Figure 5.5 shows women carrying their food aid in a cart, near a WFP food distribution point at Epworth in Harare, Zimbabwe in April 2009. **FAO** is a UN agency which leads international efforts to defeat hunger. It was established in 1945. One of the priority work areas of FAO is to increase the resilience of livelihoods from disasters. It is achieved through reducing risks and enhancing the resilience of a country's food and agriculture system. When emergencies arise, it is responsible for ensuring disaster response plans are coordinated at different levels (FAO, n.d.).

How should these health needs be addressed?

As nutritional needs are different for various groups – for example a pregnant woman may need various micronutrients for the healthy growth of the foetus – it is important to disaggregate data at least by sex and age, so that the most affected groups can be identified and the needs of vulnerable groups can be addressed appropriately, while nutritional interventions, such as general food distribution, additional micronutrients in staple foods and specific interventions, should be targeted at high risk subgroups. Optimising infant and child feeding, improving food security and ensuring access to health care are ways to reduce the risks of undernutrition. With appropriate infant and child feeding, including the promotion of breastfeeding, mortality can be reduced (WHO, HPA, & partners, 2011a). Before planning for any food relief programme, an initial rapid assessment is needed to provide a justification for intervention. During the emergency phase of a disaster, rapid nutritional needs assessments are needed at different levels, such as individual, family, vulnerable groups and general population (WHO, HPA, & partners, 2011a) (see Case Box 5.3).

In general, programmes targeting food and nutrition can be classified into two types: **general feeding programme** and **selective feeding programme**. In an emergency setting which affects a large population, ensuring basic food and nutrition is of utmost importance for basic survival. The general feeding programme aims to provide the affected population with the minimum energy, protein, fats and micronutrient requirements required for light physical activity.

A **selective feeding programme** is a more targeted food programme which aims to reduce the prevalence of malnutrition and mortality among vulnerable groups, such as pregnant women and moderately malnourished children, by providing them with additional energy and nutrients which are not provided in the general feeding programme or basic diet. It could be done by either on-site feeding or distribution of a dry ration. One of the examples of special nutritional products that are commonly used at the emergency phase is ready-to-use foods. They are provided as a supplement to children from six to 59 months who are at high risk of developing malnutrition (WHO, 2000). Note that nutritional interventions should be chosen based on the evidence and the latest best practice (WHO, HPA, & partners, 2011a).

CASE BOX 5.3 NUTRITIONAL ISSUES OF THE WENCHUAN EARTHQUAKE, 2008

The earthquake which struck Wenchuan in Sichuan Province on 12 May 2008 was the most devastating earthquake in China since 1900 in terms of both the number of people affected and the economic loss incurred, and the second deadliest following the 1976 Tangshan earthquake (Guha-Sapir, Below, & Hoyois, n.d.).

Food insecurity is common during a disaster and might even persist throughout the disaster cycle. Nevertheless, acute malnutrition, including underweight and wasting among children, was not as prevalent as expected after the Wenchuan earthquake, mainly due to the food rationing imposed by the Chinese government. After the earthquake, the government implemented a three-month general feeding programme where victims were each allowed a ration of 0.5 kg of cereals together with financial assistance of 10 renminbi (around US$1.61) per person per day.

Undoubtedly, the government's action remains an exemplar demonstrating as it does the significance of a general feeding programme. At the same time, however, the increase in cases of micronutrients deficiency after the earthquake has highlighted the importance of having a selective feeding programme as well as the general feeding programme: the nutritional status of those residing in rural areas was worse than that of the city dwellers and micronutrients deficiency was more prevalent among the former because the supply of nutritious food was disrupted. Therefore, it is essential for a selective feeding programme to be put in place together with the general one in the future. The selective feeding programme based on appropriate needs assessments should target the vulnerable populations. Lastly, improving the nutritional status during the pre-impact phase is of equal importance.

Sources: Yin et al. (2010), Zhao, Yin et al. (2010), Zhao, Yu et al. (2010), Sun et al. (2013) and Dong et al. (2014).

While there are global awareness of food and nutritional issues in emergency context, there currently are gaps in response guidelines availability for vulnerable populations, such as people with non-communicable diseases and of older age group.

Shelter and clothing

A shelter provides **thermal comfort** to a person. Shelter and clothing also **protect** people from weather changes and offer **personal safety**, **privacy** and **dignity**. In disasters, the affected population may experience the loss of shelter and personal assets, including clothing. Restoring shelter and providing adequate clothing at the emergency phase in disaster are critical for survival. Inadequate shelter and clothing, especially in extreme weather, can increase the risk of fall-ing sick. Without shelter, people might be exposed to strong prolonged sunshine, extreme temperatures and rainfall, which can cause **dehydration, sunburn, heat stroke, frostbites** and etc. Shelter and clothing also serve as barriers against vectors such as insects, rats and animals(Checchi, Gayer, Grais, & Mills, 2007). Mosquitoes, flies, fleas and lice are the most common vectors identified in overcrowded situa-tions with poor hygiene and water access. **Acute respiratory infections**, such as pneumonia and bronchitis, are also major causes of death in disasters. Poor and overcrowded shelters with indoor air pollution may contribute to the development of these illnesses.

Who are the key players?

During disasters and emergencies, the International Federation of Red Cross and Red Crescent Societies (IFRC) and the Office of the United Nations High Com-missioner for Refugees (UNHCR) co-chair the Shelter Cluster, a United Nations Inter-Agency Standing Committee (IASC) coordination mechanism. The **IFRC** is responsible for coordinating shelters in disaster contexts, while the **UNHCR** is responsible for coordinating shelters for IDPs. The **IFRC** was founded in 1919. It is currently one of the largest humanitarian organisations in the world. It carries out relief operations to assist victims of disasters, and combines this with development work to strengthen the capacities of its member national societies (IFRC, n.d.c). In a natural disaster, the IFRC usually leads the Shelter Cluster for a minimum of three months or until the end of the emergency phase (IFRC, 2012). The **UNHCR** is a UN human rights–monitoring body established under the International Cov-enant on Civil and Political Rights in 1950 and mandated to lead and coordinate international action to protect refugees and resolve refugee problems worldwide (UNHCR, n.d.a). The UNHCR leads the Shelter Cluster during man-made disas-ters and conflicts (UNHCR, n.d.b). Figure 5.6 also shows a temporary shelter for Malawi earthquake victims funded by Department for International Development (DFID), United Kingdom.

How should this need for shelter be addressed?

In the emergency context, it is important to conduct an **assessment** of local needs, capacities and resources before planning and preparation for shelter provision. Issues such as safety and security of the potential shelter building sites, availability of financial resources, building materials, technology and human resources, and institutional as well as legal capability within communities should be explored during the assessment phase. Provision of shelter depends on the destruction caused by the disaster. Repair-ing damaged homes is usually the cheapest and quickest way to provide adequate housing for the affected community. It is a less traumatic approach as well. In areas

FIGURE 5.6 A temporary shelter funded by DFID in Malawi after an earthquake in 2010

Source: Photo by Shareefa Choudhury/UK Department for International Development/CC BY 2.0 (https://www.flickr.com/photos/dfid/4992504007; https://creativecommons.org/licenses/by/2.0/deed.en 2.0 Generic license).

with minor destruction of homes and no major population displacement, housing repairs can be considered. (Barakat, 2003) However, in areas where housing repairs are not applicable, the use of emergency and temporary shelters can be considered. **Emergency and temporary shelters** are usually plastic sheeting, tents or emergency centres, which are designed to satisfy the immediate shelter needs for the early months post–disaster (see also Knowledge Box 5.5).

KNOWLEDGE BOX 5.5 PLASTIC SHEETING AS EMERGENCY SHELTER

Plastic sheeting, made from polyethylene, is one of the most commonly used temporary building materials for emergency shelters (see Figure 5.7 for an example). Although the major advantages of this kind of shelter are its versatility and low cost, plastic sheeting is supposed to be a short-term solution for sheltering and its anticipated lifetime is less than two years. In order to minimise its adverse impact on the environment, relief agencies are advised to provide framing and support along with the plastic sheeting to avoid people cutting down trees to build frames. In addition, sheeting made from non-renewable materials should have a proper disposal plan. Figure 5.8 illustrates how plastic sheeting can be used in emergency contexts.

FIGURE 5.7 Two hundred rolls of heavy-duty plastic sheeting being provided to earthquake-affected households in Nepal's Kathmandu District's Sankhu village and surrounding areas on 1 May 2015 by USAID

Source: Photo by USAID DART/Public Domain (https://www.flickr.com/photos/usembassykathmandu/17402153471/in/album-72157652684696686/).

Family shelter (A.4.1)

- Basic shelter structures
- Repair of damaged buildings
- Upgrade of tents and shelters
- Timber framed shelters

FIGURE 5.8 Using plastic sheeting for family emergency shelter

Source: Adapted from IFRC and Oxfam (2007).

Post disaster "sheltering process" is a continuum between humanitarian action and long-term development. During the construction of shelters, social and educational services, access to market and a responsible use of natural resources should be taken into consideration (IFRC, n.d.b). Humanitarian agencies who engage in post-disaster shelter building or repair should review local situations, such as disaster type, geographical conditions and cultural practices. Agencies may provide assistance, technical guidance and training as well as supply appropriate construction materials, tools and fixings, cash or vouchers, or a combination of the foregoing (The Sphere Project, 2011).

In addition to shelter, when delivering clothing and living amenities post-disaster, consideration should be given to local culture, weather, gender and age appropriateness to address the special needs of vulnerable. Special consideration should also be given to both ends of the age spectrum. For instance, since children and the elderly are more prone to heat loss, extra or thicker clothing should be provided. Gender sensitive supplies (e.g. hijabs, sanitary napkins and panties) should also be considered.

Health services

Both natural and man-made disasters pose challenges for health services. Immediately after a natural disaster, access and provision of life-saving health care services are a critical determinant for survival. Nevertheless, **damage to health infrastructure and resources** (e.g. drugs and refrigerating systems) disrupt the existing health services and the **mass influx of injured victims** coupled with the **shortage of health workers** could cause chaos in health service provision.

Who are the key players in the health sector?

In general, in addition to local residents and health care workers, **military forces** are usually the earliest medical teams that arrive in the immediate aftermath of a

---

CASE BOX 5.4   CHRONIC DISEASE CARE POST-DISASTER IN ASIA

Many relief aid organisations neglect the medical needs of those with chronic diseases during emergency situations as they mainly focus on trauma treatment and potential outbreaks of communicable diseases. The study by Chan and Sondorp (2008) highlights the importance of addressing chronic medical conditions and assessing the pre-existing health profiles of the affected population. Table 5.1 shows the overwhelming burden of chronic diseases in some of the disaster-prone countries.

TABLE 5.1 Burden of chronic diseases in selected disaster-prone countries

Country	Total number of natural disasters 2000–2008	% of chronic disease deaths (among total annual deaths)
China	235	79
India	160	53
Indonesia	133	61
Pakistan	61	42

disaster. The military medical teams have a structured approach to respond in a rapid and coordinated manner. Their local knowledge, resource access and logistics capacity (e.g. the ability to reach remote areas) is valuable for resource distribution, security services, search and rescue, medical interventions, camp settings and transportation post natural disasters. Under the Cluster Approach led by the United Nations Office for the Coordination of Humanitarian Affairs (OCHA), the World Health Organization (WHO) is the leading agency for health. **WHO** was established in 1948 and is the specialised agency within the United Nations responsible for providing leadership on global health matters. In emergencies, WHO leads the Global Health Cluster (GHC) and works together with other agencies and organisations to respond to health needs in emergencies. Apart from WHO, military, non-governmental organisations (NGOs) and civil society are also involved in providing health services during emergencies.

How should health needs be addressed in an emergency?

With limited resources during and after disasters, how medical and health services should be organised becomes a subject of important research and practical effort.

In emergency situations, **triage** prioritises victims for the appropriate medical attention based on severity and expectations for survival. Without triage, there would be confusion and chaos in the provision of health care. The basic underlying principles of triage (Du Mortier & Coninx, 2007) include: (1) with limited time, services and human resources, it is not possible to do everything for everybody; and (2) the aim therefore is to achieve the best possible results for the greatest number of people (see also Case Box 5.4).

Disasters can cause an enormous number of casualties and massive damage to the health infrastructure. As a result, the affected country and international organisations try to find ways to provide immediate medical care to the victims. Education and care facilities may turn into temporary medical centres (see Case Box 5.5). **Field hospitals** are defined as mobile, self-contained, self-sufficient health care facilities capable of rapid deployment and expansion or contraction to meet immediate emergency requirements for a specified period of time (Pan American Health Organization/WHO Regional Office for the Americas [PAHO/ WHO], 2003). According to the WHO recommendation, field hospitals should be able to (1) provide early emergency medical care (up to 48 hours after the disaster); (2) provide follow-up care for trauma cases, emergencies, routine health care and emergencies (from day 3 to day 15); and (3) act as a temporary facility to substitute damaged installations pending repair or reconstruction (usually from the second month to two years or more post-disaster). The basic requirements for field hospitals are: (1) to be fully operational within 24 hours of the disaster; (2) to be entirely self-sufficient; and (3) to offer comparable or higher standards of medical care than were available in the affected country prior to the precipitating event (PAHO/WHO, 2003).

CASE BOX 5.5 MOBILISATION OF EXISTING RESOURCES: NUTRITIONAL REHABILITATION HOME, SUNAKOTHI, LALITPUR, NEPAL

By Carol Ka Po Wong

After the Nepal earthquake on 25 April 2015, hospitals were overwhelmed by the scale of the massive disaster and the huge number of injured. Many patients had to sleep on the floor and in the tents outside the hospitals. Apart from the dire need for medical supplies and surgical equipment, there was an enormous need for beds for severely injured and surgical cases.

The Nutritional Rehabilitation Home (NRH) is one of the projects of the Nepal Youth Foundation, which aims at restoring the health of severely malnourished children as well as educating mothers about nutrition and childcare. From July 2014 to April 2015, they treated 239 malnourished children. During the course of the treatment (usually about five to six weeks), the caretakers (mostly their mothers) are taught in how to prepare nutritious meals, using foods readily available in rural areas, as well as improving their neighbours' nutrition and child care practices. The NRH was not affected by the earthquake that shook Nepal on 25 April 2015. Children and their caretakers were all safe, and the team of staff was able to deploy relief programmes within days of the earthquake. One of them was to convert the NRH into a recovery shelter, which served 285 quake-affected patients from 24 districts from 29 April to late June 2015.

One of the challenges the health authorities faced during the relief phase was to discharge patients to make room for new quake patients. The problem was that most of the patients were unable to travel long distances and still required medical attention. The staff of the NRH decided to accept some of these patients, which could satisfy the dual needs. The NRH team of 15 first expanded the initial 24-bed capacity to 65 beds by converting the children's playing room, doctors' room and training room into wards. Meanwhile, an additional three nurses and one cook joined the force so that patients could receive 24-hour nursing care and nutritious meals four times a day. As the majority of the patients referred by 12 hospitals had bone fractures and needed post-operative care, doctors' consultation sessions were available on alternate days. In addition, counsellors were ready to provide psychological support. Once the people had fully recovered, NRH also arranged transportation services to drop them home in remote areas of Nepal.

Sources: Hume (2015, April 27), Nepal earthquake: Hospitals overflowing, rural towns cut off as death toll continues to climb (2015, April 27), Birch (2015, April 29) and Nepal Youth Foundation (2015).

Mobile health unit deployment is a strategy to provide health care in remote **unstable situations**. They may be considered for a **short transition period**, before the opening or reopening of fixed health services. The services modality might offer preventive and curative services. However, several factors need to be considered before setting up mobile health units (e.g. the range of services available, the referral system associated with such services, whether they respond to the priority needs and logistic availability, and the ability to refer patients to permanent facilities (ICRC, 2006; Du Mortier & Coninx, 2007).

A **foreign medical team** is defined as a group of health professionals and supporting staff travelling outside their country of origin, aiming to provide health care to disaster-affected populations. It can involve governmental (both civilian and military), non-governmental as well as professional expertise groups (WHO, 2013).

In recent years, a global phenomenon of "disaster tourism" emerged during disaster response. **Disaster tourism** can be defined as people travelling to disaster settings to (1) see from the damaged artefact the gross intensity of the disasters; (2) experience the remnants of local treasures; (3) appreciate the reconstruction process through observing the states of the residents and the industries; (4) listen to the stories of the survivors; and (5) obtain lessons associated with the specific relief/response/reconstruction (Hiji, 2012). A disaster tourist has also been defined as a "person heading to the site of a disaster to see the destruction, take pictures, obtain bragging rights, and get the shoulder badge" (Van Hoving, Waliis, Docrat, & De Vries, 2010, p. 202). Regardless, the negativity towards disaster tourists has caused huge ethical as well as public criticism, especially when these bystanders might affect response efficiency (e.g. crowding traffic and using up valuable resources) as a result of their lack of preparedness in travelling to disaster-affected areas (see also Case Box 5.6).

CASE BOX 5.6   HAITI EARTHQUAKE 2010

The rising number of disasters globally has resulted in the emergence of international medical teams, which benefit the affected population who have no access to basic services in the immediate aftermath of disasters. The increase in international medical teams also shows global solidarity. However, many experts are concerned both about the medical teams' accountability and the standard of their care, which might not be appropriate for the local culture, and also the problem of medical disaster tourism. The Haiti earthquake in 2010 gives a different perspective on how post-disaster health services should be provided (Van Hoving et al., 2010; Welling, Ryan, Burris, & Rich, 2010; de Ville de Goyet, Sarmiento and Grünewald, 2011).

Information

Although access to essential information is one of the basic assumptions in the modern living, its needs, methods and effectiveness are often neglected and inappropriately estimated. In a disaster situation, information is essential in a disaster response for coordinating relief work, so is efficient and timely information management (e.g. management of information about relief supplies and human resource availability, dissemination of public information and management of the media). People need information to make decisions about their choice of action (see Case Box 5.7). For example, if disaster victims know what is happening and who is providing assistance, they can look for help to fulfil their basic needs. However, inaccurate information, such as rumours, may also cause insecurity, mistrust and even violence among the affected population (Bolton, 2006) (see Case Box 5.8).

Managing health–related information, such as disease monitoring and surveillance, is a vital part of a public health worker's role in a disaster response (The Sphere

---

CASE BOX 5.7   THE USE OF INFORMATION FOR CHOLERA OUTBREAK CONTROL AFTER THE HAITI EARTHQUAKE

The 2010 earthquake in Haiti was an excellent example of how information management can benefit the public's health. During the post-disaster phase of the Haiti earthquake, seven sub-clusters, including health information and disease surveillance sub-clusters, were formed under the Health Cluster leading agency Pan American Health Organization/WHO Regional Office for the Americas (PAHO/WHO). The information collected facilitated efficient and targeted interventions. Systematic disease monitoring and surveillance enabled the Health Cluster to identify the first cases of cholera reported in Artibonite, Haiti, in late October 2010. Following that, a series of actions were taken to control the spread of cholera, including disseminating relevant information on cholera treatment, prevention activities and treatment protocol through the internet, and utilising GPS technology to coordinate cholera treatment referral. These measures provided timely and updated disease information which prevented further cholera outbreaks (PAHO/WHO, 2011).

CASE BOX 5.8   THE HORROR OF THE GREAT KANTŌ EARTHQUAKE 1923 (PART 2)

In addition to the devastation caused by the earthquake and the subsequent fires bringing massive destruction to the infrastructure and the community during the Great Kantō earthquake in 1923, the disaster also illustrated the challenges that arise if there is no accurate information after a major calamity. Telephone connections and electricity were cut off, railroads were severely damaged and newsrooms were destroyed. People were not able to communicate or receive information. Thus, they were easily swayed by rumours. Some people were afraid of a second earthquake, some believed there would be tsunami, and others were worried about the eruption of Mount Fuji. Another disturbing rumour was that Korean immigrants were to blame for the fires. They were accused of planting bombs and poisoning well water. Amidst the chaos, many Koreans were killed. In Tokyo and Kanagawa, 6,000 out of the total 20,000 Koreans were massacred. Later, it was found that a can of pineapple and a bag of sugar were mistakenly identified as a bomb and poison (James, 2002; Ryang, 2003; Hays, 2009). See Case Box 2.7 for other information related to this disaster.

CASE BOX 5.9 COMMUNICATION DURING THE 2011 GREAT FLOODS IN THAILAND

By Cecilia Choi

Background

The role of the media is critically important in disaster and emergency situations since media coverage can affect a government's decisions, influence public attitudes and save lives. From late July to November of 2011, a series of floods started in Northern Thailand and swept into the Central Region, killing hundreds of people, leaving millions homeless and severely damaging the economy. These floods, the worst to hit Thailand for 50 years, affected more than 5 million people in 62 out of Thailand's 77 provinces. By mid-December 2011, 744 deaths had been reported.

Disaster communication

Approximately one-third of the media reports covering the 2011 Thailand floods were related to the business sector, focusing on the economic and financial implications of the floods. In addition, much of the coverage had a geographic bias (focusing only on Bangkok and the surrounding areas in Central Thailand and overlooking the more heavily affected north and northeast regions). Most reports of the relief effort focused on food aid rather than on health needs. There was a lack of analysis of health needs from the media reports.

To facilitate response, relief, and recovery efforts post disaster, the media reporting in the immediate aftermath of disasters and emergencies should focus on areas that are of immediate concern to the victims, including shelter, food, health, and water and sanitation.

Project, 2011) (see Case Box 5.9). Refer to Chapter 8 for how training may improve community disaster health risk literacy and approaches of how information might be disseminated in emergency situations.

Conclusion

Humanitarian principles are important values that underlie humanitarian action in disaster and emergency crisis. Basic needs for survival (e.g. water and sanitation, food, shelter, health services and information) must be addressed and secured to minimise negative impact of natural disasters on the affected population.

References

Adhikari, S., & Shrestha, N. L. (2008). School led total sanitation: A successful model to promote school and community sanitation and hygiene in Nepal. In J. Wicken, J. Verhagen, C. Sijbesma, C. Da Silva, & P. Ryan (Eds.), *Beyond construction: Use by all – A collection of case studies from sanitation and hygiene promotion practitioners in South Asia* (pp. 113–125). London, UK: WaterAid; Delft, The Netherlands: IRC International Water and Sanitation Centre.

Adhikari, S., & Shrestha, N. L. (2008, November). *School-led total sanitation (SLTS): A successful model to promote school and community sanitation and hygiene in Nepal.* Paper presented at the 3rd South Asian Conference on Sanitation (SACOSAN III) at New Delhi, India [Internet]. Retrieved from http://www.un.org.np/sacosan/uploads/document/file/SLTS%20 Paper_20120329071319.pdf

Adhikari, S., Shrestha, N. L., Malla, M., & Shrestha, G. R. (2008). *Nepal: School-led total sanitation seems unstoppable* (Sanitation and Hygiene Case Study No. 7, Soap stories and toilet tales: 10 case studies) [Internet]. Retrieved from the website of UNICEF: http://www. unicef.org/wash/files/7_case_study_NEPAL_4web.pdf

Barakat, S. (2003). *Housing reconstruction after conflict and disaster* (Network Paper No. 43) [Internet]. Retrieved from Humanitarian Practice Network, ODI website: http://odihpn. org/wp-content/uploads/2004/02/networkpaper043.pdf

Birch, J. (2015, April 29). 6 health challenges Nepal earthquake survivors now face. *Yahoo News* [Internet]. Retrieved from https://ca.news.yahoo.com/6-health-challenges-nepal-earthquake-survivors-now-face-210035832.html

Bolton, P. (2006). Managing disasters and other public health crises. In D. Pencheon, C. Guest, D. Melzer, & J.A.M. Gray (Eds.), *Oxford handbook of public health practice* (2nd ed., pp. 249–256). New York, NY: Oxford University Press.

CARE, Dubai Cares, Emory University Center for Global Safe Water, IRC International Water and Sanitation Centre, Save the Children, UNICEF, . . . WHO. (2010). *Raising clean hands: Advancing learning, health and participation through WASH in schools* [Internet]. Retrieved from the website of UNICEF: http://www.unicef.org/media/files/raising cleanhands_2010.pdf

Chan, E.Y.Y., & Sondorp, E. (2008). Including chronic disease care in emergency responses. *Humanitarian Exchange Magazine, 41*, 43–45 [Internet]. Retrieved from the website of Humanitarian Practice Network, Overseas Development Institute (ODI): http://odihpn. org/wp-content/uploads/2008/12/humanitarianexchange041.pdf

Checchi, F., Gayer, M., Grais, R. F., & Mills, E. J. (2007). *Public health in crisis-affected populations: A practical guide for decision-makers* (Network Paper No. 61) [Internet]. Retrieved from the website of Humanitarian Practice Network, ODI: http://odihpn.org/wp-content/uploads/2008/05/networkpaper061.pdf

Connolly, M. A., Gayer, M., Ryan, M. J., Salama, P., Spiegel, P., & Heymann, D. L. (2004). Communicable diseases in complex emergencies: Impact and challenges. *The Lancet, 364*, 1974–1983.

de Ville de Goyet, C., Sarmiento, J. P., & Grünewald, F. (2011). *Health response to the earthquake in Haiti January 2010: Lessons to be learned for the next massive sudden-onset disaster* [Internet]. Retrieved from the website of Pan American Health Organization/WHO Regional Office for the Americas (PAHO/WHO): http://www.paho.org/disasters/dmdocuments/HealthResponseHaitiEarthq.pdf

Dong, C., Ge, P., Ren, X., Zhao, X., Wang, J., Fan, H., & Yin, S. A. (2014). The micronutrient status of children aged 24–60 months living in rural disaster areas one year after the Wenchuan earthquake. *PLoS ONE, 9*(2), e88444.

Du Mortier, S., & Coninx, R. (2007). *Mobile health units in emergency operations: A methodological approach* (Network Paper No. 60) [Internet]. Retrieved from Humanitarian Practice Network, ODI website: http://odihpn.org/wp-content/uploads/2007/08/networkpaper060.pdf

Food and Agriculture Organization (FAO) of the United Nations. (n.d.). *About FAO.* Retrieved from http://www.fao.org/about/how-we-work/en/

Guha-Sapir, D., Below, R., & Hoyois, P. (n.d.). EM-DAT: The CRED/OFDA International Disaster Database [Internet]. Brussels, Belgium: Centre for Research on the Epidemiology of Disasters (CRED), Université Catholique de Louvain. Retrieved from www.emdat.be

Hays, J. (2009). *Great Tokyo earthquake of 1923.* Retrieved from http://factsanddetails.com/japan/cat26/sub160/item2226.html

Hiji, T. (2012). Iwate Ken Otsuchicho Ni Okeru Fukko Tourim no Kanousei [The possibility of disaster tourism in Otsuchi Town in Iwate Prefecture]. *Square, 165,* 28–31.

Hume, T. (2015, April 27). Nepal earthquake's victims overwhelm hospitals. *CNN News* [Internet]. Retrieved from http://edition.cnn.com/2015/04/27/world/nepal-earthquake-bir-hospital/

International Committee of the Red Cross (ICRC). (2006). *Mobile health units: Methodological approach* [Internet]. Retrieved from http://www.icrc.org/eng/assets/files/other/icrc_002_0886.pdf

International Federation of Red Cross and Red Crescent Societies (IFRC). (n.d.a). *The 7 fundamental principles of the Red Cross and Red Crescent movement: A historical perspective* [Internet]. Retrieved from http://www.ifrc.org/Global/Publications/principles/history.PDF

International Federation of Red Cross and Red Crescent Societies (IFRC). (n.d.b). *What is shelter & settlements?* [Internet]. Retrieved from http://www.ifrc.org/shelter

International Federation of Red Cross and Red Crescent Societies (IFRC). (n.d.c). *Who we are* [Internet]. Retrieved from http://www.ifrc.org/en/who-we-are/

International Federation of Red Cross and Red Crescent Societies (IFRC). (2012). *Shelter coordination in natural disasters* [Internet]. Retrieved from http://www.humanitarianlibrary.org/sites/default/files/2014/02/shelter_coordination_in_natural_disasters-02.pdf

International Federation of Red Cross and Red Crescent Societies (IFRC) & International Committee of the Red Cross (ICRC). (n.d.). *The Code of Conduct for the International Red Cross and Red Crescent Movement and Non-Governmental Organisations (NGOs) in Disaster Relief* [Internet]. Retrieved from http://www.ifrc.org/Global/Publications/disasters/code-of-conduct/code-english.pdf

International Federation of Red Cross and Red Crescent Societies (IFRC) & Oxfam. (2007). *Plastic sheeting: A guide to the specification and use of plastic sheeting in humanitarian relief*

[Internet]. Retrieved from http://www.humanitarianlibrary.org/sites/default/files/2014/02/IFRC-Oxfam_PlasticSheeting.pdf

James, C. D. (2002). *The 1923 Tokyo earthquake and fire* (The Earthquake Engineering Online Archive and National Information Service for Earthquake Engineering (NISEE) e-Library, Pacific Earthquake Engineering Research (PEER) Center, University of California, Berkeley) [Internet]. Retrieved from https://web.archive.org/web/20070316050633/http://nisee.berkeley.edu/kanto/tokyo1923.pdf

Leader, N. (2000). *The politics of principle: The principles of humanitarian action in practice* (HPG Report No. 2) [Internet]. Retrieved from the website of ODI: http://www.odi.org.uk/sites/odi.org.uk/files/odi-assets/publications-opinion-files/311.pdf

Mackintosh, K. (2000). *HPG report: The principles of humanitarian action in international humanitarian law* (Study 4 in: The politics of principle: The principles of humanitarian action in practice, HPG Report No. 5) [Internet]. Retrieved from the website of ODI: http://www.odi.org.uk/sites/odi.org.uk/files/odi-assets/publications-opinion-files/305.pdf

Magara, Y., & Yano, H. (2005). Management of water supplies after a disaster. In S. Kubota & Y. Tsuchiya (Eds.), *Water quality and standards* (Vol. 1, pp. 292–308). Retrieved from http://www.eolss.net/ebooklib/ebookcontents/E2–19-ThemeContents.pdf

Nepal earthquake: Hospitals overflowing, rural towns cut off as death toll continues to climb. (2015, April 27). *ABC News*. Retrieved from http://www.abc.net.au/news/2015–04–27/hospitals-overwhelmed-as-nepal-reels-in-wake-of-huge-earthquake/6423272

Nepal Youth Foundation. (2015). *Disaster relief response* [Internet]. Retrieved from http://www.nepalyouthfoundation.org/wp-content/uploads/2015/06/NYF-Disaster-Relief-Response-update-as-of-June-1–2015.pdf

Office of the United Nations High Commissioner for Refugees (UNHCR). (n.d.a). *About us* [Internet]. Retrieved from http://www.unhcr.org/pages/49c3646c2.html

Office of the United Nations High Commissioner for Refugees (UNHCR). (n.d.b). *Shelter* [Internet]. Retrieved from http://www.unhcr.org/pages/49c3646cf2.html

Oxfam. (2007). *Oxfam technical brief: Excreta disposal for people with physical disabilities in emergencies* [Internet]. Retrieved from the website of United Nations Children's Fund (UNICEF): http://www.unicef.org/cholera/Chapter_9_community/17_OXFAM_Excreta_Disposal_for_Physically_Vulnerable_People_in_Emergencies_2.pdf

Pan American Health Organization/WHO Regional Office for the Americas (PAHO/WHO). (2003). *WHO-PAHO guidelines for the use of foreign field hospitals in the aftermath of sudden-impact disasters* [Internet]. Retrieved from WHO website: http://www.who.int/hac/techguidance/pht/FieldHospitalsFolleto.pdf

Pan American Health Organization/WHO Regional Office for the Americas (PAHO/WHO). (2011). *Earthquake in Haiti – One year later: PAHO/WHO report on the health situation*. Retrieved from WHO website: http://www.who.int/hac/crises/hti/haiti_paho_jan2011_eng.pdf

Reed, Bob. (2011a). *Delivering safe water by tanker* (Technical notes on drinking-water, sanitation, and hygiene in emergencies No. 12, prepared for WHO by Water, Engineering and Development Centre (WEDC), Loughborough University) [Internet]. Retrieved from the website of WHO: http://www.who.int/water_sanitation_health/publications/2011/WHO_TN_12_Delivering_safe_water_by_tanker.pdf?ua=1

Reed, Bob. (2011b). *Technical options for excreta disposal in emergencies* (Technical notes on drinking-water, sanitation, and hygiene in emergencies No. 14, prepared for WHO by Water, Engineering and Development Centre (WEDC), Loughborough University) [Internet]. Retrieved from the website of WHO: http://www.who.int/water_sanitation_health/publications/2011/WHO_TN_14_Technical_options_for_excreta_disposal.pdf?ua=1

Ryang, S. (2003). The Great Kanto earthquake and the massacre of Koreans in 1923: Notes on Japan's modern national sovereignty. *Anthropological Quarterly, 76*(4), 731–748.

Shrestha, N. L. (n.d.). *MDG-7: Ensure Environmental Sustainability – MDG target 7.C: Halve, by 2015, the proportion of people without sustainable access to safe drinking water and basic sanitation* [Internet]. Retrieved from the website of United Nations Development Group (UNDG) website: http://mdgpolicynet.undg.org/ext/MDG-Good-Practices/mdg7/MDG7C_Nepal_School-Led_Total_Sanitation(SLTS).pdf

The Sphere Project. (2004). *Humanitarian charter and minimum standards in disaster response* [Internet]. Retrieved from http://www.refworld.org/docid/3d64ad7b1.html

The Sphere Project. (2011). *Humanitarian charter and minimum standards in disaster response* (3rd ed.) [Internet]. Retrieved from http://www.spherehandbook.org/en/the-humanitarian-charter/

The Sphere Project. (2012). *2011 edition of the Sphere Handbook: What is new?* [Internet]. Retrieved from http://www.sphereproject.org/silo/files/what-is-new-in-the-sphere-handbook-2011-edition-v2.pdf

The Sphere Project. (2012, September). *The Sphere Project: Humanitarian charter and minimum standards in disaster response* [Internet]. Retrieved from www.sphereproject.org/download/5049f50b33a50/

Sun, J., Huo, J., Zhao, L., Fu, P., Wang, J., Huang, J., . . . Ma, G. (2013). The nutritional status of young children and feeding practices two years after the Wenchuan earthquake in the worst-affected areas in China. *Asia Pacific Journal of Clinical Nutrition, 22*(1), 100–108.

United Nations. (n.d.). *International Decade for Action 'WATER FOR LIFE' 2005–2015* [Internet]. Retrieved from http://www.un.org/waterforlifedecade/index.shtml

United Nations. (1948). *The Universal Declaration of Human Rights* (General Assembly resolution 217 A) [Internet]. Retrieved from the website of Office of the United Nations High Commissioner for Human Rights (OHCHR): http://www.ohchr.org/EN/UDHR/Documents/UDHR_Translations/eng.pdf

United Nations, Department of Peacekeeping Operations. (2003). *Handbook on UN multidimensional peacekeeping operations* [Internet]. Retrieved from http://www.walterdorn.net/pdf/Peacekeeping-Handbook_UN_Dec2003.pdf

United Nations Children's Fund (UNICEF). (2005). *UNICEF water, sanitation and hygiene strategies for 2006–2015.* Retrieved from http://www.unicef.org/about/execboard/files/06–6_WASH_final_ODS.pdf

United Nations Children's Fund (UNICEF). (2009a). *Community approach to total sanitation: Based on case studies from India, Nepal, Sierra Leone, Zambia* [Internet]. Retrieved from http://www.unicef.org/innovations/files/CATS_field_note.pdf

United Nations Children's Fund (UNICEF). (2009b). *SLTS learn more* [Internet]. Retrieved from http://www.unicef.org/wash/files/SLTS_learn_more.pdf

United Nations Children's Fund (UNICEF). (2012a). *Nutrition glossary: A resource for communicators* [Internet]. Retrieved from http://www.unicef.org/lac/Nutrition_Glossary_%283%29.pdf

United Nations Children's Fund (UNICEF). (2012b). *UNICEF's work in water, sanitation, and hygiene (WASH) in humanitarian action 2012.* Retrieved from http://www.unicef.org/wash/files/UNICEF_WASH_Humanitarian_final.pdf

United Nations Inter-Agency Standing Committee (IASC). (2005). *Guidelines for gender-based violence interventions in humanitarian settings: Focusing on prevention of and response to sexual violence in emergencies* [Internet]. Retrieved from the website of United Nations Office for the Coordination of Humanitarian Affairs (OCHA): https://docs.unocha.org/sites/dms/Documents/GBV%20Guidelines%20%28English%29.pdf

United Nations Office for the Coordination of Humanitarian Affairs (OCHA). (2010). *OCHA on message: Humanitarian principles* [Internet]. Retrieved from https://docs.unocha.org/ sites/dms/Documents/OOM_HumPrinciple_English.pdf

United Nations Office for Disaster Risk Reduction (UNISDR). (2011). *Global assessment report on disaster risk reduction* [Internet]. Retrieved from http://www.preventionweb.net/ english/hyogo/gar/2011/en/home/download.html

United Nations Water (UN Water). (2013). *Water and disasters* [Internet]. Retrieved from http://www.unwater.org/fileadmin/user_upload/watercooperation2013/doc/Fact sheets/water_disasters.pdf

Valent, F., Little, D., Bertollini, R., Nemer, L. E., Barbone, F., & Tamburlini, G. (2004). Burden of disease attributable to selected environmental factors and injury among children and adolescents in Europe. *The Lancet, 363*(9426), 2032–2039.

Van Hoving, D. J., Waliis, L. A., Docrat, F., & De Vries, S. (2010). Haiti disaster tourism – A medical shame. *Prehospital and Disaster Medicine, 25*(3), 201–202.

Welling, D. R., Ryan, J. M., Burris, D. G., & Rich, N. M. (2010). Seven sins of humanitarian medicine. *World Journal of Surgery, 34*(3), 466–470.

World Food Programme (WFP). (n.d.a). *About WFP* [Internet]. Retrieved from http://www. wfp.org/about

World Food Programme (WFP). (n.d.b). *UN Humanitarian Air Service* [Internet]. Retrieved from https://www.wfp.org/logistics/aviation/unhas-current-operations

World Health Organization (WHO). (2000). *The management of nutrition in major emergencies* [Internet]. Retrieved from http://whqlibdoc.who.int/publications/2000/9241545208. pdf?ua=1

World Health Organization (WHO). (2012). *10 Facts on Nutrition* [Internet]. Retrieved from http://www.who.int/features/factfiles/nutrition/facts/en/

World Health Organization (WHO). (2013). *Classification and minimum standards for foreign medical teams in sudden onset disaster* [Internet]. Retrieved from http://www.who.int/hac/ global_health_cluster/fmt_guidelines_september2013.pdf

World Health Organization (WHO), United Kingdom Health Protection Agency (HPA), & partners. (2011a). *Disaster risk management for health: Nutrition* [Internet]. Retrieved from http://www.who.int/hac/events/drm_fact_sheet_nutrition.pdf

World Health Organization (WHO), United Kingdom Health Protection Agency (HPA), & partners. (2011b). *Disaster risk management for health: Water, sanitation and hygiene* [Internet]. Retrieved from http://www.who.int/hac/events/drm_fact_sheet_wash.pdf

Yin, S., Zhao, X. F., Zhao, L. Y., Fu, P., Zhang, J., & Ma, G. S. (2010). The nutrition status of women of reproductive ages in the areas affected by Wenchuan earthquake after one year. *Zhonghua yufang yixue zazhi [Chinese Journal of Preventive Medicine], 44*(8), 686–690.

Zhao, L. Y., Yu, D. M., Huang, J., Zhao, X. F., Li, J. W., Du, W. W., . . . Yin, S. A. (2010). The nutrition status of special population living in the areas affected by Wenchuan earthquake after 3 months. *Zhonghua yufang yixue zazhi [Chinese Journal of Preventive Medicine], 44*(8), 701–705.

Zhao, X. F., Yin, S., Zhao, L. Y., Fu, P., Zhang, J., & Ma, G. S. (2010). The nutrition status of children under 60 months in the rural areas affected by Wenchuan earthquake after one year. *Zhonghua yufang yixue zazhi [Chinese Journal of Preventive Medicine], 44*(8), 691–695.

6

CURRENT AND LIKELY MEDICAL AND PUBLIC HEALTH THREATS AND CHALLENGES FOR DISASTER RESPONSE IN THE TWENTY-FIRST CENTURY

Current and likely health threats

Disaster subtypes, demographic characteristics (size, age and gender composition), general sociopolitical context, underlying health problems experienced by the population, and potential risks to environment, security and lifeline services are all threats that might affect the health outcomes of a disaster-struck population. This chapter provides an overview of the health threats and the likely public health challenges after natural disasters in the twenty-first century.

Threats to physical health

Injury and violence

Injuries constitute a major disease burden and health needs in the natural disaster-affected community (see Knowledge Box 6.1). Although injury patterns might vary according to disaster subtypes (refer to Chapter 4), unintentional injuries are more likely to occur in natural disasters than intended injuries (i.e. those resulting from violence). Proper and timely injury and trauma care will save lives and enhance recovery and the mental well-being of the affected community. Untreated wounds and improper injury care may result in avoidable mortality, morbidity and permanent disabilities which affect post-disaster livelihoods.

Although intentional injuries are less likely to occur after a natural disaster than after a conflict or war, domestic violence, gender-based violence (forced and early marriage, sexual assault and rape), assault, self-harm, suicide and trafficking are commonly reported as a result of the stress and social disruption in emergencies, particularly during the acute emergency phase of a natural disaster when law and social order are compromised. The vulnerable subgroups (the very elderly, unaccompanied children and women) must be protected from further abuses.

KNOWLEDGE BOX 6.1   TYPICAL INJURIES IN EARTHQUAKES

Collapsed buildings and fallen objects following earthquakes might cause deaths and severe musculoskeletal injuries that require emergency surgery and repeated operations. Table 6.1 summarises typical profile of injuries in earthquakes.

TABLE 6.1 Typical profile of injuries in earthquakes in descending order of proportion

Profile of injuries	Proportion (%)
Lower limb	30
Upper limb	20
Multiple site	15
Face	13
Scalp	11
Back	8
Chest	2
Abdomen	1
Burns	0.25

Source: Adapted from Li and Redmond (2016, p. 84).

To address these challenges, surveillance and monitoring of trauma service needs, implementation of proper therapeutic and curative trauma care, and ensuring the availability and accessibility of multidisciplinary rehabilitation support (e.g. physiotherapy and occupational therapy and psychological service) are all important response dimensions to be considered during the acute response stage. Following acute emergency phase, long-term clinical realignment, such as medical infrastructure and resources support, and community-based rehabilitation (CBR considers the environmental and social aspects for disabled individuals to help them participate fully in the life of their community) are important approaches to be considered after natural disasters.

Communicable diseases

With major population displacements, collapse and disruption of life-supporting services and disease control programmes, poorer access to health care services, medical resources and coordination, increased mortality and morbidity from communicable diseases are common after natural disasters. Disaster-affected populations are vulnerable to waterborne, vector-borne, vaccine-preventable diseases as well as diseases that are associated with overcrowding, such as acute respiratory infections, meningococcal diseases, tuberculosis, diarrhoea and skin diseases. Of note, malaria is endemic in 80% of the high-risk natural disaster zones of the world. Diarrhoeal diseases (cholera, typhoid fever, shigellosis, hepatitis E in pregnant women and leptospirosis after floods in rodent endemic areas), acute respiratory infections, measles and vector-borne diseases (malaria and dengue) are the most common types of infectious diseases found in disasters. In addition, sexually transmitted infections (STIs) and HIV may be important health risks within a disaster context when there is a disruption of community and health infrastructure. Population movement, the breakdown of social networks which render greater exposure to sexual violence and transaction sex and the reduced access to prevention health services will put the health of vulnerable population groups at risk.

The key factors associated with communicable disease risks include the availability of adequate water and functional latrines, vaccination coverage, the nutritional status of the affected population and access to health care services. The main response should be to ensure safe water and sanitation, immunisation, primary-care services availability, surveillance and an intact early warning system plus infection control of vector-borne diseases (in areas with endemic malaria and dengue fever) (see Knowledge Box 6.2).

Non-communicable diseases

Non-communicable conditions are a major disease burden in this century. Natural disasters can worsen a person's existing chronic disease by causing physical and mental stress that put additional pressure on the cardiovascular system (raising blood pressure and thus precipitating heart attacks and strokes) or disrupt the supply of drugs needed to treat his/her disease (e.g. insulin for diabetics) (see Knowledge Box 6.3). People who suffer from non-communicable diseases (NCDs), such as cardiovascular disease, chronic lung diseases and diabetes, are more vulnerable to disruption and stress induced by disasters (Chan & Sondorp, 2007; The Hurricane

KNOWLEDGE BOX 6.2   STEPS TO INFECTIOUS DISEASE CONTROL

Infectious disease control is one of the common health strategies public health workers apply to protect population health. The following four steps are the basic principles of infectious disease control which apply to both non-emergency and disaster settings.

1 Identification of an outbreak

An outbreak is a limited epidemic presenting as a localised increase in the incidence of an infection or infectious disease (Sleigh, 2005). Clinical symptoms, the epidemiology of the disease and laboratory findings are the three key dimensions that should be considered.

2 Determination of the cause of an outbreak

A thorough understanding of factors inducing the outbreak is essential for planning control measures. Key issues include: identification of the source of the agent, potential vectors, route of transmission, exposure characterisation and detection of specific host factors (Rand, 2008).

3 Implementation of control measures

After confirming the cause of the outbreak, appropriate control measures should be applied immediately (Council to Improve Foodborne Outbreak Response [CIFOR], 2009). Provision of safe drinking water and ensuring proper hygiene and sanitation are often the most important preventive measures (World Health Organization [WHO], United Kingdom Health Protection Agency [HPA], & partners, 2011a). Other common control measures include health advice, vaccination, vector elimination, individual protection, community restriction, such as isolation and quarantine, and early treatment of patients (Lewis, Sheringham, Kalim, & Crayford, 2011).

4 Risk communication

Providing accurate and timely information related to the outbreak is essential. Effective risk communication facilitates the dissemination of related health information and keeps the public updated about the outbreak situation (Hyer & Covello, 2005). The mass media is a common tool used in risk communication.

Of note, the four steps are not necessarily sequential; the measures are taken according to the evolving needs and circumstances of the actual situations.

KNOWLEDGE BOX 6.3   SHOULD COMMUNICABLE DISEASES ALWAYS BE MANAGED AS ACUTE DISEASES?

In general, although the impact of communicable diseases on people is mostly short-term in nature, HIV/AIDS, TB and certain vector-borne diseases (e.g. malaria) are examples of infections that might affect population groups in a lifelong or recurrent manner. The chronicity of these diseases has prompted a rethink of the management implications in an emergency. For example, following a disaster, with a compromised immune system, a person living with HIV may not be able to recover from a simple chest infection if he/she cannot get his/her usual antiretroviral drugs to manage the underlying conditions.

Katrina Advisory Group & Kessler, 2007; Chan & Kim, 2011; The Sphere Project, 2011). NCDs can also affect treatment and recovery from an injury or illness caused by the natural disaster. Surgical repair of a fractured bone may become very high-risk if the individual's blood pressure is unstable. A diabetic patient may face poor wound healing if his/her diabetes is not being controlled through the usual diet control or medication. A significant proportion of deaths in post-disaster phases can result from the failure of health care services provision for patient with chronic disease needs (WHO, HPA, & partners, 2011c). Disasters may also cause stress and lifestyle disruptions that reveal previously unknown pre-existing chronic diseases. Table 6.2 gives further examples of how disasters result in problems with chronic disease.

TABLE 6.2 The relationship between natural disasters and chronic diseases

Chronic disease	Nature	Mechanism	Outcome
Cardiovascular disease/ hypertension	Non-communicable	Disaster-induced stress directly worsens condition – e.g. raised blood pressure and heart arrhythmias	• Increase in heart attacks (Suzuki et al., 1997; Ogawa, Tsuji, Shiono, & Hisamichi, 2000)
		(Kario, Matsuo, Shimada, & Pickering, 2001; Parati, Antonicelli, Guazzarotti, Paciaroni, & Mancia, 2001; Gerin et al., 2005).	• Increase in strokes (Kario, McEwen, & Pickering, 2003) • Unsafe to operate on injuries
Diabetes	Non-communicable	Inappropriate diet and lifestyle post-disaster and lack of usual medication leave blood sugar levels high and erratic	• Complications of diabetes – e.g. kidney disease (Kamoi et al., 2006)
		(Kirizuka et al., 1997; Kamoi, Tanaka, Ikarashi, & Miyakoshi, 2006).	• Complications of any injuries – e.g. wound infection, unsafe to operate on injuries
HIV/AIDS	Communicable	Lack of usual medication Poor general health Lack of condoms Sexual violence	• Increased death and illness (e.g. infections) • Increased transmission of disease (Spiegel, 2004)
Tuberculosis (TB)	Communicable	Lack of treatment and monitoring	• Increased death and illness • Increased risk of multi-drug-resistant TB

Source: Chan and Southgate (2014, p. 79).

The recent literature on public health has suggested that chronic disease needs are still largely neglected post–disaster (Wells, 2005; Chan, 2008; Chan & Sondorp, 2008; Chan, 2009; Chan & Kim, 2011; Zhang, Liu, Liu, & Zhang, 2011). Case Box 6.1 discusses why NCDs continue to be ignored in major earthquake relief operations such as 2008 Wenchuan earthquake in Sichuan Province of China.

CASE BOX 6.1   THE 2008 SICHUAN EARTHQUAKE

An earthquake with a magnitude measuring 7.9 on the Richter scale occurred on 12 May 2008 in Wenchuan County in Sichuan Province in southwestern China. The earthquake killed more than 87,000 and affected 45 million people. The death toll ranks eighth among all earthquakes recorded in history (Centre for Research on the Epidemiology of Disasters [CRED], 2013).

Although the complications associated with prolonged entrapment in collapsed buildings were expected to be high, the prevalence of crush syndrome was reported to be only around 1% among the physical trauma and injury cases (Zhang et al., 2012). Yet, timely medical response, especially carrying out surgery within the first week of the earthquake, was hindered by the prevalence of chronic non-communicable diseases (NCDs) among the victims: close to 38% of them required management of their pre-existing, unstable chronic medical conditions before surgery. In the second week, more than 50% of the injured victims required treatment for preventing the exacerbation of underlying conditions.

Technically, standard guidelines and medication are required for NCD management after disasters. The lack of an operational mandate, competing field priorities and a general lack of awareness and expertise for chronic medical management were consistently reported by the responders. Although the patient-to-doctor ratio was 1:3 in many disaster response sites, 80% of the doctors were orthopaedic surgeons and there was a lack of general internal medicine and primary care professionals to manage underlying common chronic medical conditions (Chan, 2008). There was also a resistance to treating patients with chronic conditions because of a limited understanding of the treatment implications and long-term financial constraints.

Even if there might be willingness to manage chronic disease post–natural disasters, there was another major concern about sustainability. Hung (2010; Hung, Lam, Chan, & Graham, 2013) describes the dilemma that his team faced when diagnosing hypertension after the earthquake. His team questioned that once the consultation drug supply was used up, the drugs were either too expensive or just not available to the patient to allow long-term treatment. They therefore questioned whether they should treat, or even look for raised blood pressures at all.

Why are chronic diseases still being forgotten?

Although typical natural disaster emergency health responses include emergency (often surgical) treatment for injuries, basic care for communicable diseases, such as diarrhoea and respiratory infections, surveillance of and response to communicable disease outbreaks, nutritional support and provision of water and sanitation (Landesman, 2001; The Sphere Project, 2011), the management of non-communicable chronic disease remains neglected (Ford et al., 2006; Kwak, Shin, Kim, Kwon, & Suh, 2006; Guha-Sapir, van Panhuis, & Lagoutte, 2007; Chan, 2008; Chan & Griffiths, 2009; Chan & Kim, 2010a, 2010b). Case Box 6.2 discusses some factors that lead to chronic diseases are still forgotten notwithstanding the evidence.

CASE BOX 6. 2   WHY ARE CHRONIC NON-COMMUNICABLE DISEASES FORGOTTEN?

The lack of an operational mandate and guidelines, the inflexible established practices and concern about sustaining the provision of chronic medication after natural disasters remain the major challenges (Chan & Sondorp, 2007; Spiegel, Checchi, Colombo, & Paik, 2010). Minimum standards, with the exception of those of the Sphere Project (2011), are virtually non-existent (HelpAge International, 2005; Wells, 2005). There are multiple reasons for such neglect of chronic disease, some of which are listed in Table 6.3.

TABLE 6.3 Reasons why different responders often neglect chronic diseases after a disaster

Lack of awareness
Lack of operational mandate
Not part of established practices
Lack of relevant skills and expertise to detect and manage chronic diseases in a post-disaster setting and resistance to external pressure to change among local health systems and stakeholders lacking understanding of the problem
Lack of knowledge of local demographic and epidemiological characteristics among outside response organisations and alternative financial incentives among local care providers
Lack of resources for managing chronic diseases in relief settings
Lack of standardised protocols or guidelines for the management of chronic diseases in the post-disaster context
Lack of cooperation/coordination
Issue of sustainability

Source: Adapted from Chan and Sondorp (2007).

Some progress is being made to raise the profile of chronic diseases post-disaster. The most recent version of the Sphere standards says that people should "have access to essential therapies to reduce morbidity and mortality due to acute complications or exacerbation of their chronic health condition" and that "people who were previously on anti-retroviral therapy continue to receive treatment." Key indicators, such as "all primary health care facilities have clear standard operating procedures for referrals of patients with NCDs to secondary and tertiary care facilities," are also proposed (The Sphere Project, 2011, pp. 336, 329, 337). Evidence-based clinical guidelines are now being developed. For example, for hypertension, some technical groups recommend frequent home blood pressure measurement, good sleep quality, hydration and physical activity (Kario, Shimada, & Takaku, 2005). Continued advocacy in the published literature will raise awareness of the issue but chronic medical conditions are becoming too significant a disaster disease burden to be ignored in the coming decades.

Primary care approach in disaster medical and public health responses

Field studies have indicated that the most common medical treatments required in a post–natural disaster clinic were antibiotics (20.2%), analgesia (17.1%), tetanus vaccine (15.5%) and wound care (14.2%) (Nufer, Wilson-Ramirez, Shah, Hughes, & Crandall, 2006). The health infrastructure and systems with disaster-resilience features (protection of essential equipment and stockpiling of essential medicines) can maintain the continuity of care for a population with chronic disease needs. Not only can the primary care approach tackle these immediate needs, non-communicable disease management needs may also be addressed through primary care service approach, which deals with the range of service needs across the pathway of care (see Chapter 2) from prevention, diagnosis and treatment to rehabilitation and palliative care. A primary care unit, with its underlying knowledge and information of the prevalence of pre-emergency NCD patterns, NCD treatment protocols and guidelines in emergencies, clinical assessment and audit tools to monitor diseases as well as the availability of relevant equipment and medication for NCD management are all important elements to ensure the success of a programme. Active health education and promotion activities may also be conducted during the relief phase to raise awareness of these issues among the public, including the appropriate diet and family support for target groups.

Threats to mental health

The World Health Organization defines mental health as "a state of well-being in which every individual realises his or her own potential, can cope with the normal stresses of life, can work productively and fruitfully, and is able to make a contribution to her or his community" (WHO, 2014). In ordinary circumstances, people

KNOWLEDGE BOX 6.4 GLOBAL PATTERN OF MENTAL HEALTH PROBLEMS

Mental disorders are prevalent in all regions of the world and are major contributors to global morbidity and mortality. More than 10% of the global burden of disease, measured in disability-adjusted life years (DALY), is attributed to mental disorder.

generally make three fundamental assumptions about the world, that: (1) the world is essentially a good place, (2) life and events have meaning and purpose; and (3) they are valuable and worthy (Janoff-Bulman, 1992).

Not all distress is abnormal and a large portion of distress is a normal human reaction in times of critical incidents (Williams & Alexander, 2009). However, in disasters, traumatic experiences challenge individuals' perception about the world and themselves and such stressors are known risk factors for mental health problems, the impact of which could be far-reaching (see Knowledge Box 6.4).

Normal reaction after disasters

After the occurrence of a disaster (i.e. impact), it is normal for an affected population to experience distress. Such distress usually peaks within the first week of the incident and then the level gradually drops as the post-disaster time passes. Figure 6.1

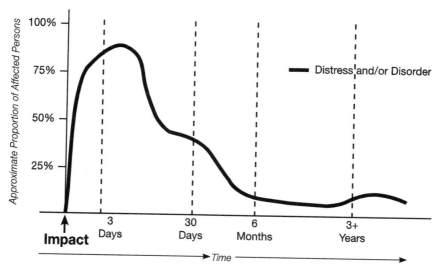

FIGURE 6.1 Post-disaster mental impact over time

Source: Adapted from Williams and Alexander (2009).

shows the (approximate) proportion of people who will develop distress and/or a disorder after a disaster over time.

Major adverse psychological outcomes after a disaster

Mental health consequences of disasters are influenced by psychological and social factors *before, during and after* the disastrous event. These factors are interconnected, and they are also affected by the availability of humanitarian assistance, such as providing food security, shelter, water and sanitation (WHO, HPA, & partners, 2011b). There are three important groups of factors associated with **psychological outcomes** in a disaster context: (1) pre-existing (pre-impact) conditions, such as a severe mental disorder, depression and substance abuse; (2) those induced by the emergency situation, such as grief, non-pathological distress, alcohol and other substance use, depression and anxiety disorders, including post-traumatic stress disorder (PTSD); and (3) those arising from circumstances created as a result of humanitarian aid, such as anxiety due to lack of information about food distribution.

People develop different kinds of psychosocial distress after a disaster. A United States National Survey reported that more than 18% of men and 15% of women were exposed to a natural disaster in their life (North et al., 1999; Norris et al., 2002; Galea, Nandi, & Vlahov, 2005). Common types of psychological disorders after disasters include **acute stress disorder**, which is characterised by acute stress reactions manifested between two days and four weeks after experiencing traumatic or stressful events (Bryant, Friedman, Spiegel, Ursano, & Strain, 2011); **generalised anxiety disorder**, characterised by excessive anxiety lasting over six months (Andrews et al., 2010); **major depressive disorder**, which is a condition marked by a depressed mood and/or loss of interest for at least two weeks and at least five of the following symptoms: persistent low mood, diminished interest in all activities, significant unintentional weight loss or gain, insomnia or sleeping too much, agitation or psychomotor retardation noticed by others, fatigue or loss of energy, excessive guilt, diminished ability to concentrate and recurrent thoughts of death (American Psychiatric Association [APA], 2000); and **PTSD**, which is very similar to acute stress disorder and is characterised by recurrent flashbacks about a traumatic event and other acute stress symptoms (a diagnosis used for individuals who present with the symptoms for more than one month) (APA, 2000). Among all these adverse mental health outcomes, it is important to point out that PTSD is the most reported psychological disorder identified among the victims. The prevalence of PTSD among direct victims ranges between 30% and 40%, while the rate among the general population ranges between 5% and 10% (Neria, Nandi, & Galea, 2008). Table 6.4 describes the mental health impact of various types of disaster. In general, man-made disasters appear to affect the mental health of the affected population more severely.

Vulnerable populations, such as people who have an underlying history of mental health problems and those who are socially isolated and marginalised, are

TABLE 6.4 Mental health impact and types of disaster

	Minimal impairment (%)	Moderate impairment (%)	Severe impairment (%)	Very severe impairment (%)
Natural disaster	10.2	55.7	21.6	12.5
Man-made disaster	0	33.3	27.8	38.9
Technological disaster	14.8	46.3	18.5	20.4

Source: Norris et al. (2002).

CASE BOX 6.3   AN EXAMPLE OF HOW TO UPGRADE AN EMERGENCY MEDICAL KIT TO CATER TO "NON-LIFE-THREATENING" HEALTH NEEDS

The Interagency Emergency Health Kit is a box with medicines and medical supplies designed to meet the expected primary health care needs of people exposed to major humanitarian emergencies. However, previous editions of the kit only included three psychotropic medicines (chlorpromazine injections, diazepam injections and phenobarbital tablets), were not well equipped to assist people with severe depression and psychosis. Adopting a definition of health that encompasses physical, mental and social aspects, the current version of the Interagency Emergency Health Kit now includes one medicine for each of the five classes of psychotropic medicines, including anti-depressant and anti-psychotic medications. Table 6.5 summarises the change in psychotropic medicine in the Emergency Health Kit.

TABLE 6.5 The Interagency Emergency Health Kit

	The Interagency Emergency Health Kit	
	3rd Edition	4th Edition
Anti-epileptic	Phenobarbital	
Anti-psychotic	Chlorpromazine (injectable)	Haloperidol (injectable and oral)
Anxiolytic	Diazepam (injectable)	Diazepam (injectable and oral)
Anti-depressant	N/A	Amitriptyline
Anti-Parkinson	N/A	Biperiden

Source: van Ommeren et al. (2011).

more likely to experience mental health impact in disasters than the general population. Poor mental health outcomes post-disaster are associated with domestic violence, unemployment, dropping out early from school, divorce and poorer health outcomes (Prince et al., 2007). A review found that youths, people living in developing context and those who experienced mass violence (e.g. terrorism and shooting sprees rather than natural or technological disasters) are associated with more severe adverse mental health outcomes. Among adult victims, more severe exposure, female gender, middle age, ethnic minority status, secondary stressors, prior psychiatric problems and weak or deteriorating psychosocial resources most consistently increased the likelihood of adverse outcomes (Norris et al., 2002) (see Case Box 6.3).

Mental health response

Mental health needs in a post-disaster setting can be addressed by using a **psychosocial approach**. The "four-layer pyramid" (Figure 6.2) illustrates how mental health and psychosocial needs might be addressed in emergencies (United Nations Inter-Agency Standing Committee [IASC], 2008). The bottom layer shows that the provision of security and services targeting basic physical needs is required to meet broad-based general psychosocial needs. Community and family support constitutes the second layer, which demonstrates why relief measures should attempt to assist victims to reunite with families and encourage the reactivation of social networks. The third layer shows that only a small proportion of the affected population might need psychosocial interventions and support from non-specialised community mental health workers and primary health care workers. The top layer highlights a very small subset within the disaster-affected population who may experience real mental health difficulties and thus require specialised psychological and psychiatric support from professional health workers (see Case Box 6.4).

Addressing the spectrum of mental health needs after natural disasters requires robust general basic services, community support networks, psychological first aid, mental health care and psychosocial support incorporation within education, integration of mental health services in general health service delivery and primary health care and access to specialist care and medication for people with severe mental disorders (WHO, HPA, & partners, 2011b). In addition, the following considerations should be taken into account when planning for psychosocial interventions:

1   Disaster psychosocial support interventions should be tailored to the intended communities (Oriol, 1999).
2   Interventions should focus on local capacity building and strengthening of self-help abilities (IASC, 2010).
3   Psychosocial support programme should be incorporated into existing system or programme as far as possible to enhance programme sustainability and reduce social stigma (IASC, 2010).

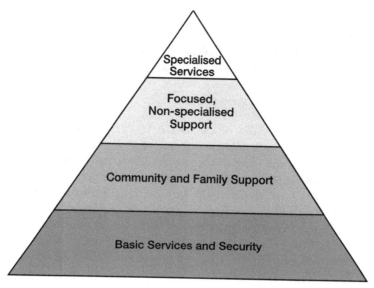

FIGURE 6.2 Four-layer pyramid of needs for mental health and psychosocial support in emergencies

Source: Adapted from IASC (2008).

As discussed earlier in this section, the greatest mental health needs usually present in the first days immediately after the disaster and it is believed that if appropriate action is taken during this period, severe psychiatric disorder or mental health distress can be prevented.

Critical incident stress debriefing

This is a method developed in the 1970s which was widely used in the past. It consists of a seven-phase group discussion which is conducted between two and ten days after a traumatic experience. This model encourages participants to express their emotions and thoughts about the trauma to facilitate reprocessing. However, in recent years, this model has been criticised for creating re-traumatisation of the participants if not delivered with follow-up support. And thus, this model is no longer being advocated and used as common in post-disaster settings.

Psychological first aid

Psychological first aid (PFA) is a skill set that limit distress and negative health behaviour, and help people cope with stressful and traumatic events in life. The Institute of Medicine, National Institute of Mental Health and the WHO have recommended

CASE BOX 6.4 PSYCHOLOGICAL SUPPORT AS ONE OF THE PILLARS IN THE CONTROL OF THE WEST AFRICA EBOLA VIRUS DISEASE OUTBREAK

By Eliza Cheung with Hong Kong Red Cross

The Ebola epidemic in West Africa from 2013–2015 has been considered as "the most severe acute public health emergency seen in modern times" according to the World Health Organization (2014, September 3). The epidemic has taken 11,298 lives, with the total cumulative cases having reached over 27,000 (WHO, 2015, August 12). According to the International Federation of Red Cross and Red Crescent Societies (IFRC), psychosocial support is one of the five essential pillars for the entire Ebola operation, among other measures including clinical case management, safe and dignified burials, social mobilisation and beneficiary communication, and tracing and monitoring contacts (IFRC, 2014, September 18).

Various psychosocial issues in Ebola-affected communities were identified as having an impact on the effectiveness of outbreak control including the intense fear in local communities, the spread of rumours, frontline workers working under enormous stress and stigmatisation, and health measures interfering with traditional burial rituals (Cheung, 2015). For instance, those involved in the safe and dignified burials worked under tremendous stress. This level of stress posed a significant risk to these workers since the smallest mistake in their work could prove fatal. This psychosocial support to these frontline workers is not a luxury – it is a matter of life and death.

The lessons and good practices learned from frontline experiences were included and discussed in the provisional Psychological First Aid (PFA) guide (adapted for the Ebola context) that was published by the WHO and partner organisations (WHO, Christoffel-Blindenmission [CBM], World Vision International, & United Nations Children's Fund [UNICEF], 2014).

this method of intervention to be used during or immediately after a disaster (Institute of Medicine, 2003). The concept of psychological first aid is similar to physical first aid. The skills can be applied to everyone, and should be taught to individuals without specialised mental health training, including public health practitioners, responders in disasters, military personnel and community volunteers (see Case Boxes 6.5 and 6.6).

In summary, people with pre-existing social or psychological conditions who are exposed to mass casualties and violence are at higher risk of poor mental health outcomes. Although the majority of mental health consequences subside over time, a small but substantial proportion require continuous specialised care to avoid far-reaching consequences in other areas of life.

CASE BOX 6.5 PRE-DISASTER PSYCHOLOGICAL FIRST AID TRAINING AMONG RESPONDERS IN A VESSEL COLLISION ACCIDENT ON NATIONAL DAY IN HONG KONG

By Eliza Cheung and Emily Ying Yang Chan

Mental and psychosocial problems are one of the major consequences of disasters and critical incidents. Although disaster responders are also affected, their mental health and psychosocial needs are usually overlooked (Norris et al., 2002). On the National Day of the People's Republic of China in 2012, the deadliest maritime disaster in Hong Kong in 40 years resulted in 39 deaths and more than 100 injured. First aiders of the Auxiliary Medical Service (AMS) of the Hong Kong SAR government responded quickly and provided physical and psychological first aid (PFA) support to survivors and their families at the hospitals and the morgues. A study investigated the effectiveness of pre-disaster PFA training in protecting the post-disaster mental health of first responders.

Findings supported the potential beneficial impact of PFA training to responders' own mental health, including better coping, resilience, life satisfaction and perceived social support from friends. Trained PFA responders also showed a better capacity to provide support to disaster victims, as shown by more knowledgeable in disaster mental health and PFA and higher self-efficacy in offering emotional support to survivors (Cheung, Chan, Sin, & Wong, 2014; Cheung, 2014b).

CASE BOX 6.6 PSYCHOLOGICAL SUPPORT SERVICE AMID POLITICAL PROTESTS

By Eliza Cheung with Hong Kong Red Cross

The protests that took place in Hong Kong in 2014 were also known as the Umbrella Movement or Occupy Movement by local and international media. Tens of thousands of citizens flooded the areas around the government headquarters and occupied busy commercial hubs in the city for 79 days calling for universal suffrage for the Hong Kong Chief Executive election in 2017 (Hong Kong protests: Timeline of the occupation, 2014, December 11). Clashes and violence between the police and protestors broke out. The Hong Kong Red Cross (HKRC), its headquarters located right in the middle of the occupation as shown in Figure 6.3, had been providing physical first aid and a psychological support service since the first day of the protest; these services were also provided round-the-clock during times that were particularly tense (Cheung, 2014a).

FIGURE 6.3 Occupy Central

While the physical first aid providers handled the physical injuries, volunteers in the Psychological Support Service (PSS) team comforted those who presented various psychological reactions, including fear, anger, and disbelief, with individual or group psychological first aid. Another psychological hotline service was also launched by HKRC to support the general public who might be directly or indirectly affected by the incident.

Many callers to the hotline reported emotional disturbance or personal relationship problems due to increasingly sharp divergence in political views. Families and friends reported heated arguments, leading to the abrupt ending of personal relationships. Over half of the callers who sought support from the hotline also suffered from various stress reactions after seeing news reports of the violence from various media channels.

Threats to social health

Although much less documented when compared with physical and mental health outcomes, social well-being is an important dimension to be addressed post disaster. For **social well-being**, risk factors associated with adverse outcomes include: (1) pre-existing (pre-impact) problems, such as belonging to a marginalised group or political oppression; these vulnerabilities may be exacerbated in an emergency situation; (2) risks as the result of an emergency, such as reduced safety, separation from family members, destruction of livelihoods and the destruction of community structures; and (3) circumstances created as a result of humanitarian aid – for example overcrowding or lack of privacy in camps, aid dependency and undermining of local capacity. Case Box 6.7 and Knowledge Box 6.5 highlight some important social dimensions of disaster needs and responses.

CASE BOX 6.7 TSUNAMI MARRIAGE IN ISLAMIC INDONESIA

By Christy Chan

On 26 December 2004, Banda Aceh, Indonesia suffered a devastating tsunami that killed more than 160,000 people (or about 4% of the Aceh population). There were more women than men among the deceased in this disaster because most of the men were out working in the fields or fishing at sea, while women and children stayed at home. In four villages in the Aceh Besar district, only 189 out of 676 survivors were female. Similar figures were also recorded in the Lampu'uk subdistrict, where only 40 out of the 750 survivors were women. In heavily damaged zones, 6.12% of the men lost their wives while only 3.86% women were widowed.

Under Shari'ah, women are maritally disadvantaged in disasters as they are not allowed to remarry within three months after their spouses' death, while men can remarry any time. In one case, a man married his sister-in-law one week after his wife's disappearance in the tsunami only to find his wife reappeared one month later.

In addition, the phenomenon of involuntary marriages became prevalent as men and women from different families were being sheltered temporarily in the same tents after the tsunami, and women were under social pressure to marry men staying in the same tents. This is a result of the formal establishment of Shari'ah in Aceh, which enforces Islamic principles in people's everyday life such as death rituals, ceremonies, and marriage rituals. Younger women tend to be more susceptible to forced marriage. After this disaster, the average age gap between husbands and wives has increased by five years from eight to 13 years. This forced marriage may have implications on women's well-being, livelihood and education opportunities.

Sources: Oxfam International (2005), United Nations Population Fund (UNFPA) (2005) and Burrows, Frankenberg, Katz, Sikoki, and Thomas (2012).

KNOWLEDGE BOX 6.5   DEAD BODY MANAGEMENT

The popular media has often postulated that the sudden increase in dead bodies after a disaster will inevitably cause epidemics (Morgan, 2004). The mythical association between dead bodies and epidemics puts pressure on the government to perform unnecessary dead body management, such as spraying "disinfectants" and rapid mass burials. Media photos of a dead body similar to Figure 6.4 add to this panic. In reality, the main causes of death in a natural disaster are injury, drowning or fire and the health conditions of the deceased are likely to be similar to those who survived the disaster. It is thus rare that the victims carry epidemic-causing infectious diseases at the time of death. Even if some of them did carry infectious diseases at death, most infectious organisms (with the notable exception of HIV) are unable to survive beyond 48 hours and, therefore, the risk of having a cadaver-induced epidemic is relatively low.

Nevertheless although cadavers rarely cause epidemics after disasters, a proper cadaver management system is still needed when an emergency arises. Burial sites should be at least 200 metres away from drinking water sources as gastroenteritis might become a problem if water sources become contaminated by dead bodies (Morgan, Tidball-Binz, & van Alphen, 2006). In addition, when managing the dead bodies, attention should be paid to the

FIGURE 6.4   A dead body in a school parking area after New Orleans was struck by the Hurricane Katrina disaster in 2005

Source: Photo by ioerror/Jacob Appelbaum/CC BY-SA 2.0 (https://commons.wikimedia. org/wiki/File:AlgiersKatrinaCorpseIoerrorA.jpg; https://creativecommons.org/licenses/ by-sa/2.0/deed.en).

ethical, religious and cultural practices of the local community. Rapid mass burials, for instance, may cause long-term harm to the mental health of the victims' relatives (Pan American Health Organization/WHO Regional Office for the Americas [PAHO/WHO], 2004). Thus, proper cadaver management with good communication is important for the psychosocial well-being of survivors (WHO, HPA, & partners, 2011b).

Special health needs post-disaster

A **special needs population** is any individual, group or community whose circumstances create barriers to: (1) obtaining or understanding information, or (2) the ability to react in the same way as the general population. Circumstances that may create barriers include: age, physical, mental, emotional or cognitive status, culture, ethnicity, religion, language, citizenship and socio-economic status (Ford, n.d.). Vulnerable special needs populations can be divided into physical, psychological and social categories. People with physical needs include pregnant women, infants, disabled people, people with chronic illness and those living with an immunodeficiency syndrome. People with psychological needs include those with chronic mental illness, alcohol addiction, substance abuse and suicidal thoughts or actions. In the social domain, vulnerable populations include the homeless, those left behind, alone or orphaned, those in abusive families and refugees.

Extremes of age: children

In disasters, children are more vulnerable than adults because of their limited opportunity and ability to survive. Save the Children has reported that more than half of the people affected by disaster globally are children (United Nations Office for Disaster Risk Reduction [UNISDR], 2011) (see Knowledge Box 6.6). In the 1971 Bangladesh cyclone, half of all deaths were children under ten years of age, and in the 1976

KNOWLEDGE BOX 6.6   CHILDREN IN DISASTERS

Children require special attention in disasters. In general, 30 to 50% of fatalities in natural disasters are children. Although it varies with the legal, cultural and historical development of a country, a child is defined as a person below the age of 18 (United Nations, 1989). As minors, they are entitled to the protection of their rights and vulnerabilities. The main causes of mortality for children are the same as those that cause morbidity in non-emergency settings. The excess mortality comes from the vulnerability presented by their physiological as well as social vulnerability (e.g. dependency on access to services, resources and entitlements).

Guatemala earthquake, child mortality was considerably higher than adult mortality (Seaman & Maguire, 2005). As in non-emergency settings, most fatalities in children during disasters result from diarrhoea, measles, respiratory diseases and malaria (WHO, HPA, Save the Children & partners, 2011). Immature immune systems, together with the lack of immunisation, poor sanitation levels and inadequate food supplies, make them more susceptible to communicable diseases. Young children require less daily calorific intake but more frequent meals than adults. The lack of nutritious food can lead to malnutrition, micronutrient deficiency, underweight and stunting in children. Psychosocially, children are highly dependent on their families; the separation of children from parents can cause emotional insecurity and lack of access to resources. In resource-scarce settings, children are easily exploited or taken away from home or school for financial reasons. Case Boxes 6.8 and 6.9 discuss children's experiences in disasters.

CASE BOX 6.8   THE HEALTH IMPACT OF RECURRENT FLOODS ON CHILDREN IN BANGLADESH

Two-thirds of Bangladesh's land area is no higher than 5 meters above sea level. The country is susceptible to flash floods and storm surges that result from tropical cyclones. The bulk of the land consists of the floodplains of three major rivers that drain into the Bay of Bengal: the Padma, the Jamuna and the Meghna. These rivers carry rainfall from India, Nepal, Bhutan and China, in addition to the snowmelts from the Himalayas. Around 30% of the country is affected by floods annually.

Studies indicate that 55% of children under five are underweight in areas that experience recurrent floods, compared with the national average of 41%. In fact, children exposed to recurrent floods have a seven-time higher risk of wasting than unexposed children even after the flood seasons. The problem of underweight and stunting in children, combined with poor access to health care services, increases the risk of other diseases among children in areas with recurrent floods. Households exposed to recurrent floods practise altered dietary behaviour. To manage the risk of lowered food supply during flood seasons, these households lower their food consumption by exchanging rice with wheat, as well as reducing consumption of fruit, vegetables and milk due to the high cost and scarcities. Many households continue to reduce their daily caloric intake even after the flood period is over; on average they consume less than 1,818 calories per person per day.

As the health impact of floods is not always immediate, and not necessarily directly attributable to the natural hazard itself, the long-term impact of other types of recurrent disasters in communities deserves further study.

Source: del Ninno, Dorosh, Smith, and Roy (2001).

CASE BOX 6.9 CHILD SOLDIER

In 2001, UNICEF estimated that there were about 300,000 soldiers younger than 18 years of age in more than 50 countries around the world. Many were refugees from natural disasters or conflicts, orphans separated from their families at very young age, or simply recruited coercively. These "child soldiers" often take up the roles of porters, cooks, spotters, spies, human shields, or even suicide bombers. A study by Bayer, Klasen, and Adam (2007) found that three-fourths of 169 former child soldiers experienced one or more of the following brutalities: threats of being killed, serious injuries, committing murder, and witnessing a friend or family member being killed. The post-traumatic stress they suffered may hinder them from using peaceful ways to resolve conflicts. Former child soldiers often report that their greatest concern is their reintegration into society as they are often denied equal educational opportunities. They desire to return to school, but are usually too old or have no resources. Governments and the international community need to pay more attention to the effort of reintegrating this specific group into society. The protection of unaccompanied children after natural disasters and emergencies is thus an important measure to prevent young children entering into a vicious cycle of violence and abuse.

Source: Anda et al. (2006).

Extremes of age: older people

Older people generally suffer from poorer health than younger people. They are more susceptible to diseases because of poor immune systems and minor conditions can easily become major problems (e.g. not having a blanket while sleeping can cause hypothermia in the elderly as they are more vulnerable to heat and cold). With age, an individual decreases in sight, hearing, muscle strength and mobility, which results in difficulties accessing health services, queuing up to receive food or getting to the toilet. The loss of hearing makes it difficult for them to hear warning messages. The lack of physical energy makes them more vulnerable because they are not able to collect firewood and water or cook food. They often lack teeth, leading to difficulties in digesting food. Dental health is usually not available in emergency situations. They often suffer joint pain, especially in the hips, knees and back. Furthermore, chronic diseases, such as hypertension, diabetes mellitus and respiratory diseases, are common in the elderly. In disasters, older people with chronic diseases may suffer if they lose their routine medications and are not able to seek medical help (see also Knowledge Box 6.7).

In terms of social and psychological aspects, older people may face social exclusion and suffer from a breakdown of their social support networks because they may

KNOWLEDGE BOX 6.7   FACTS AND TRENDS OF OLDER PEOPLE IN THE TWENTY-FIRST CENTURY

The United Nations defines an elderly person as someone over 60 years of age, while the term "oldest-old" refers to those over 80 years. However, the concept of an older person may differ between regions, depending on the context and culture. In less-developed countries, people in their fifties can be considered elderly because they cannot do physical work anymore and are more prone to develop various chronic conditions. The number of people aged over 60 is expected to reach almost 2 billion people, or 22% of the world's population in 2050. Over 80% of them will be living in developing countries. The oldest-old group constitutes the fastest growing old-age group, at a rate of 3.8% per year, exceeding the 60–79 age groups at 2.0% a year. Figure 6.5 shows the increasing number of elderly people and decreasing number of young people globally.

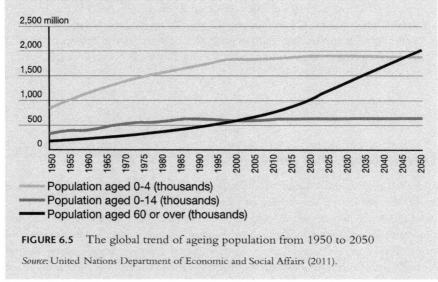

FIGURE 6.5   The global trend of ageing population from 1950 to 2050

Source: United Nations Department of Economic and Social Affairs (2011).

be separated from their families, peers or caregivers. In the 2006 Lebanon War, 68% of older persons were depressed or showed probable depression. Inaccessibility to information, language and literacy barriers, social isolation and lack of separation of the sexes make them vulnerable to different kinds of abuses, such as rape, gender-based violence and theft.

Due to the physiological changes and various barriers (e.g. the inability to access technology), special needs assessment protocol, guidelines and programmes might need to be developed to effectively understand and address the needs of older people after disasters (WHO, HPA, & partners, 2011d) (see also Case Boxes 6.10 and 6.11).

CASE BOX 6.10   AFTER THE 2005 PAKISTANI KASHMIR EARTHQUAKE: THE FORGOTTEN HEALTH NEEDS OF THE ELDERLY

On 8 October 2005, an earthquake measuring 7.6 on the Richter scale hit the Pakistan-administered part of Kashmir. More than 79,000 deaths were recorded in Pakistan. About 3.7% of Pakistan's population of 158 million were over 65 years of age at that time. To understand more about the health needs and health outcomes of older people in disasters, a study about the health needs of older people was conducted in both rural and urban areas of the Neelum Valley of Pakistani Kashmir in February 2006, four months after the earthquake.

The most common diseases reported by the elderly population included upper respiratory tract infection, pneumonia, arthralgia, backache and skin infections (such as scabies). Increased age disparities in access to care for chronic medical conditions were also observed and 25%–38% of the respondents reported at least one unmanaged, underlying medical problem. Geographic access was also found to be one of the main barriers for old people to obtain health services, especially in remote rural areas. The clinic utilisation rate of old people was lower for remote mountainous clinics than clinics in internally displaced person (IDP) camps near cities. A difference in gender health service utilisation among the elderly was also observed. In remote rural areas, men were the main users of health services, but had a limited or no access to psychological health services since most programmes targeted women and children. No medical relief group regarded old people as a need group; hence there were no targeted interventions.

It is essential for relief agencies to be sensitive towards the elderly population. Targeted needs assessments should be conducted at the initial post-disaster phase to address the specific needs of old people (WHO, HPA, & partners, 2011d). Establishing a long-term NCD management strategy among the elderly population in the post-disaster phase could fill in the current gap in relief work.

Source: Chan and Griffiths (2009).

Reproductive health

Sexual and reproductive health is a human right and presents significant public health challenges to be addressed in both emergency and non–emergency settings. In general, timely interventions (safe pregnancies and childbirth) may prevent adverse outcomes in reproductive health. Knowledge Box 6.8 and Case Box 6.12 below discuss some important issues in reproductive health.

Natural disasters have affected women and girls disproportionately. For example, in the 1991 cyclone in Bangladesh, women and girls accounted for nearly 90%

CASE BOX 6.11 CHILD-FRIENDLY SPACE: AN INTERGENERATIONAL APPROACH

By Christy Chan

During a disaster, people often underestimate what old people can contribute and treat them as "invisible" as a result of their vulnerabilities, such as illiteracy, physical weakness and limited language abilities. However, old people can play a key role in emergency situations. An estimation in 2007 suggested that more than half of the children in the north of Uganda were cared for by their grandparents and up to 60% of orphans in sub-Saharan Africa live in grandparent-headed households; old people's committees in Bangladesh actively disseminated early warning messages to the elderly and their families and notified people when and where to receive relief goods after the 2007 Cyclone Sidr.

Child-friendly spaces (CFSs) have been widely used in emergencies to help and protect children since UNICEF launched the CFS initiative in Albania in 1999. Different agencies may use different terms, such as safe spaces, child-centred spaces and emergency spaces for children, but they are all intended to address the psychosocial needs of vulnerable children and provide them with long-term support through activities like storytelling, playing and learning. Together with HelpAge in Pakistan, UNICEF and its partners agreed to adopt an intergenerational approach, which encouraged old people to participate in CFSs. Old people were invited to attend a CFS for half an hour once a week. This idea turned out to be a great success. Some old people even turned up at the CFS every day to tell stories, organise activities and take care of the equipment.

Sources: Day, Pirie, and Roys (2007), UNICEF (2011) and Ager and Metzler (2012).

---

of the deaths. During the 2003 European heatwave, more women died than men (Pirard et al., 2005). Young women also face increased vulnerability to exploitation, violence and transactional sex. An increase in risk-taking behaviour might occur because of the breakdown in youth–adult partnerships and the distortion of future perspectives. The disruption to the provision of basic contraceptive methods and the lack of emergency contraceptive methods during disasters may lead to an increased risk of unplanned pregnancies and an increased risk of unsafe abortions. There could also be the potential danger of a situation developing where rape and sexual violence are rampant.

During disasters, pregnant women are at risk of various gestational problems and a wide range of adverse preventable obstetric outcomes if they do not receive timely

KNOWLEDGE BOX 6.8 FACTS AND TRENDS OF WOMEN IN DISASTERS

According to the International Union for Conservation of Nature, women and children are 14 times more likely to die than men during a disaster. Women are more vulnerable to disaster-related afflictions than men because in many countries they are considered second-class citizens with restricted mobility, fewer education opportunities and poorer employment (UNISDR, 2011). Pregnant women who were caught in crisis thus face disproportionate risk and vulnerability. An estimated 3,580,000 maternal deaths occur annually. Ninety-nine per cent occur in the developing world, with 87% in sub-Saharan Africa and South Asia. Countries in conflict or experiencing other forms of instability often experience the highest rates of maternal and neonatal mortality. In any emergency situation, one in five women of childbearing age is likely to be pregnant. Therefore, reproductive health is an essential component to public health and medical humanitarian response in crisis.

provision of health care services by trained professionals with adequate facilities (WHO, HPA, & partners, 2011e). Poor access to skilled care for childbirth, obstetrics and neonatal care support will increase the risk of maternal death. In addition, it is necessary to support the social well-being of women past puberty by providing sanitary supplies and facilities. The case ahead will give us a glimpse of how a disaster can affect women in other ways.

There are regular reports of women being the victims of rape, physical abuse, sexual assault and increased domestic violence after disasters. In the aftermath of the 2004 Sri Lanka tsunami, there were incidents of gang rape and molestation by male residents in temporary shelters (Oxfam International, 2005). Unprotected coitus puts women at a high risk of unwanted pregnancies and **sexually transmitted infections**. In some countries, violence against women is regarded as a private issue that cannot be discussed with other people.

It is important to also point out, however, that access to health/medical services for gender-specific health needs and vulnerabilities should not be limited to women only. Men (who might be excluded from the traditional "vulnerability focus"–based psychosocial service) and people from the homosexual and transgender community might face further barriers (social, cultural and legal norms) to access to care and services.

To respond comprehensively to reproductive needs after disasters, the Minimum Initial Service Package (MISP) for reproductive health is being advocated by the Sphere Project. It argues that primary care services should always attempt to include reproductive health services, with an emphasis on prevention and management of excess maternal and neonatal morbidity and mortality, planning of

CASE BOX 6.12 DISASTER PREPAREDNESS PLAN NEEDED FOR MATERNAL CARE, NEPAL EARTHQUAKE 2015

By Eva Chor-chiu Lam

Nepal was struck by an earthquake measuring 7.8 magnitude on 25 April 2015 and another earthquake with a magnitude of 7.3 in less than three weeks. More than 8,800 people died in the two earthquakes, over 22,000 were injured and over 600,000 houses were destroyed. Up to 2015, the most severe earthquake in Nepal was that in 1934, which caused the deaths of more than 10,000 (Government of Nepal, n.d; United Nations Office for the Coordination of Humanitarian Affairs & Office of the Resident and Humanitarian Coordinator in Nepal, 2015, June; USGS, 2016, April). According to health assessment reports conducted by various international aid organisations, pregnant women were among the most vulnerable after the catastrophe. The UNFPA estimated that of the 8 million people affected by the quakes, more than 126,000 were pregnant women and two million were of reproductive age (UNFPA, 2015, May 26). WHO estimated that 10,000 babies were delivered every month across the 14 most severely affected districts (WHO Country Office for Nepal, 2015).

Without the village health posts, village people had to walk along hill trails for several hours to reach the nearest health facilities. After the quake, pregnant women were forced to face the risks of landslides as they walked on the quake-damaged trails from their hill villages to reach delivery facilities. As disaster preparedness plans or prepositioned delivery kits for maternal care after disasters were not present in those villages, although there might have been trained birth attendants, emergency delivery kits were not available for them to take care of pregnant women.

In Melamchi village in the Sindhupalchok district, the Red Cross medical outreach team found many totally collapsed or destroyed health posts in the affected hill villages. A 28-year-old pregnant woman who was about to go into labour was found by the Red Cross outreach team in a village where the health post had collapsed. The Red Cross team escorted her to the primary health care centre and the baby was delivered safely ('Miracle baby' for Nepal earthquake victim, 2015, May 13). After the emergency, the Red Cross team coordinated the supply of emergency delivery kits to village health posts. In countries where pregnant women are among the most vulnerable groups after disasters, an emergency preparedness plan for pregnant women at family and community levels can provide maternal care support to pregnant women after disasters. Creating home delivery plans, promoting group support and training community health workers are some components of emergency preparedness plans for maternal care after disasters (Haeri & Marcozzi, 2015).

reproductive-related services, reduction of HIV/STIs and proactive prevention and management of the consequences of sexual violence.

People with disabilities

In addition, according to the World Health Organization (WHO, 2013), around 15% of the world's population live with some form of disability and they have to face greater barriers to access basic survival needs and health services in disasters.

In the 2013 first-ever UN global survey of people with disabilities in disaster, it was found that these vulnerable people were rarely consulted about their disaster needs and mostly had not participated in community disaster management and risk reduction processes, and thus being excluded from relevant decision making and planning (UNISDR, 2014). Most of these 5,717 respondents do not have a personalised disaster preparedness plan and very few were aware of a national or communal disaster risk reduction or disaster management plan. Very few people living with disabilities were confident that they could evacuate without difficulty in disaster and some would not be able to evacuate at all. A majority of them did not think or did not know the Hyogo Framework for Action had addressed their disaster needs.

Some respondents to the survey suggested setting up an annually-updated national or communal register of those who may need assistance in disaster, and the training for all emergency responders in augmentative and alternative communication skills.

Knowledge Box 6.9 highlights guidelines and fact sheets developed by WHO for special population subgroups mentioned above.

KNOWLEDGE BOX 6.9 WORLD HEALTH ORGANIZATION GUIDELINES AND FACT SHEETS IN DISASTER

Responding to health and medical implications of disasters requires a good understanding of the nature of the disaster and the relevant needs of the survivors during emergencies. The World Health Organization has published a series of fact sheets that highlight essential health domains as part of disaster management, which cover disaster risk management, chemical safety, child health, climate risk management and communicable diseases. They also include people with disabilities and older people, mass casualty management, mass fatalities/dead bodies, mental health, natural hazards, NCDs, nutrition, radiation emergencies, safe hospitals, sexual and reproductive health and water, sanitation and hygiene.

Source: WHO (n.d.).

Conclusion

Disasters not only lead to increased population risk and exposure to injury, communicable diseases and non-communicable conditions, but they also pose other threats to the population.

Demographic make-up, pre-existing epidemiological patterns, environmental context, field security and response capacity of the affected community are all important considerations when determining current and likely health threats post-disaster. The health needs of vulnerable populations, such as elderly people, children, women, the disabled, as well as the health needs of internally displaced persons (IDPs) and refugees, all deserve special attention when prioritising medical and humanitarian disaster relief programmes. Attention should also be paid to the mental and social health needs of patients, their families and frontline relief workers and the provision of rehabilitation or palliative care in accordance with the pathway of care approach to protect health.

References

Ager, A., & Metzler, J. (2012). *Child friendly spaces: A structured review of the current evidence-base*. Retrieved from the website of World Vision International: http://www.wvi.org/sites/default/files/CFS%20Literature%20Review%20final%20Aug%202012.pdf

American Psychiatric Association (APA). (2000). *Diagnostic and statistical manual of mental disorders* (4th ed.). Washington, DC: American Psychiatric Association.

Anda, R. F., Felitti, V. J., Bremner, J. D., Walker, J. D., Whitfield, C., Perry, B. D., . . . Giles, W. H. (2006). The enduring effects of abuse and related adverse experiences in childhood: A convergence of evidence from neurobiology and epidemiology. *European Archives of Psychiatry and Clinical Neuroscience, 256*(3), 174–186.

Andrews, G., Hobbs, M. J., Borkovec, T. D., Beesdo, K., Craske, M. G., Heimberg, R. G., . . . Stanley, M. A. (2010). Generalized worry disorder: A review of DSM-IV generalized anxiety disorder and options for DSM-V. *Depression and Anxiety, 27*(2), 134–147.

Bayer, C. P., Klasen, F., & Adam, H. (2007). Association of trauma and PTSD with openness to reconciliation and feelings of revenge among former Ugandan and Congolese child soldiers. *Journal of the American Medical Association, 298*(5), 555–559.

Bryant, R. A., Friedman, M. J., Spiegel, D., Ursano, R., & Strain, J. (2011). A review of acute stress disorder in DSM-5. *Depression and Anxiety, 28*(9), 802–817.

Burrows, M., Frankenberg, E., Katz. P., Sikoki, B., & Thomas, D. (2012). *Family formation in Indonesia after the 2004 Indian Ocean Tsunami*. Paper presented at Population Association of America 2012 Annual Meeting, San Francisco, CA [Internet]. Retrieved from http://paa2012.princeton.edu/papers/122142

Centre for Research on the Epidemiology of Disasters (CRED). (2013). *People affected by conflict 2013: Humanitarian needs in numbers*. Retrieved from http://reliefweb.int/sites/reliefweb.int/files/resources/PubID303ConflictReport.pdf

Chan, E.Y.Y. (2008). The untold stories of Sichuan earthquake. *The Lancet, 372*(9636): 359–362

Chan, E.Y.Y. (2009). Why are older people health needs forgotten post-natural disaster relief in developing countries? A healthcare provider survey of 2005 Kashmir, Pakistan earthquake. *American Journal of Disaster Medicine, 4*(2), 107–112.

Chan, E.Y.Y., & Griffiths, S. (2009). Comparison of health needs of older people between affected rural and urban areas after the 2005 Kashmir, Pakistan earthquake. *Prehospital and Disaster Medicine, 24*(5), 365–371.

Chan, E.Y.Y., & Kim, J. J. (2010a). Characteristics and health outcomes of internally displaced population in unofficial rural self-settled camps after the 2005 Kashmir, Pakistan earthquake. *European Journal of Emergency Medicine, 17*(3), 136–141.

Chan, E.Y.Y., & Kim, J. J. (2010b). Remote mobile health service utilization post 2005 Kashmir-Pakistan earthquake. *European Journal of Emergency Medicine, 17*(3), 158–163.

Chan, E.Y.Y., & Kim, J. (2011). Chronic health needs immediately after natural disasters in middle-income countries: The case of the 2008 Sichuan, China earthquake. *European Journal of Emergency Medicine, 18*(2), 111–114.

Chan, E.Y.Y., & Sondorp, E. (2007). Natural disaster medical intervention: Missed opportunity to deal with chronic medical needs? An analytical framework. *Asia Pacific Journal of Public Health, 19*(Special Issue), 45–51.

Chan, E.Y.Y., & Sondorp, E. (2008). Including chronic disease care in emergency responses. *Humanitarian Exchange Magazine, 41* [Internet]. Retrieved from Humanitarian Practice Network website: http://odihpn.org/magazine/including-chronic-disease-care-in-emergency-responses/

Cheung, E.Y.L. (2014a). Neutrality crucial amidst political controversies. *Coping with Crisis, 2,* 26–27 [Internet]. Retrieved from the website of Psychosocial Centre, International Federation of Red Cross and Red Crescent Societies (IFRC): http://pscentre.org/wp-content/uploads/Coping2–2014-med.pdf

Cheung, E.Y.L. (2014b). *Psychological first aid as a public health disaster response preparedness strategy for responders in critical incidents and disasters* (Unpublished doctoral dissertation). The Chinese University of Hong Kong, Hong Kong, China. Retrieved from http://search.proquest.com/docview/1691127433

Cheung, E.Y.L. (2015). An outbreak of fear, rumours, and stigma: Psychosocial support for Ebola virus disease outbreak in West Africa. *Intervention, 13*(1), 45–84.

Cheung, E.Y.L., Chan, E.Y.Y., Sin, C.K.M., & Wong, A. H. (2014, October). *Impact of Psychological First Aid training on disaster responding aid workers' mental well-being: A cross-sectional study two months after the vessel collision accident on the National Day.* Paper presented at the 6th Global Conference of the Alliance for Healthy Cities, Hong Kong, China.

Council to Improve Foodborne Outbreak Response (CIFOR). (2009). *Guidelines for foodborne disease outbreak response* (2nd ed.) [Internet]. Atlanta, GA: Council of State and Territorial Epidemiologists. Retrieved from http://www.cifor.us/documents/CIFOR%20Industry%20Guidelines/CIFOR-Industry-Guideline.pdf

Day, W., Pirie, A., & Roys, C. (2007). *Strong and fragile: Learning from older people in emergencies* [Internet]. Retrieved from the website of HelpAge International: www.helpage.org/download/4c754e9356cc6

del Ninno, C., Dorosh, P. A., Smith, L. C., & Roy, D. K. (2001). *The 1998 floods in Bangladesh: Disaster impacts, household coping strategies, and response* (Research Report 122) [Internet]. Washington, DC: International Food Policy Research Institute. Retrieved from https://www.ifpri.org/cdmref/p15738coll2/id/125308/filename/125309.pdf

Ford, E. S., Mokdad, A. H., Link, M. W., Garvin, W. S., McGuire, L. C., Jiles, R. B., & Balluz, L. S. (2006). Chronic disease in health emergencies: In the eye of the hurricane. *Preventive Chronic Disease, 3*(2) [Internet]. Retrieved from http://www.cdc.gov/pcd/issues/2006/apr/pdf/05_0235.pdf

Ford, K. (n.d.). *Emergency planning for people with disability* [Internet]. Retrieved from the website of Iowa Department of Public Health: https://idph.iowa.gov/Portals/1/Files/DisabilityHealthProgram/emergency_planning.pdf

Galea, S., Nandi, A., & Vlahov, D. (2005). The epidemiology of post-traumatic stress disorder after disasters. *Epidemiologic Reviews, 27*(1), 78–91. doi:10.1093/epirev/mxi003

Gerin, W., Chaplin, W., Schwartz, J. E., Holland, J., Alter, R., Wheeler, R., . . . Pickering, T. G. (2005). Sustained blood pressure increase after an acute stressor: The effects of the 11 September 2001 attack on the New York City World Trade Center. *Journal of Hypertension, 23*(2), 279–284.

Government of Nepal, Nepal Disaster Risk Reduction Portal. (n.d.). Nepal earthquake 2015: Country profile [Internet]. Retrieved from http://drrportal.gov.np/ndrrip/main.html?id=0

Guha-Sapir, D., van Panhuis, W. G., & Lagoutte, J. (2007). Short communication: Patterns of chronic and acute diseases after natural disasters – A study from the International Committee of the Red Cross field hospital in Banda Aceh after the 2004 Indian Ocean tsunami. *Tropical Medicine & International Health, 12*(11), 1338–1341. doi:10.1111/j.1365–3156.2007.01932.x

Haeri, S., & Marcozzi, D. (2015). Emergency preparedness in obstetrics. *Obstetrics & Gynecology, 125*(4), 959–970. doi:10.1097/AOG.0000000000000750

HelpAge International. (2005). *The impact of the Indian Ocean tsunami on older people: Issues and recommendations* [Internet]. Retrieved from http://www.helpage.org/silo/files/the-impact-of-the-indian-ocean-tsunami-on-older-people-issues-and-recommendations.pdf

Hong Kong protests: Timeline of the occupation. (2014, December 11). *BBC News* [Internet]. Retrieved from http://www.bbc.com/news/world-asia-china-30390820

Hung, K. K. C. (2010). *Disease pattern in a rural setting three weeks after the 2008 Sichuan, China earthquake: Hong Kong Red Cross basic health clinic in Yanmen town* (Unpublished master's thesis). Universita Del Piemonte Orientale, Alessandria, Novara and Vercelli, Italy; and Vrije Universiteit, Brussels, Belgium.

Hung, K. K. C., Lam, E. C. C., Chan, E. Y. Y., & Graham, C. A. (2013). Disease pattern and chronic illness in rural China: The Hong Kong Red Cross basic health clinic after 2008 Sichuan earthquake. *Emergency Medicine Australasia, 25*(3), 252–259. doi:10.1111/1742–6723.12080

The Hurricane Katrina Community Advisory Group, & Kessler, R. C. (2007). Hurricane Katrina's impact on the care of survivors with chronic medical conditions. *Journal of General Internal Medicine, 22*(9), 1225–1230. doi:10.1007/s11606–007–0294–1

Hyer, R. N., & Covello, V. T. (2005). *Effective media communication during public health emergencies: A WHO handbook*. Retrieved from the website of World Health Organization: http://www.who.int/csr/resources/publications/WHO%20MEDIA%20HANDBOOK.pdf

Institute of Medicine, Committee on Responding to the Psychological Consequences of Terrorism. (2003). *Preparing for the psychological consequences of terrorism: A public health strategy*. Washington, DC: National Academies Press.

International Federation of Red Cross and Red Crescent Societies (IFRC). (2014, September 18). *Emergency appeal operation update: Africa-Ebola coordination and preparedness* (Operations update No. 1) [Internet]. Retrieved from http://adore.ifrc.org/Download.aspx?FileId=64340

Janoff-Bulman, R. (1992). *Shattered assumptions: Towards a new psychology of trauma*. New York, NY: Free Press.

Kamoi, K., Tanaka, M., Ikarashi, T., & Miyakoshi, M. (2006). Effect of the 2004 Mid Niigata Prefecture earthquake on glycemic control in type 1 diabetic patients. *Diabetes Research and Clinical Practice, 74*(2), 141–147. doi:10.1016/j.diabres.2006.03.028

Kario, K., Matsuo, T., Shimada, K., & Pickering, T. G. (2001). Factors associated with the occurrence and magnitude of earthquake-induced increases in blood pressure. *The American Journal of Medicine, 111*(5), 379–384. doi:10.1016/S0002–9343(01)00832–4

Kario, K., McEwen, B. S., & Pickering, T. G. (2003). Disasters and the heart: A review of the effects of earthquake-induced stress on cardiovascular disease. *Hypertension Research, 26*(5), 355–367. doi:10.1291/hypres.26.355

Kario, K., Shimada, K., & Takaku, F. (2005). Management of cardiovascular risk in disaster: Jichi Medical School (JMS) proposal 2004. *Japan Medical Association Journal, 48*(7), 363–376.

Kirizuka, K., Nishizaki, H., Kohriyama, K., Nukata, O., Arioka, Y., Motobuchi, M., . . . Tsuboi, S. (1997). Influences of the Great Hanshin-Awaji earthquake on glycemic control in diabetic patients. *Diabetes Research and Clinical Practice, 36*(3), 193–196. doi:10.1016/S0168–8227(97)00030–2

Kwak, Y. H., Shin, S. D., Kim, K. S., Kwon, W. Y., & Suh, G. J. (2006). Experience of a Korean disaster medical assistance team in Sri Lanka after the South Asia tsunami. *Journal of Korean Medical Science, 21*(1), 143–150.

Landesman, L. Y. (2001). *Public health management of disasters: The practice guide.* Washington, DC: American Public Health Association.

Lewis, G. H., Sheringham, J., Kalim, K., & Crayford, T. J.B. (2011). *Mastering public health: A postgraduate guide to examinations and revalidation.* London, UK: Edward Arnold.

Li, W., & Redmond, A. (2016). Individual preparedness in disaster response. In N. Wolfson, A. Lerner, & L. Roshal (Eds.), *Orthopedics in disasters: Orthopedic injuries in natural disasters and mass casualty events* (pp. 83–95). Springer-Verlag Berlin Heidelberg.

'Miracle baby' for Nepal earthquake victim. (2015, May 13). *BBC News.* Retrieved from http://www.bbc.com/news/world-asia-32730294

Morgan, O. (2004). Infectious disease risks from dead bodies following natural disasters. *Revista Panamericana de Salud Pública, 15*(5), 307–312.

Morgan, O., Tidball-Binz, M., & van Alphen, D. (2006). *Management of dead bodies after disasters: A field manual for first responders* [Internet]. Retrieved from the website of Pan American Health Organization/WHO Regional Office for the Americas (PAHO/WHO):http://www.paho.org/disasters/index.php?option=com_docman&task=doc_download&gid=29&Itemid=

Neria, Y., Nandi, A., & Galea, S. (2008). Post-traumatic stress disorder following disasters: A systematic review. *Psychological Medicine, 38*(4), 467–480.

Newnham, E. A., McBain, R. K., Hann, K., Akinsulure-Smith, A. M., Weisz, J., Lilienthal, G. M., . . . Betancourt, T. S. (2015). The youth readiness intervention for war-affected youth. *Journal of Adolescent Health, 56*(6), 606–611. doi:10.1016/j.jadohealth.2015.01.020

Norris, F. H., Friedman, M. J., Watson, P. J., Byrne, C. M., Diaz, E., & Kaniasty, K. (2002). 60,000 disaster victims speak: Part I. An empirical review of the empirical literature, 1981–2001. *Psychiatry, 65*(3), 207–239.

North, C. S., Nixon, S. J., Shariat, S., Mallonee, S., McMillen, J. C., Spitznagel, E. L., & Smith, E. M. (1999). Psychiatric disorders among survivors of the Oklahoma City bombing. *Journal of the American Medical Association, 282*(8), 755–762. doi:10.1001/jama.282.8.755

Nufer, K. E., Wilson-Ramirez, G., Shah, M. B., Hughes, C. E., & Crandall, C. S. (2006). Analysis of patients treated during four Disaster Medical Assistance Team deployments. *Journal of Emergency Medicine, 30*(2), 183–187.

Ogawa, K., Tsuji, I., Shiono, K., & Hisamichi, S. (2000). Increased acute myocardial infarction mortality following the 1995 Great Hanshin-Awaji earthquake in Japan. *International Journal of Epidemiology, 29*(3), 449–455. doi:10.1093/ije/29.3.449

Oriol, W. E. (1999). *Psychosocial issues for older adults in disasters.* Rockville, MD: Center for Mental Health Services, Substance Abuse and Mental Health Services Administration, U.S. Department of Health and Human Services.

Oxfam International. (2005). *The tsunami's impact on women* (Oxfam briefing note). Retrieved from http://www.oxfam.org/sites/www.oxfam.org/files/women.pdf

Pan American Health Organization/WHO Regional Office for the Americas (PAHO/WHO). (2004). *Management of dead bodies in disaster situations* (Disaster Manuals and

Guidelines Series No. 5) [Internet]. Retrieved from http://www.who.int/hac/techguidance/management_of_dead_bodies.pdf

Parati, G., Antonicelli, R., Guazzarotti, F., Paciaroni, E., & Mancia, G. (2001). Cardiovascular effects of an earthquake: Direct evidence by ambulatory blood pressure monitoring. *Hypertension, 38*, 1093–1095. doi:10.1161/hy1101.095334

Pirard, P., Vandentorren, S., Pascal, M., Laaidi, K., Le Tertre, A., Cassadou, S., & Ledrans, M. (2005). Summary of the mortality impact assessment of the 2003 heat wave in France. *Euro Surveillance, 10*(7), 153–156.

Prince, M., Patel, V., Saxena, S., Maj, M., Maselko, J., Phillips, M. R., & Rahman, A. (2007). No health without mental health. *The Lancet, 370*(9590), 859–877. doi:10.1016/S0140–6736(07)61238–0

Rand, E. C., (Ed.). (2008). *The Johns Hopkins and International Federation of Red Cross and Red Crescent Societies public health guide for emergencies* (2nd ed.). Geneva, Switzerland: Johns Hopkins Bloomberg School of Public Health and the International Federation of Red Cross and Red Crescent Societies.

Seaman, J., & Maguire, S. (2005). ABC of conflict and disaster: The special needs of children and women. *British Medical Journal, 331*, 34–36. doi:10.1136/bmj.331.7507.34

Sleigh, A. (2005). Outbreaks, epidemics and clusters. In P. Webb, C. Bain, & S. Pirozzo (Eds.), *Essential epidemiology: An introduction for students and health professionals* (pp. 249–257). Cambridge, UK; New York, NY: Cambridge University Press.

The Sphere Project. (2011). *Humanitarian charter and minimum standards in disaster response* (3rd ed.) [Internet]. Retrieved from http://www.spherehandbook.org/en/the-humanitarian-charter/

Spiegel, P. B. (2004). HIV/AIDS among conflict-affected and displaced populations: Dispelling myths and taking action. *Disasters, 28*(3), 322–339. doi:10.1111/j.0361–3666.2004.00261.x

Spiegel, P. B., Checchi, F., Colombo, S., & Paik, E. (2010). Health-care needs of people affected by conflict: Future trends and changing frameworks. *The Lancet, 375*(9711), 341–345. doi:10.1016/S0140–6736(09)61873–0 http://www.healthynewbornnetwork.org/sites/default/files/resources/Spiegel_conflict.pdf

Suzuki, S., Sakamoto, S., Koide, M., Fujita, H., Sakuramoto, H., Kuroda, T., . . . Matsuo, T. (1997). Hanshin-Awaji earthquake as a trigger for acute myocardial infarction. *American Heart Journal, 134*(5), 974–977. doi:10.1016/S0002–8703(97)80023–3

United Nations. (1989). *Convention on the Rights of the Child* [Internet]. Retrieved from the website of Office of the United Nations High Commissioner for Human Rights: http://www.ohchr.org/Documents/ProfessionalInterest/crc.pdf

United Nations Children's Fund (UNICEF). (2011). *Guidelines for child friendly spaces in emergencies* [Internet]. Retrieved from http://www.unicef.org/protection/Child_Friendly_Spaces_Guidelines_for_Field_Testing.pdf

United Nations Department of Economic and Social Affairs (UNDESA), Population Division. (2011). *World population prospects: The 2010 revision* [Internet]. Retrieved from http://www.un.org/en/development/desa/population/publications/trends/population-prospects_2010_revision.shtml

United Nations Inter-Agency Standing Committee (IASC). (2008). *IASC guidelines on mental health and psychosocial support in emergency settings: Checklist for field use* [Internet]. Retrieved from https://interagencystandingcommittee.org/system/files/legacy_files/Checklist%20for%20field%20use%20IASC%20MHPSS.pdf

United Nations Inter-Agency Standing Committee (IASC), Reference Group for Mental Health and Psychosocial Support in Emergency Settings. (2010). *Mental health and psychosocial support in humanitarian emergencies: What should humanitarian health actors know?*

Retrieved from https://interagencystandingcommittee.org/system/files/legacy_files/IASC%20RG%20doc%20health%20audience.pdf

United Nations Office for the Coordination of Humanitarian Affairs & Office of the Resident and Humanitarian Coordinator in Nepal. (2015, June). *Nepal: Earthquake 2015* (Situation Report No. 20) [Internet]. Retrieved from http://reliefweb.int/sites/reliefweb.int/files/resources/OCHANepalEarthquakeSituationReportNo.20%283June2015%29_Final.pdf

United Nations Office for Disaster Risk Reduction (UNISDR). (2011). *Disaster through a different lens: Behind every effect, there is a cause: A guide for journalists covering disaster risk reduction* [Internet]. Retrieved from http://www.unisdr.org/files/20108_mediabook.pdf

United Nations Office for Disaster Risk Reduction (UNISDR). (2014). *Living with disability and disasters: UNISDR 2013 survey on living with disabilities and disasters - Key findings.* Retrieved from http://www.unisdr.org/2014/iddr/documents/2013DisabilitySurveryReport_030714.pdf

United Nations Population Fund (UNFPA). (2005). *Gender-based violence in Aceh, Indonesia: A case study* [Internet]. Retrieved from http://pdfsr.com/check_download/gender-based-violence-in-aceh-indonesia

United Nations Population Fund (UNFPA). (2015, May 26). *Infograph on Nepal earthquake* [Internet]. Retrieved from http://www.unfpa.org/sites/default/files/resource-pdf/Nepal_Infographic_26%20May%202015.pdf

United States Geological Survey (USGS). (2016, April). Historic earthquakes: Bihar, India - Nepal (1934 January 15 08:43 UTC - Magnitude 8.1) [Internet]. Retrieved from http://earthquake.usgs.gov/earthquakes/world/events/1934_01_15.php

van Ommeren, M., Barbui, C., de Jong, K., Dua, T., Jones, L., Perez-Sales, P., . . . Saxena, S. (2011). If you could only choose five psychotropic medicines: Updating the Interagency Emergency Health Kit. *PLoS Medicine, 8*(5), e1001030. doi:10.1371/journal.pmed.1001030

Wells, J. (2005). *Protecting and assisting older people in emergencies* (Network Paper No. 53) [Internet]. Retrieved from the website of Humanitarian Practice Network, Overseas Development Institute (ODI): http://odihpn.org/wp-content/uploads/2005/12/networkpaper053.pdf

Williams, R., & Alexander, D. (2009). Psychosocial resilience and distress in the face of adversity, conflict, terrorism, or catastrophe. In A.P.C.C.H. Hopperus Buma, D. G. Burris, A. Hawley, J. M. Ryan, & P. F. Mahoney (Eds.), *Conflict and catastrophe medicine: A practical guide* (2nd ed., pp. 360–373). London, UK: Springer.

World Health Organization (WHO). (n.d.). Humanitarian health action: Resources and links [Internet]. Retrieved from http://www.who.int/hac/techguidance/preparedness/resources_links/en/

World Health Organization (WHO). (2013). *Guidance note on disability and emergency risk management for health* [Internet]. Retrieved from http://apps.who.int/iris/bitstream/10665/90369/1/9789241506243_eng.pdf?ua=1

World Health Organization (WHO). (2014). *Mental health: A state of well-being* [Internet]. Retrieved from http://www.who.int/features/factfiles/mental_health/en/

World Health Organization (WHO). (2014, September 3). *Media Centre: UN senior leaders outline needs for global Ebola response* [Internet]. Retrieved from http://www.who.int/mediacentre/news/releases/2014/ebola-response-needs/en/

World Health Organization (WHO). (2015, August 12). *Ebola situation report* [Internet]. Retrieved from http://apps.who.int/iris/bitstream/10665/182071/1/ebolasitrep_12Aug2015_eng.pdf?ua=1&ua=1

World Health Organization (WHO), Christoffel-Blindenmission (CBM), World Vision International, & UNICEF. (2014, September). *Psychological first aid during Ebola virus disease outbreaks* (provisional version) [Internet]. Retrieved from WHO website: http://apps. who.int/iris/bitstream/10665/131682/1/9789241548847_eng.pdf?ua=1

World Health Organization (WHO), United Kingdom Health Protection Agency (HPA), & partners. (2011a). *Disaster risk management for health: Communicable diseases* [Internet]. Retrieved from http://www.who.int/hac/events/drm_fact_sheet_communicable_diseases. pdf?ua=1

World Health Organization (WHO), United Kingdom Health Protection Agency (HPA), & partners. (2011b). *Disaster risk management for health: Mental health and psychosocial support* [Internet]. Retrieved from http://www.who.int/hac/events/drm_fact_sheet_mental_ health.pdf?ua=1

World Health Organization (WHO), United Kingdom Health Protection Agency (HPA), & partners. (2011c), *Disaster risk management for health: Non-communicable diseases* [Internet]. Retrieved from http://www.who.int/entity/hac/events/drm_fact_sheet_non_commu nicable_diseases.pdf?ua=1

World Health Organization (WHO), United Kingdom Health Protection Agency (HPA), & partners. (2011d). *Disaster risk management for health: People with disabilities and older peo- ple* [Internet]. Retrieved from http://www.who.int/entity/hac/events/drm_fact_sheet_ disabilities.pdf?ua=1

World Health Organization (WHO), United Kingdom Health Protection Agency (HPA), & partners. (2011e). *Disaster risk management for health: Sexual and reproductive health* [Internet]. Retrieved from http://www.who.int/hac/events/drm_fact_sheet_sexual_and_reproductive _health.pdf?ua=1

World Health Organization (WHO), United Kingdom Health Protection Agency (HPA), Save the Children, & partners. (2011). *Disaster risk management for health: Child health* [Internet]. Retrieved from http://www.who.int/hac/events/drm_fact_sheet_child_ health.pdf?ua=1

World Health Organization (WHO) Country Office for Nepal. (2015). *Humanitarian cri- sis after the Nepal earthquakes 2015: Initial public health risk assessment and interventions* [Internet]. Retrieved from http://www.searo.who.int/entity/emergencies/phra_nepal_ may2015.pdf

Zhang, L., Fu, P., Wang, L., Cai, G., Zhang, L., Chen, D., . . . Chen, X. (2012). The clinical features and outcome of crush patients with acute kidney injury after the Wenchuan earthquake: Differences between elderly and younger adults. *Injury*, *43*, 1470–1475. doi:10.1016/j.injury.2010.11.036

Zhang, L., Liu, Y., Liu, X., & Zhang, Y. (2011). Rescue efforts management and characteristics of casualties of the Wenchuan earthquake in China. *Emergency Medicine Journal*, *28*(7), 618–622. doi:10.1136/emj.2009.087296

7

RESOURCES FOR DISASTER RESPONSE AND BEYOND

For any disaster, in order to effectively respond, all members of the at-risk/affected community should be involved in its preparedness, response and recovery process. This chapter will discuss and highlight the issues and challenges of disaster responses in the twenty-first century.

Key stakeholders in disaster response

KNOWLEDGE BOX 7.1   KEY DISASTER RESPONSE AGENCIES

TABLE 7.1 Key stakeholders in international disaster response

Abbreviation	Agency
CIDA	Canadian International Development Agency
DFID	Department For International Development, United Kingdom
FAO	Food and Agriculture Organization of the United Nations
GAIN	Global Alliance for Improved Nutrition, United Nations
GAVI	Global Alliance for Vaccines and Immunizations
GFATM	Global Fund to Fight AIDS, Tuberculosis and Malaria
IAEA	International Atomic Energy Agency
ICRC	International Committee of the Red Cross
IDA	International Development Association, World Bank Group
IFAD	International Fund for Agricultural Development, United Nations

(Continued)

TABLE 7.1 (Continued)

Abbreviation	Agency
IFRC	International Federation of the Red Cross and Red Crescent Societies
ILO	International Labour Organization, United Nations
IMF	International Monetary Fund
MSF	Doctors without Borders/Médecins Sans Frontières
NIH	National Institutes of Health, United States Department of Health and Human Services
OHCHR	Office of the United Nations High Commissioner for Human Rights
UN	United Nations
UNAIDS	Joint United Nations Programme on HIV/AIDS
UNDCP	United Nations Drug Control Programme
UNDP	United Nations Development Programme
UNEP	United Nations Environment Programme
UNESCO	United Nations Educational, Scientific and Cultural Organization
UNFPA	United Nations Population Fund
UN-Habitat	United Nations Human Settlements Programme
UNHCR	Office of the United Nations High Commissioner for Refugees
UNICEF	United Nations Children's Fund
UNIDO	United Nations Industrial Development Organization
UNIFEM	United Nations Development Fund for Women
UNRWA	United Nations Relief and Works Agency for Palestine Refugees in the Near East
USAID	United States Agency for International Development
WFP	World Food Programme, United Nations
WHI	Women's Health Initiative, United States Department of Health and Human Services
WHO	World Health Organization, United Nations
WIPO	World Intellectual Property Organization, United Nations
WTO	World Trade Organization

The cluster approach

As there are many stakeholders involved in disaster response (see Table 7.1) (see also Knowledge Box 7.1), the **cluster approach** is a system for coordinating

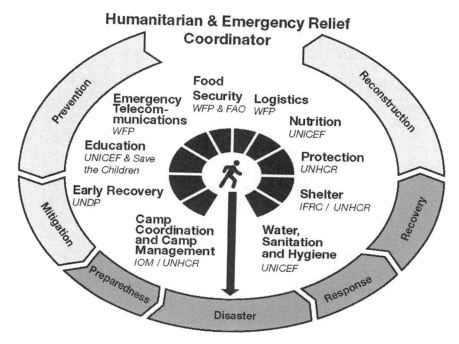

FIGURE 7.1   Cluster approach: 11 clusters and their corresponding leading agencies

Source: Adapted from the United Nations Office for the Coordination of Humanitarian Affairs (OCHA) (n.d.).

humanitarian actors by sector. Launched in 2005 by the United Nations Inter-Agency Standing Committee (IASC), it aims to improve the effectiveness, predictability and accountability of humanitarian responses (Fredriksen, 2012). Each cluster comprises organisation groups in a specific sector and aims to coordinate operational activities (IFRC, 2012). A total of 11 clusters are included in the response system and Figure 7.1 shows the clusters and their corresponding global leading agencies. The leading agencies report to the United Nations Emergency Relief Coordinator (ERC) (see Case Box 7.1).

The cluster approach functions at multiple levels. At the global level, it aims to strengthen systematic preparedness and technical capacity in humanitarian emergencies. Leading agencies of the global clusters are responsible for setting standards and policy-setting, building response capacity and carrying out operational support (IASC, 2006). At the country level, clusters are established when there is a humanitarian need with sufficient scale and complexity to justify a multi-sectoral response. Country-level clusters known as "sectoral groups" work with the global leaders to ensure a coherent and effective emergency response (WHO, 2007).

CASE BOX 7.1 THE 2009 WEST SUMATRA EARTHQUAKE IN INDONESIA

By Cecilia Choi

FIGURE 7.2 The 2009 earthquake on Sumatra

Source: Adapted from www.mapsofworld.com.

An earthquake measuring 7.6 on the Richter scale hit the West Sumatra Province of Indonesia on 30 September 2009 (see Figure 7.3). The earthquake, which was followed by two major aftershocks and landslides, caused more than 1,000 deaths, injured more than 3,000 people and damaged nearly 400,000 buildings. Figure 7.2 shows an example of the destruction caused. Thirteen districts were affected and the earthquake was also felt in the surrounding areas, including Riau, North Sumatra Province, Singapore, Malaysia and Jakarta, located 922 kilometres away. The government of Indonesia, UN organisations, non-governmental organisations (NGOs) and different bilateral agencies worked together on the immediate relief and long-term recovery works.

Cluster approach

The humanitarian clusters were activated within 48 hours of the disaster. The relief efforts were organised into 10 clusters: agriculture; coordination and safety; education; food and nutrition; health; logistics and telecommunications; protection; shelter; water, sanitation and hygiene; and early recovery. Below is a selection of cluster activities.

Health cluster

This was led by the WHO and the Ministry of Health. In the early response stages, 3,000 health workers were deployed and five field hospitals were set

FIGURE 7.3   Aftermath of the 2009 West Sumatra earthquake in Indonesia

Source: Photo by AusAID/CC BY 2.0 (https://www.flickr.com/photos/dfataustralian aid/10691196073; https://creativecommons.org/licenses/by/2.0/deed.en).

up. Fifty-three organisations participated in five sub-cluster areas: immunisation, psychosocial and mental health; mobile clinic, injury surveillance and rehabilitation; nutrition, maternal and child health; health facility support and environmental health. The cluster responded to the emergency situation in a timely manner and coordinated with nearly all (90%) of the partners in the field. They worked closely with the Indonesian Army and the relief kits were delivered to remote areas using helicopters. Fifteen maternal health posts were established in the areas where community health centres were damaged. Within one month, they had provided 535 antenatal services, 222 delivery assistances and 760 family planning services.

Food and nutrition cluster

UNICEF and WFP coordinated the provision of food and the response nutritional needs during the emergency situation. The cluster distributed supplementary foods through 62 community health centres and 698 primary schools to reach 114,873 children under the age of five, 42,340 pregnant and lactating women, 111,577 students and 5,697 teachers in six districts. WFP distributed 1,090 metric tons of fortified foods and noodles. The local government coordinated the distribution of staple food and provided emergency public kitchens. At the end of the emergency period, no severe case of malnutrition was identified and the cluster seemed to have achieved its objective.

Water, sanitation and hygiene (WASH) cluster

UNICEF, along with the Public Work Department and PDAM, the Indonesian regional water utility company, coordinated the cluster to prevent the water- and sanitation-related diseases. The initial response of the WASH cluster was to distribute water storage tanks, hygiene kits, water purification units, water bladders, and water trucking, particularly in areas directly affected by the disaster. By the beginning of 2010, 69,992 hygiene kits, 36,495 jerry cans, 43 water treatment plants, 196 public water points, four pipe systems, and 37 wells had reached 90% of the affected population.

Shelter cluster

The main activities in this cluster were providing temporary shelters, per- manent housing support, training and outreach to the community. During the emergency phase, the IFRC first led the cluster, followed by the Early Recovery Shelter Cluster Coordination Team (SCCT) and finally passed to UN-Habitat and Early Recovery Network in April 2010. The initial response included some key challenges such as the lack of local skilled workers (such as carpenters), impact on environment, sustainability, the lack of under- standing of government policies, and the communication coordination among the agencies. In addition, with a large number of women-headed households, gender-specific training was conducted to ensure the acces- sibility to all assistance to these female-headed households. By the end of April 2010, 75% of the damaged houses (135,755 out of 181,066) in seven districts had been repaired or rebuilt with the support from the government and relief agencies.

In summary, the 2009 West Sumatra earthquake shows how the Cluster Approach allowed regular meetings and exchanges of information among the various agencies to sustain the collaboration, resulting in the successes achieved in each of the clusters.

Sources: OCHA (2009), OCHA, UN Resident and Humanitarian Coordinator for Indonesia (2009, 2011), WHO (2009, November), Government of Indonesia (2011) and IFRC (2011).

Refugees and internally displaced persons

Social instability and insecurity after a disaster may cause large–scale population displacement. An **internally displaced person (IDP)** is someone who has been forced to flee his/her home for the same reasons as a refugee, but has not crossed an internationally recognised border. A **refugee** is someone who,

KNOWLEDGE BOX 7.2   FACTS AND TRENDS

Refugees and **IDPs** are people displaced by natural disasters and conflicts. They may suffer from direct health impacts (e.g. deaths, injuries, mental distress and post-traumatic stress disorder) and indirect health impacts caused by poor living conditions. In general, displaced populations in camps face difficulties in access to basic needs, including shelter, clean water and sanitation, food, health services and access to information. They are vulnerable to communicable disease outbreaks and prolonged health impacts, such as malnutrition and mental health problems. High mortality rates (under-five mortality rate and crude mortality rate), acute malnutrition (global acute malnutrition, GAM) and poor measles vaccination coverage (MVC) illustrate the vulnerability of a population living in camps compared to one living in a regular habitat.

owing to a well-founded fear of being persecuted for reasons of race, religion, nationality, membership of a particular social group, or political opinion, is outside the country of his nationality and is unable to or, owing to such fear, is unwilling to avail himself of the protection of that country.

(UNHCR, 2011)

The biggest difference between IDPs and refugees is that IDPs are under the legal protection of their own government despite the fact that said government might be the cause of their displacement (see Knowledge Box 7.2).

Although IDPs face similar challenges to refugees, IDPs cannot invoke the same legal protection as refugees. According to the UNHCR, there are more IDPs in the world than refugees. Globally, there were an estimated 20.8 million IDPs in mid-2013, compared with 11.1 million refugees (UNHCR, 2013). In general, the health impact on IDPs is more severe than refugees. They are almost twice as likely as refugees to die from conflict-related causes, especially disease and starvation. To fill the health inequity gaps, specific interventions should be conducted in response to the needs of IDPs (see Case Box 7.2).

Challenges in responding to disaster and humanitarian medical needs

In the twenty-first century, climate change, environmental degradation, poverty and urbanisation have posed many challenges for disaster response stakeholders.

Emerging trends of disasters result from: (1) Climate change: global average combined land and ocean surface temperature, as calculated based on a linear trend, showed a warming of 0.85 °C, over the period 1880–2012. Heatwave frequency has increased since 1950 in large parts of Europe, Asia and Australia (Intergovernmental Panel on Climate Change [IPCC], 2013); (2) **Environmental degradation**: humans extract

---

CASE BOX 7.2 HEALTH OUTCOMES OF THE INTERNALLY DISPLACED PERSONS (IDPS) AFTER THE 2005 PAKISTANI KASHMIR EARTHQUAKE

On 8 October 2005, an earthquake struck Pakistan-administered Kashmir. Many people were displaced into official internally displaced person (IDP) camps, coordinated and supported by relief agencies, and a substantial number of people lived in clusters of unofficial IDP camps of various sizes. A field-based health study was conducted four months after the earthquake and found significant differences in demographic characteristics and physical and psychological health outcomes among residents of IDP camps of different sizes.

When compared with official camps, unofficial camps were more likely to be headed by women, and have a larger family size and a higher percentage of old people. Residents in official camps generally reported better overall self-reported well-being and a lower incidence of injuries inflicted in the earthquake than those in smaller, unofficial self-settled camps. Residents of unofficial camps experienced a higher percentage of gastrointestinal symptoms, skin infections, self-reported depression, helplessness and poor appetite. Inhabitants of the smaller, unofficial self-settled camps also suffered more severe property loss in the earthquake and were less likely to keep contact with their families.

While relief groups may choose to focus on offering assistance to residents in larger official camps for logistic or political reasons, certain subgroups such as the inhabitants of smaller, unofficial self-settled camps may be more vulnerable to undesirable physical and mental health outcomes because of their ineligibility to receive official aid and services. Relief agencies that aim to cater for the most vulnerable should target IDPs residing in unofficial camp settings and remote areas (Chan & Kim, 2010).

---

and use around 50% more natural resources than 30 years ago, estimated at about 60 billion tonnes of raw materials a year (Sustainable Europe Research Institute [SERI], Global, 2000, & Friends of the Earth Europe, 2009); (3) **Poverty**: by 2030, between 176 and 319 million extremely poor people living in 45 countries will be most exposed to drought, extreme temperature and flood hazards (Shepherd et al., 2013); and (4) **Rapid urbanisation**: by 2025, around two-thirds of the world's population will reside in urban areas. In the early 2010s, up to 3,351 cities around the world were located in low-lying coastal zones. Six out of the ten largest cities in the world were located along seismic fault lines (de Zeeuw, 2011; UNISDR, 2012; World Bank, 2014).

Climate change

Reports of extreme weather events and natural disasters have tripled since the 1960s. Climate change–related hazards, such as floods, droughts and storms, accounted for the majority of the emergency humanitarian responses. The increased extreme

FIGURE 7.4 Flooding in Venice

Source: Photo by Wolfgang Moroder/CC BY-SA 3.0 (https://commons.wikimedia.org/wiki/Category:Floods_in_Venice#/media/File:Acqua_alta_in_Piazza_San_Marco.jpg; http://creativecommons.org/licenses/by-sa/3.0/).

Note: Flooding in Venice is not uncommon these days. Tourists still gather at the square, despite the flood.

weather event frequency also raises the risk of water insecurity, drought and food shortages and, as a result, the likelihood of malnutrition and diarrhoeal and vector-borne diseases (e.g. malaria) (World Health Organization [WHO], United Kingdom Health Protection Agency [HPA], & partners, 2011). Climate change has also created new kinds of hazards, such as melting glaciers and the resulting sea-level rises (Knutson et al., 2010; Gencer, 2013). Populations living in high mountain ranges, such as the Kingdom of Bhutan, and low-lying and coastal areas, such as the Maldives and Venice (see Figure 7.4), are particularly vulnerable (Rahmstorf, 2012). The Intergovernmental Panel on Climate Change predicts sea-level rise will increase the severity and likelihood of flash floods as well as coastal floods resulting from storm surges (Bigio, 2003; Klein, Nicholls, & Thomalla, 2003; Church et al., 2013) (see also Case Boxes 7.3 and 7.4).

Environmental degradation

The ecosystem serves as a buffer to protect communities from natural hazards and mitigates disaster risk by absorbing sudden changes in climatic, geological or biological systems. For example, wetlands can store water, stabilise shorelines and control soil erosion, which helps mitigate the risk of floods. However, the rapid population growth coupled with increased unsustainable human activities, such as unplanned urbanisation, intensification of agriculture and increased use of non-renewable energy, has caused environmental degradation and reduced the natural disaster resilience of communities (Alo, 2008). Deforestation, where massive areas of forested land have been destroyed for agricultural and domestic use (e.g. for cooking and heating), also produces secondary effects and exacerbates soil erosion, which will increase the risk of floods, mudslides and landslides (Dolcemascolo, 2004; United Nations Inter-Agency Secretariat of the International Strategy for Disaster Reduction [UN/ISDR], 2004).

CASE BOX 7.3   WILL HONG KONG SINK UNDER THE SEA?

Hong Kong has a coastline of approximately 730 km and consists of 260 islands. Only 25% of its land is developed, resulting in heavy urban development with 7 million people living in low-lying areas and on reclaimed land. The mean sea level in Victoria Harbour, Hong Kong, rose at a rate of 30 mm per decade on average between 1954 and 2014. Under the high greenhouse gas (GHG) emission scenario, the annual mean sea level in Hong Kong may rise by 0.63 to 1.07 m in the period 2081 to 2100 relative to the average between 1986 and 2005 (Figure 7.5). With an expected rise in mean sea-levels and storm surges, Hong Kong is seriously threatened by increased risk of coastal flooding, and its urban coastal-based residents might need to adapt to these environmental challenges.

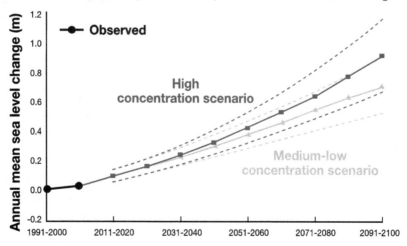

FIGURE 7.5   Observed and projected annual mean sea level in Hong Kong Projected mean sea level in Hong Kong relative to the average of 1986–2005: high (black), medium–low (grey) greenhouse gas emission scenarios (solid line indicates the mean value, while dashed lines show the likely range).

Source: Adapted from Hong Kong Observatory. Observed climate change in Hong Kong: Mean sea-level (http://www.hko.gov.hk/climate_change/proj_hk_msl_e.htm).

CASE BOX 7.4   SEA LEVEL RISE IN BANGLADESH

Bangladesh is one of the world's poorest and most populous regions. It is known to be vulnerable to cyclones and sea-level rises as many regions are located just one to three metres above mean sea level in the low-lying deltas of the Ganges, Brahmaputra and Meghna rivers. These deltas are inundated with saline water by daily high tides. Tropical cyclones and monsoon rainfalls intensify inundation and there are no adequate coastal defences. Future sea-level rises are likely to increase the height of daily tides and of storm surges during cyclones. Furthermore, a rise of one metre in the sea level would make nearly 20% of Bangladesh people "environmental refugees".

Drinking water may become extremely salinated as water supplies in coastal areas may be contaminated with seawater. An epidemiological study found a clear dose-response relationship between drinking water salinity and the risk of pre-eclampsia and hypertension in pregnant women. This indicates that the saltier their drinking water was, the more likely they were to develop hypertensive disorders during pregnancy. Currently more than 70% of the coastal population rely on unprotected water sources; thus health risks associated with the excessive salt intake from drinking water in these areas will continue to increase.

Source: GRID-Arendal (2001).

Poverty

People living in poverty are disproportionally affected by disasters as they tend to live in the areas where environmental hazards might be most intense. Poverty-stricken people have limited coping and adaptation capacities. Without targeted disaster preparedness or risk reduction action, disasters will force underprivileged groups into a vicious downward spiral of chronic poverty (UNISDR, 2003). Loss of assets and sources of income as well as the cost of recovery can lead to bankruptcy. Exposure to frequent disasters also slows down the progress of a country's poverty reduction. In 2008, Cyclone Nargis killed 138,000 people in Myanmar, while a storm of similar strength, Hurricane Gustav, killed 153 in the Caribbean and the United States (Shepherd et al., 2013) (see Knowledge Box 7.3).

Developing countries also have a limited capacity for prevention since the priority of disaster preparedness and risk reduction is low in comparison with other development goals, such as economic development (World Bank, 2006). Infrastructure in developing countries in general is poor in quality. Houses in unplanned settlements (e.g. slums) are more likely to be poorly constructed and buildings are likely to collapse in disasters. The remoteness of settlements also limits people's access to public services and resources.

KNOWLEDGE BOX 7.3   FACTS AND TRENDS OF POPULATIONS LIVING IN POVERTY/ RESOURCE-DEFICIT SETTINGS

Globally, there are 3 billion people with incomes less than US$2 per day and 1.3 billion on less than US$1 per day. According to UN-Habitat, almost 3 billion people will be living in slums by 2030. Poorer nations had more disaster casualties and have accumulated 3.3 million deaths in the past 40 years. Poor people have no insurance and experience more difficulties in recovering from disaster. They often lose their homes, jobs and livelihoods (UNISDR, 2011).

Urbanisation

Since 1950, although developing countries in Africa, Asia and Latin America have showed a sixfold increase in the number of medium-sized cities (Gencer, 2013), these urban environments are rarely prepared for the influx. Many urban areas, such as Ho Chi Minh City in Vietnam, Kathmandu in Nepal and Dhaka in Bangladesh (World Bank, 2010), are located in disaster-prone areas near seismic fault lines or in low-lying coastal regions (Gencer, 2013). Poor or absent building codes and regulations and inadequate basic infrastructure and facilities in slums will increase residents' risk of exposure to flash floods in cyclone seasons (UNISDR, 2003). In addition, migrants and job seekers from rural areas face a disproportional risk during and after disasters as they may be forced to live in unplanned, informal settlements like slums (such as Dharavi slum shown in Figure 7.6) with inadequate access to clean water, sanitation, transportation and other public services (Herrmann & Khan, 2008, July) (see also Knowledge Box 7.4 and Case Box 7.5).

KNOWLEDGE BOX 7.4   FACTS AND TRENDS: DISASTER RESPONSE IN URBAN VERSUS RURAL SETTINGS

Although rural populations experience more disasters, urban disaster response systems are usually more organised while the technical, human and resource inadequacy in rural communities limits their response capacity. Moreover, the lack of media attention to rural disasters might result in a reporting bias towards disaster responses in urban areas rather than the more disaster-prone rural areas and might mask the adverse disaster impact on rural areas (Iqbal, Ali, Khursheed, & Saleem, 2014).

FIGURE 7.6 Asia's largest slum: Dharavi slum in Mumbai of India
This image illustrates how rapid and unplanned urbanisation results in the expansion of slums in urban areas.

Source: Photo by Erin Lee from Evanston/CC BY 2.0 (https://www.flickr.com/photos/74852128@N00/3128320636; https://creativecommons.org/licenses/by/2.0/deed.en).

CASE BOX 7.5   THE 2010 FLOODING IN HAINAN ISLAND, CHINA

By Crystal Yingjia Chu

On the evening of 30 September 2010, torrential rainfall struck Hainan, an island province of China at the country's southernmost point. The two rounds of torrential rain, the longest recorded since 1961, brought devastating damage to the island. Four people died, more than 700,000 people were evacuated and nearly 4 million residents were affected by the floods. The floodwater inundated 1,160 villages and 90% of the island was flooded. The disaster damaged over 20,000 houses and caused more than 10 billion renminbi of economic loss.

Although Hainan has enjoyed rapid economic growth in recent decades, the local government paid limited attention to developing the drainage system. Compared with the national level, Hainan lagged behind in the density of sewage pipes. Hainan had an area of 33,920 *square kilometre*, but only some 2,286 km of sewage pipes in 2009. In comparison, Jiangsu and Zhejiang, two other coastal provinces in China, had 0.417 km and 0.240 km of sewage pipes per *square kilometre* while in Hainan, only 0.067 km per square kilometre was reported. Poor infrastructure, such as the inadequate drainage system and numerous outdated reservoirs, greatly hampered the resilience of the province during flooding. In some locations, the construction of buildings might have even blocked the original drainage lines. During the period of torrential rain, although the 179 reservoirs that had been reinforced were all safe, the rest posed a huge risk. As a result, a total of 43 small reservoirs, 601 watertight barriers and 183 dams collapsed under the immense weight of water and were eventually destroyed. Hence, improving the drainage system would increase the communities' resilience, particularly during floods.

Source: Collaborating Centre for Oxford University and CUHK for Disaster and Medical Humanitarian Response [CCOUC] (2011).

Key challenges to effective relief

Despite increasing efforts of working together and advances in information technology, there are currently no internationally standardised methods to measure the performance of relief efforts (Guha-Sapir & Below, 2000) (see Case Box 7.6).

What are the gaps in providing effective relief?

Accountability: There are two different types of accountability: (1) accountability to donors, and (2) accountability to the beneficiaries of aid. Accountability to donors includes the responsibility to deliver aid in an efficient and cost-effective manner, while accountability to beneficiaries requires feedback mechanisms from the communities.

Coordination: Sudden massive aid relief will create problems if there is a lack of good coordination and communication. For instance, in 2005 the government in Vietnam received 791 visits from donors, which amounted to more than two a day on average. Without proper coordination and sufficient capacity, it is difficult to control and monitor aid flow (see also Case Box 7.7).

Professionalism: New humanitarian actors usually emerge in a disaster situation. Some may not have proper training and understanding of humanitarian principles. However, there are no mechanisms that can rule out an unqualified organisation (Deutscher & Fyson, 2008; VanRooyen, 2013) (see Case Box 7.8).

CASE BOX 7.6   RELIEF AID EFFECTIVENESS IN ACEH, INDONESIA, AFTER THE 2004 TSUNAMI

On 26 December 2004, an undersea earthquake with a magnitude of 9.0 on the Richter scale struck Indonesia's Aceh province. The tsunami killed more than 150,000 people and displaced more than 700,000. Two days later, the Indonesian government declared that the province would require international assistance. The damages and losses, including the reconstruction and development costs, reached US$7.7 billion. Some 133 countries and 16,000 foreign military personnel participated in the immediate emergency response, as exemplified in Figure 7.7. By the end of 2007, more than 2,000 projects had been implemented in Aceh by 463 organisations.

Aid effectiveness

Although the massive influx of aid and assistance was effective in ensuring the immediate survival needs, there was no standardised relief assessment or programme. As a result, the information was confused and it was difficult to maintain coordination and communication among organisations. Another problem was the miscommunication between the relief agencies and the community. For instance, an agency provided ten boats for local fishermen but none of them was used for fishing. The local fishermen explained that

FIGURE 7.7   Relief aid in the wake of the 2004 Indian Ocean tsunami

Source: Photo by Department of Foreign Affairs and Trade, Australia/Lorrie Graham/ CC BY 2.0 (https://www.flickr.com/photos/dfataustralianaid/10673961123; https:// creativecommons.org/licenses/by/2.0/deed.en).

"the boats have many structural problems and are not the usual boats we use here. It would be dangerous to use these boats beyond the river."

Conclusion

The Indonesia case illustrates that understanding the general conditions of the population, including their culture and customs, is essential for the provision and delivery of relief post-disaster.

Sources: Eye on Aceh (2006) and Masyrafah and McKeon (2008).

CASE BOX 7.7   HOW PUBLIC-PRIVATE PARTNERSHIPS BETWEEN TELECOMMUNICATIONS AND HUMANITARIAN AGENCIES CAN SAVE LIVES

With 89% mobile penetration in the developing world, aid groups increasingly recognise that information and the ability to communicate are as important as physical aid. In 2013 Oxfam used mobile money to send cash to 1,700 families and after the 2010 earthquake in Haiti, the Red Cross reached out to half a million affected through SMS. The humanitarian partnership between Inmarsat and Télécoms Sans Frontières (TSF) provided the hospital serving refugee camps on the Thai-Burmese border with a vital satellite internet connection and communication base – facilitating faster, more efficient aid and mobile health (mHealth) services.

Source: Aid and International Development Forum (2015, March 17).

CASE BOX 7.8   TAIWAN'S DEADLY TYPHOON MORAKOT: THE INADEQUATE DISASTER PREPAREDNESS, MANAGEMENT, COMMUNICATIONS AND CULTURALLY SENSITIVE RESPONSE

By Chi Shing Wong

Taiwan was struck by Typhoon Morakot, the deadliest and wettest in half a century, on 8 August 2009. It brought record-breaking rainfall of more than 2,700 mm in 72 hours, triggered landslides and severe flash flooding, and claimed almost 500 lives with 200 people missing (Yu & Hung, 2010; Cheng, 2013).

Overall, the government was criticised for its unpreparedness and slow disaster response. There was a general lack of "standby preparedness", such as the absence of full-time employees and volunteers, and failure in crisis-stage communication efforts, e.g. the poor dissemination of information regarding evacuation orders, the scope of the damage, sheltering places and medical treatment. Initial deployment for such a large-scale disaster only involved 2,100 soldiers. There were no cargo helicopters to carry large earth diggers and other machinery to its remote mountainous areas in the central and southern region. Foreign aid was at first rejected and there was a three-day delay in calling a special national security meeting to coordinate relief efforts, which led to the failure to evacuate victims early enough. The poor response had caused the premier and his cabinet to resign within a month of the disaster (Hsu & Ko, 2009, August 19; Siu, 2009, August 14; Cheng, 2013).

Typhoon Morakot also highlighted the often neglected cultural aspect of disaster response. According to government statistics, nearly half of the typhoon victims were aborigines, who make up a mere 2% of the island's total population while mostly living in remote mountainous areas. Many aborigines refused evacuation for fear of losing their lands permanently, and thus their way of life and cultural heritage (Shih & Wang, 2009, August 27; Cheng, 2013). The earlier study of Elliott and Pais (2006) into Hurricane Katrina has also shown a tendency for minorities to be reluctant to evacuate. Some disaster studies (Burby & Strong, 1997; Spence, Lachlan, & Griffin, 2007) argue that this reluctance to follow evacuation instructions among vulnerable populations may arise from their distrust of government to protect their health and safety. A similar reluctance to evacuate could occur where the legal protection of property and residence rights is ambiguous and the legitimacy of the government is weak.

Cost of disasters

Not only do disasters lead to a negative short-term economic impact, such as a decline in GDP and loss of assets (Benson & Clay, 2004), but also their long-term negative consequences affect a country's development (Refer to Figure 2.12). Direct human losses, the destruction of infrastructure, demolition of the physical capital that leads to industrial output reduction and disruption in the market supply chain (Asian Development Bank, 2013) are all important factors that affect economic outcomes. Although short-term absolute economic losses in these countries might be small when compared with developed countries (Benson & Clay, 2004), their loss in relation to the country's GDP is the greatest. In short, the least-developed countries with simple economic structures suffer the most in disasters. With the increasing cost of technology development, infrastructure and human capital, economic costs associated with disasters are expected to increase in the coming decades. Effective

---

CASE BOX 7.9   THE COST OF EBOLA

In 2014 and 2015, Ebola was one of the most catastrophic disasters affecting the global community. In Africa, Ebola caused massive casualties in Sierra Leone, Liberia and Guinea during the 18 months of the epidemic. In terms of the human toll, it has claimed the lives of 11,000 people including over 500 health care workers. National health systems are devastated and the associated damage is alarming. The loss of an average of 80 doctors, nurses and midwives from each of the three countries translated into a 75% increase in maternal mortality for instance. With this immense destruction of health systems, the routine malaria-related health services in 2014 were disrupted. Increases in untreated malaria cases of 45%, 88% and 140% were reported in Guinea, Sierra Leone and Liberia respectively. An additional 10,000 deaths can be attributed to the epidemic. The societal and economic damage of this epidemic is not to be underestimated. Schools were forced to shut down, agricultural productivity dropped substantially and all the cross-border trade was cut off.

Source: Mullan (2015).

---

disaster risk reduction (DRR) that might protect a community will bring a high economic return to the community (Vorhies, 2012). The United Nations Development Programme (UNDP) has estimated that economic losses from disasters can be reduced by US$7 dollars for every US$1 spent on DRR measures (UNDP, 2007). Unfortunately, less than 0.7% of relief aid globally has gone to DRR-related activities in the past 20 years (see also Case Box 7.9).

Disaster response planning

Given the potential cost of disasters, disaster response planning is crucial to maximising the cost-effectiveness of response. In response planning, the potential health needs of the affected population would need to be addressed (see Case Box 7.10). In principle, health needs may be defined in four ways: (1) **normative need** – need as defined by expert opinion based on research, (2) **felt need** – what people in a community say they want or feel they need, (3) **expressed need** – which can be inferred about the health need of a community by observation of the community's utilisation of services and (4) **comparative need** – usually derived from examining the services provided to a population in one area and using this information as the basis to determine the type of services required in another area with a similar population make-up (Hawe, Degeling, & Hall, 1990). As outcomes of needs assessment might vary with the approach or perspective adopted during the assessment, stakeholders should reach a consensus before engaging in assessment and relevant planning (see Knowledge Box 7.5).

KNOWLEDGE BOX 7.5   A SAMPLE PROGRAMME PLANNING TOOL

Situation analysis
- Who chooses the information?
- Whose views should be taken into consideration?
- Which information source should be emphasised?

Priority setting
- Whose view should be taken into consideration?
- What view of health is chosen, by whom?
- What are the criteria or factors to be considered in setting priorities?

Option appraisal
- Who chooses the available options and who limits them?
- How are options being appraised and by whom?

Evaluation
- Who is involved in the evaluation?
- What are the criteria for evaluation?
- What is the standard used to evaluate programmes?

Situational analysis

Situational analysis focuses on understanding the context, mapping out the needs of the population and analysis of the currently available resources or services and other factors that would hinder the operation or implementation of potential programmes in the intermediate term and long term. Regardless of methods, key information collected during the situational analysis stage might include:

1   Population characteristics
   a   demographic
   b   religion
   c   culture
   d   education level
2   Area characteristics and infrastructure
   a   geographic and topographic characteristics
   b   infrastructure
   c   socio-economic background, information from the public and private sectors
3   Policy and political environment
   a   overall national policies and existing health policies
   b   political and ideological environment

4 Health needs
    a   individual perceived medical needs
    b   community perceived health needs
    c   epidemiological patterns of common diseases and causes of death
5 Services provided by health and non-health sectors
    a   health services: facilities, utilisation, service gaps, health service organisation arrangements
    b   resources: financial, personnel, buildings, land, equipment, vehicles and other supplies
6 Efficiency, effectiveness, equity and quality of the current services

---

CASE BOX 7.10 PUBLIC HEALTH FINDINGS FROM THE 2013 TYPHOON HAIYAN IN THE PHILIPPINES

On November 8, 2013, the Philippines was hit by a category 5 hurricane, Typhoon Haiyan, which affected 18 million people (WHO, 2013, November). International relief teams including the IFRC responded soon after the disaster to supply the basic needs of the affected population. The Japanese Red Cross Society (JRCS) Basic Health Care Emergency Reponses Unit (BHC ERU) was one of the teams deployed to the affected areas. Rapid assessments were conducted in the Daanbantayan district at the northern tip of Cebu Island. The total population in Daanbantayan is about 86,000 (22,000 households) with 20 local government units (LGUs, local name: barangays) in total. More than 90% of houses were destroyed or partially damaged. This case study describes the situation observed in Daanbantayan and discusses the public health findings within the first month of the disaster.

Public health findings

By maintaining a close working relationship with the community health workers at the various levels, narrative and basic statistics were obtained and analysed to identify the health needs. Methodologies used included interviews with midwives and barangay/neighbourhood health workers (BHWs), analysis of descriptive statistics from fixed and mobile clinics, and a survey study consisted of 13 questions. Interviews revealed that the poor sanitation and shelter conditions had made communicable disease a looming health threat. Open defecation was practiced and many households lacked a secure water source. Meanwhile although infectious diseases, including respiratory infections and skin infections, were common, non-communicable diseases (NCD) contributed to the highest number of emergencies. Survey results showed knowledge gaps in tuberculosis (Q6), sexual health (Q7), NCD (Q10) and mental health (Q12). A summary of respondents' performance can be found in Figure 7.8.

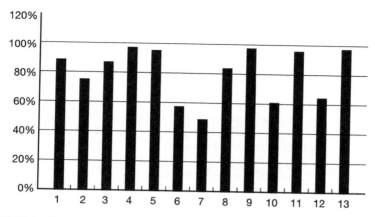

FIGURE 7.8 Percentage of respondents giving a correct answer to each question in the knowledge-attitude-practice (KAP) survey

Although community health centres were central to health activities in the communities, many were badly destroyed. Public health programmes and some maternal antenatal checks and activities were suspended due to lack of health structures.

Health care services include general first aid and wound management, tetanus injection and treatment of common illnesses are the keys for people in evacuation centres during the emergency phase. Training gaps among midwives and other BHWs identified include relevant disaster training, use of equipment and medicines.

Conclusion

Although the cluster approach launched in 2005 by the Inter-Agency Standing Committee has facilitated disaster response for the past decade, local response still faces the lack of standardised, measurable performance indicators for reporting, accountability, coordination and professionalism of relief efforts. As securing resources for addressing disaster response will rely heavily on the pre-existing commitment of governments and external agencies, local pre-disaster planning and preparedness are crucial community protection mechanism to enhance disaster response effectiveness.

References

Aid & International Development Forum. (2015, March 17). [Infographic] *How PPPs between telecommunications and humanitarian agencies can save lives* [Internet]. Retrieved from http://www.aidforum.org/disaster-relief/infographic-how-ppps-between-telecommunications-and-humanitarian-agencies-c

Alo, B. I. (2008). Contribution of road transportation to environmental degradation in Nigeria's urban cities. *Proceedings of the 2008 LAMATA Annual National Conference on Public Transportation, Lagos, Nigeria*, 1–19.

Asian Development Bank. (2013). *Investing in resilience: Ensuring a disaster-resistant future.* Retrieved from http://www.adb.org/sites/default/files/publication/30119/investing-resilience.pdf

Benson, C., & Clay, E. J. (2004). *Understanding the economic and financial impacts of natural disasters* (Disaster Risk Management Series No. 4). Retrieved from the website of World Bank: http://www-wds.worldbank.org/servlet/WDSContentServer/WDSP/IB/2004/04/20/000012009_20040420135752/Rendered/PDF/284060PAPER0Disaster0Risk0no.04.pdf

Bigio, A. G. (2003). Cities and climate change. In A. Kreimer, M Arnold, & A. Carlin (Eds.), *Building safer cities: The future of disaster risk* (Disaster Risk Management Series No. 3, pp. 91–99). Retrieved from the website of World Bank: http://www-wds.worldbank.org/servlet/WDSContentServer/WDSP/IB/2003/12/05/000012009_20031205154931/Rendered/PDF/272110PAPER0Building0safer0cities.pdf

Burby, R., & Strong, D. (1997). Coping with chemicals: Blacks, whites, planners, and industrial pollution. *Journal of American Planning Association, 63*(4), 469–480. doi:10.1080/01944369708975940

Chan, E.Y.Y., & Kim, J. J. (2010). Characteristics and health outcomes of internally displaced population in unofficial rural self-settled camps after the 2005 Kashmir, Pakistan earthquake. *European Journal of Emergency Medicine, 17*(3), 136–141. doi:10.1097/MEJ.0b013e32832fca1c

Cheng, S. S. (2013). Crisis communication failure: A case study of Typhoon Morakot. *Asian Social Science, 9*(3), 18–32. doi:10.5539/ass.v9n3p18

Church, J. A., Clark, P. U., Cazenave, A., Gregory, J. M., Jevrejeva, S., Levermann, A., . . . Unnikrishnan, A. S. (2013). Sea level change supplementary material. In T. F. Stocker, D. Qin, G.-K. Plattner, M. Tignor, S. K. Allen, J. Boschung, . . . P. M. Midgley (Eds.), *Climate change 2013: The physical science basis* (Contribution of Working Group I to the Fifth Assessment Report of the Intergovernmental Panel on Climate Change). Retrieved from the website of Intergovernmental Panel on Climate Change (IPCC): http://www.ipcc.ch/pdf/assessment-report/ar5/wg1/supplementary/WG1AR5_Ch13SM_FINAL.pdf

Collaborating Centre for Oxford University and CUHK for Disaster and Medical Humanitarian Response (CCOUC). (2011). *The 2010 Hainan flood: Loopholes in flood preparedness* (CCOUC Disaster Case Studies Series). Hong Kong, China: Author.

Deutscher, E., & Fyson, S. (2008). Improving the effectiveness of aid. *Finance and Development, 45*(3). Retrieved from the website of International Monetary Fund: https://www.imf.org/external/pubs/ft/fandd/2008/09/deutscher.htm

de Zeeuw, H. (2011). Cities, climate change and urban agriculture. *Urban Agriculture, 25* (September), 39–42.

Dolcemascolo, G. (2004). *Environmental degradation and disaster risk.* Retrieved from http://www.gdrc.org/uem/disasters/disenvi/Environmental-Degradation-and-Disaster-Risk.pdf

Elliott, J. R., & Pais, J. (2006). Race, class and Hurricane Katrina: Social differences in human responses to disaster. *Social Science Research, 35*(2), 295–321. doi:10.1016/j.ssresearch.2006.02.003

Eye on Aceh. (2006). *A people's agenda? Post-tsunami aid in Aceh.* Retrieved from http://reliefweb.int/sites/reliefweb.int/files/resources/0ECAB7B7E4ABD4D549257126002DA37F-eoa-idn-28feb.pdf

Fredriksen, A. (2012). *Making humanitarian spaces global: Coordinating crisis response through the cluster approach* (Doctoral dissertation). Retrieved from Columbia University Academic Commons website: http://hdl.handle.net/10022/AC:P:14511

Gencer, E. A. (2013). Natural disasters, urban vulnerability, and risk management: A theoretical overview. In *The interplay between urban development, vulnerability, and risk management: A case study of the Istanbul Metropolitan Area* (SpringerBriefs in Environment, Security, Development and Peace: Mediterranean Studies, Vol. 7, pp. 7–43). New York, NY: Springer.

Government of Indonesia (National Disaster Management Agency (BNPB), National Development Planning Agency (Bappenas), & the provincial governments of West Sumatra and Jambi). (2011). The West Sumatra earthquake. In *West Sumatra and Jambi natural disasters: Damage, loss and preliminary needs assessment* (pp. 1–16). Retrieved from http://www-wds.worldbank.org/external/default/WDSContentServer/WDSP/IB/2009/11/03/000334955_20091103042447/Rendered/PDF/514090WP0Box34110DALA0West0Sumatera.pdf

GRID-Arendal. (2001). *Vital climate graphics: Potential impact of sea-level rise on Bangladesh* [Internet]. Retrieved from http://www.grida.no/publications/vg/climate/page/3086.aspx

Guha-Sapir, D., & Below, R. (2000). *The quality and accuracy of disaster data: A comparative analyses of three global data sets.* ProVention Consortium & The Disaster Management Facility, The World Bank. Retrieved from www.unisdr.org/2005/task-force/working%20groups/wg3/Comparative_Analysis_of_3_Global_Data_Sets.pdf

Hawe, P., Degeling, D., & Hall, J. (1990). *Evaluating health promotion: A health worker's guide.* Sydney, Australia: MacLennan & Petty.

Herrmann, M., & Khan, H. A. (2008, July). *Rapid urbanization, employment crisis and poverty in African LDCs: A new development strategy and aid policy* (MPRA Paper No. 9499). Retrieved from Munich Personal RePEc Arhive (MPRA) website: http://mpra.ub.uni-muenchen.de/9499/

Hsu, J. W., & Ko, S. L. (2009, August 19). Morakot: The aftermath: MOFA's Hsia tenders resignation. *Taipei Times.* Retrieved from http://www.taipeitimes.com/News/front/archives/2009/08/19/2003451520

Intergovernmental Panel on Climate Change (IPCC). (2013). *Climate Change 2013: The Physical Science Basis.* Contribution of Working Group I to the Fifth Assessment Report of the Intergovernmental Panel on Climate Change [Stocker, T. F., D. Qin, G.-K. Plattner, M. Tignor, S. K. Allen, J. Boschung, A. Nauels, Y. Xia, V. Bex and P. M. Midgley (eds.)]. Cambridge, England: Cambridge University Press.

International Federation of Red Cross and Red Crescent Societies (IFRC). (2011). *Shelter Cluster review: 2009 Indonesia earthquakes.* Retrieved from http://www.ifrc.org/docs/Evaluations/Evaluations2011/Asia%20Pacific/Indonesia_SC_review_Jan2011.pdf

International Federation of Red Cross and Red Crescent Societies (IFRC). (2012). *Shelter coordination in natural disasters.* Retrieved from http://humanitarianlibrary.org/sites/default/files/2014/02/shelter_coordination_in_natural_disasters-02.pdf

Iqbal, M. J., Ali, F. M., Khursheed, M. B., & Saleem, S. (2014). Analysis of role of media in disaster reporting in Pakistan [Special edition]. *European Scientific Journal, 1,* 570–575.

Klein, R. J. T., Nicholls, R. J., & Thomalla, F. (2003). The resilience of coastal megacities to weather-related hazards. In A. Kreimer, M. Arnold, & A. Carlin (Eds.), *Building safer cities: The future of disaster risk* (Disaster Risk Management Series No. 3, pp. 101–120). Retrieved from the website of World Bank: http://www-wds.worldbank.org/servlet/WDSContentServer/WDSP/IB/2003/12/05/000012009_20031205154931/Rendered/PDF/272110PAPER0Building0safer0cities.pdf

Knutson, T. R., McBride, J. L., Chan, J., Emanuel, K., Holland, G., Landsea, C., . . . Sugi, M. (2010). Tropical cyclones and climate change. *Nature Geoscience*, *3*(3), 157–163. doi:10.1038/NGEO779

Masyrafah, H., & McKeon, J.M.J.A. (2008). *Post-tsunami aid effectiveness in Aceh: Proliferation and coordination in reconstruction* (Wolfensohn Center for Development Working Paper No. 6). Retrieved from the website of The Brookings Institution: http://www.brookings. edu/~/media/research/files/papers/2008/11/aceh%20aid%20masyrafah/11_aceh_aid_ masyrafah.pdf

Mullan, Z. (2015). The cost of Ebola. *The Lancet Global Health*, *3*(8), e423. doi: http://dx.doi. org/10.1016/S2214-109X(15)00092-3

Office of the United Nations High Commissioner for Refugees (UNHCR). (2011). *The 1951 convention relating to the status of refugees and its 1967 protocol*. Retrieved from http:// www.unhcr.org/4ec262df9.html

Office of the United Nations High Commissioner for Refugees (UNHCR). (2013). *UNHCR mid-year trends 2013*. Retrieved from http://unhcr.org/52af08d26.pdf

Rahmstorf, S. (2012). Modeling sea level rise. *Nature Education Knowledge*, *3*(10), 4. Retrieved from the website of Nature Education Knowledge Project: www.nature.com/scitable/ knowledge/library/modeling-sea-level-rise-25857988

Shepherd, A., Mitchell, T., Lewis, K., Lenhardt, A., Jones, L., Scott, L., & Muir-Wood, R. (2013). *The geography of poverty, disasters and climate extremes in 2030*. Retrieved from the website of ODI: http://www.odi.org.uk/sites/odi.org.uk/files/odi-assets/publications-opinion-files/8633.pdf

Shih, H., & Wang, F. (2009, August 27). Liu seeks input from aboriginal heads. *Taipei Times*. Retrieved from http://www.taipeitimes.com/News/taiwan/archives/2009/08/27/2003452098

Siu, C. (2009, August 14). Taiwan mudslide death toll rises. *BBC News*. Retrieved from http://news.bbc.co.uk/2/hi/asia-pacific/8200833.stm

Spence, P. R., Lachlan, K. A., & Griffin, D. R. (2007). Crisis communication, race, and natural disasters. *Journal of Black Studies*, *37*(4), 539–554. doi:10.1177/0021934706296192

Sustainable Europe Research Institute (SERI), Global 2000, & Friends of the Earth Europe. (2009). *Overconsumption? Our use of the world's natural resources* [Internet]. Retrieved from http://www.foe.co.uk/sites/default/files/downloads/overconsumption.pdf

United Nations Development Programme (UNDP). (2007). *Fighting climate change: Human solidarity in divided world* (Human development report 2007/2008). Retrieved from http:// hdr.undp.org/sites/default/files/reports/268/hdr_20072008_en_complete.pdf

United Nations Inter-Agency Secretariat of the International Strategy for Disaster Reduction (UN/ISDR). (2004). *Living with risk: A global review of disaster reduction initiatives*. Retrieved from www.unisdr.org/files/657_lwr1.pdf

United Nations Inter-Agency Standing Committee. (IASC). (2006). *Guidance note on using the Cluster Approach to strengthen humanitarian response*. Retrieved from https://interagency standingcommittee.org/system/files/legacy_files/Cluster%20implementation%2C%20 Guidance%20Note%2C%20WG66%2C%2020061115-.pdf

United Nations International Strategy for Disaster Reduction (UNISDR). (2003). *Disaster reduction and sustainable development: Understanding the links between vulnerability and risk to disasters related to development and environment*. Retrieved from http://www.gdrc.org/uem/ disasters/disenvi/DR-and-SD-English.pdf

United Nations International Strategy for Disaster Reduction (UNISDR). (2011). *Disaster through a different lens: Behind every effect, there is a cause: A guide for journalists covering disaster risk reduction*. Retrieved from http://www.unisdr.org/files/20108_mediabook.pdf

United Nations Office for Disaster Risk Reduction (UNISDR). (2012). *Making cities resilient report 2012*. Geneva, Switzerland: Author.

United Nations Office for the Coordination of Humanitarian Affairs (OCHA). (n.d.). Humanitarian response: What is the Cluster Approach? [Internet]. Retrieved from https://www.humanitarianresponse.info/clusters/space/page/what-cluster-approach

United Nations Office for the Coordination of Humanitarian Affairs (OCHA). (2009). *Indonesia: West Sumatra earthquake, 30 September 2009* [Infographic]. Retrieved from http://reliefweb.int/sites/reliefweb.int/files/resources/AD7D7D011EEBEBE9C1257642002
3EA63-map.pdf

United Nations Office for the Coordination of Humanitarian Affairs (OCHA), UN Resident and Humanitarian Coordinator for Indonesia. (2009). *West Sumatra earthquake: Humanitarian response plan in coordination with the Government of Indonesia*. Retrieved from http://www.who.int/hac/crises/idn/indonesia_response_plan_2009.pdf

United Nations Office for the Coordination of Humanitarian Affairs (OCHA), UN Resident and Humanitarian Coordinator for Indonesia. (2011). *Cluster ATLAS: 2009 West Sumatra earthquake response*. Jakarta, Indonesia: Author.

VanRooyen, M. (2013). Effective aid. *Harvard International Review, 35*(2). Retrieved from http://hir.harvard.edu/vanrooyen-effective-aid/

Vorhies, F. (2012). *The economics of investing in disaster risk reduction*. Retrieved from the website of UNISDR: http://www.unisdr.org/files/32357_drreconomicsworkingpaperfinal3.pdf

World Bank. (2010). *Climate risks and adaptation in Asian coastal megacities: A synthesis report*. Retrieved from http://siteresources.worldbank.org/EASTASIAPACIFICEXT/Resources/
226300–1287600424406/coastal_megacities_fullreport.pdf

World Bank. (2014). Urban development [Internet]. Retrieved from http://data.worldbank.org/topic/urban-development

World Bank, Independent Evaluation Group. (2006). *Hazards of nature, risks to development: An IEG evaluation of World Bank assistance for natural disasters*. Retrieved from http://www-wds.worldbank.org/external/default/WDSContentServer/WDSP/IB/2006/06/29/00016001
6_20060629133433/Rendered/PDF/366150Hazards0and0risks01PUBLIC1.pdf

World Health Organization (WHO). (2007). The Cluster Approach. In *Managing WHO humanitarian response in the field handbook* (Annex 7). Retrieved from http://www.who.int/hac/techguidance/tools/manuals/who_field_handbook/annex_7/en/

World Health Organization (WHO). (2009, November). *Earthquake in Padang, West Sumatra Province, Republic of Indonesia* (Emergency Situation Report (ESR-16)). Retrieved from http://reliefweb.int/sites/reliefweb.int/files/resources/B0B55046F387C12385257685
007A657B-Full_Report.pdf

World Health Organization (WHO). (2013, November). *Public health risk assessment and interventions: Typhoon Haiyan Philippines*. Retrieved from http://www.wpro.who.int/philippines/typhoon_haiyan/media/Philippines_typhoon_haiyan_ph_risk_assessment_
16Nov2013_FINAL.pdf

World Health Organization (WHO), United Kingdom Health Protection Agency (HPA), & partners. (2011). *Disaster risk management for health: Communicable diseases* [Internet]. Retrieved from http://www.who.int/hac/events/drm_fact_sheet_communicable_diseases.
pdf?ua=1

Yu, J., & Hung, C. H. (2010). Jiangyuliang chongxianqi tuigu zhi tantao – Yi Molake taifeng Jiaxian yuliangzhan weili [An exploration of rainfall return period estimation: The case of Jiaxian rainfall station in Typhoon Morakot]. *Bulletin of Taiwan Association of Hydraulic Engineer Science, 13*, 34–43. Retrieved from http://www.hydraulic.org.tw/admin/post2/
pic2/34–43.pdf

8

FROM PUBLIC HEALTH EMERGENCY PREPAREDNESS TO RESILIENCE

Climate change is expected to cause more severe and more frequent natural hazards. As our cities and coasts grow more vulnerable, these hazards can lead to disasters that are far worse than those we have seen to date.
—Ban Ki-moon, Secretary General of the United Nations
(United Nations International Strategy for Disaster Reduction [UNISDR], 2007)

This chapter discusses the concepts of disaster preparedness, resilience, prevention as well as some case examples of how preparedness efforts are currently being applied at the individual, household, community and global levels. Key international strategies and policies such as Hyogo Framework for Action, the human security approach and the Sendai Framework for Disaster Risk Reduction 2015-2030 will be highlighted.

Disaster preparedness and resilience

Disaster preparedness is the term for "activities taken in advance of a disaster to ensure an effective response to the impact of hazards, including issuing timely and effective early warnings and the temporary evacuation of people and property from threatened locations" (The Sphere Project, 2011). **Resilience** is the ability of a system, community or society that is exposed to hazards to resist, absorb, accommodate to and recover from the effects of a hazard in a timely and efficient manner (UNISDR, 2009).Raising disaster preparedness increases resilience, but other circumstances, such as previous exposures to disasters or having a stable health care workforce, are also factors that enhance resilience. Figure 8.1 displays the functional areas of disaster resilience and their relationship with other domains across communal, organisational and individual levels.

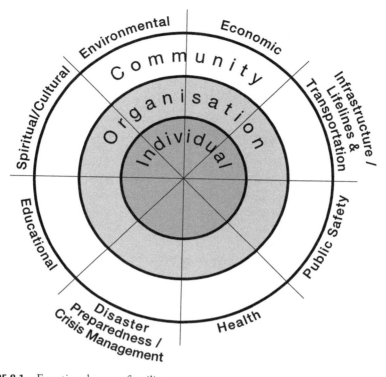

FIGURE 8.1 Functional areas of resilience

Source: Adapted from Neighbourhood Empowerment Network (http://empowersf.org/wp-content/uploads/2014/04/RBV-Program-Guide.pdf).

CASE BOX 8.1   DO PEOPLE WITH PREVIOUS DISASTER EXPERIENCE HAVE BETTER PREPAREDNESS THAN PEOPLE WITHOUT ANY PREVIOUS DISASTER EXPERIENCE?

The study by Chan, Kim, Lin, Cheung, and Lee (2014) suggests that although an association was found between previous disaster exposure and disaster preparedness in Western urban communities, previous disaster experience alone is not necessarily a predictor for disaster preparedness in rural settings of Asia. Local culture and customs, the level of education, policies and regulations targeting the hazard also played important roles.

Since the twentieth century, environmental degradation, climate change, poverty and income disparity as well as the rapid global urbanisation are all important risks associated with adverse human outcomes in disasters. (Benson & Clay, 2004;

Vorhies, 2012). Case box 8.1 describes the study findings of how previous experience alone cannot predict preparedness.

Disaster resilience is multifaceted and requires collaborative efforts among international organisations, local governments and civil societies. "Health" is considered as one of the core resilience dimensions and the health sector's core responses usually took place during emergencies and disasters.

The prevention concept

As highlighted in Chapter 1, public health adopts the concept of "prevention is better than cure" as its underlying principle of action. When applied in disaster/emergency context, disaster prevention refers to "[t]he outright avoidance of adverse impacts of hazards and related disasters . . . through actions taken in advance" (UNISDR, 2009, p. 22). The notion suggests that it is always possible to minimise the adverse impact of disasters.

Three levels of prevention may be considered during action planning. Primary prevention refers to activities that aim to prepare and enhance resilience before the disaster. Secondary prevention actions proactively address the health risk and response during the disaster. Tertiary prevention actions focus on minimising the health impact and damage after the disaster (see also Section 1.10, "Hierarchy of Prevention"). Case Box 8.2 describes a study conducted to understand health and environmental behaviours and practice. Most of the behaviours are related to climate change which can impact on disasters.

CASE BOX 8.2   MITIGATION STRATEGY: HEALTH CO-BENEFITS OF COMBINING ENVIRONMENTALLY FRIENDLY MEASURES AND HEALTH RISK ISSUES

CCOUC conducted a territory-wide random sampling telephone survey in Hong Kong between January and February 2016 to understand local patterns of carbon-reducing behaviours that could also benefit health. The results (See Figure 8.2) show that Hong Kong people had quite high awareness and practice of some of these behaviours, but relatively low of others. For example, 70% of the respondents often used less packing and shopping bags and only 3% had no awareness while only 5.8% often had at least one vegetarian meal every week and 49% had never considered. There is also a discrepancy between awareness and practice in some behaviours like using less air-conditioning or heating: a mere 9.2% of the respondents had no awareness of this behaviour, but only 44.1% actually practised it often. The promotion of awareness and practice of environmentally friendly behaviours may be facilitated if the health co-benefits of these behaviours can be highlighted. In the case of reducing air-conditioning and heating use and reducing electricity consumption, not only can air pollution and greenhouse gas emission from fossil fuels power plants be alleviated, but also reduce the risks of stroke, heart disease, lung cancer and chronic lower respiratory diseases. Likewise, having vegetarian meal and consuming less meat do not only cut greenhouse gas produced by livestock like cattle and conserve water resources to produce crops for feeding livestock, but also reduce the risks of colorectal cancer, cardiovascular diseases and diabetes. These potential health gains could also offset the cost of mitigation action. Many indirect health co-benefits may also arise from action taken in the non-health sectors. For example, well-planned land-use management may help prevent other environmental health risks arising from flooding, increased water run-off and water contamination. Well-planned climate mitigation strategies may create opportunities for health protection in a community through improved rural health infrastructure, access to renewable energy for health facilities and environmentally friendly and disaster-resilient buildings (World Health Organization [WHO], 2014).

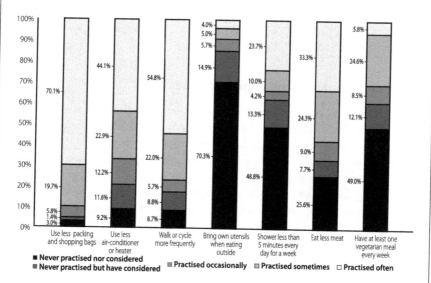

FIGURE 8.2 Awareness and practice of environmentally friendly behaviours with health co-benefits in Hong Kong

Source: Selected results from Chan, Chan, et al. (2016, p. 53).

Since the millennium, the climate change mitigation policies with anticipated health co-benefits are likely to gain widespread public support. However, to ensure "health" and "health co-benefits from environmentally friendly behaviours" are integrated into planning and implementation of these climate change mitigation efforts, technical knowledge, strong political will, good multi-sectoral partnerships and proactive leadership are needed. Mitigation actions with the most benefits to health should be prioritised over other competing issues. The potential long-term mitigation cost is relatively small when compared to an anticipated cost-saving in health systems from the health benefits, such as prevented deaths, diseases and disabilities (WHO, 2014). Proactive inclusion and engagement of the health sector are a key strategy to ensure a fair assessment of costs can be conducted. Cost-benefit assessments are important for policy decision-making and health benefits should be considered as "offsets" or "trade-offs" from the initial cost of mitigation investment.

Although mitigation strategies can bring many benefits, especially those for the climate-related disasters, the main barrier to mitigation may be the lack of awareness and the affordability of related policy implementation, particularly in developing countries. With limited financial resources and competing priorities, mitigation actions are often sidelined because they lack immediate results. Second, for sustainability, mitigation strategies require long-term planning, training and human resources. Without the supporting systems, the technology is neither functional nor sustainable. In addition, while benefits from some adaptation strategies can be immediate and obvious, the mitigation effects, such as lower CO_2, may not be noticeable for long periods (Klein et al., 2007). This could be a major challenge to sustaining political will.

Building resilience through preparedness

Globally, there have been significant discussions about promoting resilience through preparedness in the health sectors. Such strategies might be broadly categorised into two major approaches – namely "top-down" and "bottom-up". "**Top-down**" approaches involve policy initiatives, legislative development and implementation by governments and regional or international agencies. While governments have important responsibilities to maintain functional infrastructures and other social services, such as roads, communications and health care, policy making should involve key frontline and community stakeholders to maximise effectiveness and coordination. "**Bottom-up**" approaches involve action taken by local communities and individuals to increase disaster resilience in response to the unique disaster risks they face. These approaches show that the surge of volunteers in an emergency situation can be beneficial to improving the disaster response (see Case Box 8.3).

Three important challenges exist in community disaster response in the twenty-first century. First and foremost, there are uncertainties of community **disaster literacy and preparedness in civil society**. Knowledge, skills, community attitude and actual behavioural uptake vary in disaster-prone communities. Hence, the same response in all communities to the same disaster warning message cannot be

---

CASE BOX 8.3 BOTTOM-UP RESILIENCE: COORDINATION OF MILLIONS OF VOLUNTEERS IN DISASTER RESPONSE IN CHINA

In addition to government efforts, effective disaster response also requires contribution from the local community and the volunteer sector. In the 2008 Wenchuan earthquake in China, 13 million volunteers all over the country were reported to have taken part in the relief efforts, among whom 3 million worked on the frontline in Sichuan Province. In 2011, it was estimated that there were more than 60 million community volunteers in China, but only around 20 million were formally registered under various government-led community volunteer systems such as the China Red Cross. Moreover, these volunteers have not been taken into account in the current national disaster-response policies, and their role has never been clearly defined. Instead of being a contributing force, an influx of uncoordinated and untrained volunteers without clearly-defined role, proper protection and accountability for their actions into the disaster site could hamper the response effectiveness and efficiency. Finding ways to identify and properly mobilise these unregistered volunteers in a productive way poses a big challenge to national and local governments.

Source: Chan (2013).

---

assumed. Second, there is an urgent need to identify approaches to effectively **manage volunteers**. However, most stakeholders lack the experience and expertise to address, coordinate and mobilise relevant community volunteers. Community capacity building is urgently needed to address the increased hazards and disaster risks with urban living and the impact of climate change. Accountability for volunteer actions (e.g. performing clinical duties by non-clinically trained volunteers) becomes a major challenge for the management of volunteers in disaster-affected sites. Last but not least, stakeholders need to reconsider the best way to mobilise **technology such as the Internet and social media** to support preparedness and responses. Information inaccuracy and the lack of accountability in social media and civil discussion platforms might sometimes confuse and hamper effective action by responders and affected communities.

Preparedness at the individual level

Disaster risk literacy refers to an individual's ability to acquire and comprehend disaster risk information, which might enhance disaster resilience capacity. The underlying idea is that evidence-based interventions should be conducted to enhance individuals' capacity to initiate self-help behaviours to mitigate and respond to disasters (see Knowledge Box 8.1).

KNOWLEDGE BOX 8.1   LITERACY AND DISASTER HEALTH RISK LITERACY

Before approaching the subject of disaster risk literacy, it is first necessary to understand the concepts of **literacy** and **health literacy**. UNESCO (2004, p. 13) defines **literacy** as the "ability to identify, understand, interpret, create, communicate and compute, using printed and written materials associated with varying contexts". It involves a continuum of learning tangible skills and cognitive skills, particularly reading, writing and basic arithmetic. Functionally literate people can develop their knowledge and potential and participate fully in their communities. **Health literacy** is defined as "the degree to which individuals have the capacity to obtain, process, and understand basic health information and services needed to make appropriate health decisions" (Ratzan & Parker, 2000). It is composed of four elements: cultural and conceptual knowledge – that is the ability to understand health and illness, and to conceptualise the risks and benefits of potential interventions and outcomes; listening and speaking skills – that is effective public health communication and patient-provider communication (e.g. being able to report symptoms and understand the physician's instructions); writing and reading skills, such as the ability to understand food labelling and health education brochures; and numeracy skills, such as the ability to calculate nutrition values, compare health product packages and determine proper dosage and timing of medicines. Health literacy emphasises empowering people to make effective use of health information. It is a composite term used to describe a range of measurable outcome indicators in health education and interventions (Nutbeam, 2000).

   Disaster health risk literacy refers to the ability of individuals to acquire, evaluate and comprehend basic disaster information in order to prepare for disasters, respond to emergencies and mitigate disaster risks. Key components of disaster health risk literacy include: (1) cultural and conceptual knowledge – the ability to conceptualise and understand disaster risk and its impact on health; (2) listening and speaking literacy (oral literacy) – the ability to understand and describe disaster-related information orally; (3) writing and reading literacy (print literacy) – the ability to understand disaster warnings, disaster-related information brochures and written contingency plans; and (4) numeracy literacy – the ability to compare different disaster risks and probabilities (Chan & Yue, 2012).

Preparedness at the household level

In modern era, the household is one of the basic functional social units in communities. Household preparedness is especially critical for remote areas where official external help is limited in crises. In countries where rapid urbanisation has led to major socio-economic disparity, household preparedness might be the only way rural communities may rely on in the face of disasters. Unfortunately, knowledge about effective preparedness at the household level is limited, and academic research is still in its infancy in this area. Case Boxes 8.4A, 8.4B and 8.5 illustrate household-level preparedness in Asia (see also Knowledge Box 8.2).

CASE BOX 8.4A   PREPAREDNESS IN URBAN SETTINGS: HONG KONG

Studies indicate that urban communities in general have a low level of disaster preparedness. In New South Wales, Australia, less than one-fifth of the households in a townhouse-based community reported preparation of radio and compatible batteries, mobile phones, emergency contact lists and first aid kits in case of disasters (Cretikos et al., 2008). Another study by Bethel, Foreman, and Burke (2011) in the United States yielded similar results. In Hong Kong, a cross-sectional telephone survey revealed that 87.2% of the respondents did not perceive Hong Kong to be susceptible to natural disasters. Basic supplies such as face masks, adhesive bandages and basic medication such as anti-pyretic drugs were reportedly available in over 90% of interviewed households. However, first aid kits (49.3%) and non-perishable food and drinking water (57.3%) were less commonly reported (Chan, Yue, Lee,& Wang, 2016).

CASE BOX 8.4B   PREPAREDNESS IN RURAL SETTINGS: THE ETHNIC MINORITY HEALTH PROJECT IN CHINA

Globally, China suffers the highest frequency and the greatest impact on human health from natural disasters. There is difference in household-level disaster preparedness between urban and rural communities and information is limited about preparedness in rural communities. The rural communities, in particular those which are ethnic-minority-based and living in extreme poverty (less than US$1.25 per person per day), face higher natural disaster risks and have limited knowledge and resources for disaster preparedness. Since 2009, the Collaborating Centre for Oxford University and Chinese University of Hong Kong for Disaster and Medical Humanitarian Response (CCOUC) (n.d.a) has been developing the Ethnic Minority Health Project (EMHP) to investigate general public health and disaster preparedness in rural China. Health education and disaster preparedness interventions have been carried out in dozens of remote disaster-prone, extremely poor and geographically remote ethnic minority communities across eight inland provinces of China (see Figure 8.3). These include Dai (at the origin of the Yangtze River), Hui (along the Loess Plateau of the Yellow River), Yi, Li, Naxi, Zhuang, Miao, Tujia, Dong (on the highlands of three main rivers in southwestern provinces), Buyi and Tibetan minorities. The targeted sites are prone to various natural disasters, e.g. rainstorms, earthquakes, snowstorms, fires, droughts, and floods.

Site selection follows four key principles: remoteness, minority ethnicity, economic vulnerability and disaster-proneness. After a site is selected, a health needs assessment is conducted through household surveys, focus group discussions and stakeholder interviews. Information on households' health status, disaster preparedness and their access to health services is gathered. Three months after the assessment, health interventions (e.g. how to prepare a disaster preparedness kit, manage diarrhoeal problems by making oral rehydration solutions, and reduce health risk related to post-disaster situations) are performed in the community through health education campaigns. Evaluation is carried out immediately after intervention and one year post-intervention by making a comparison with the baseline assessment before the intervention.

FIGURE 8.3   Visited sites of CCOUC Ethnic Minority Health Project

Source: CCOUC (n.d.b).

CASE BOX 8.5   IMPACT OF DISASTER PREPAREDNESS INTERVENTION IN YI MINORITY COMMUNITY IN SICHUAN PROVINCE, CHINA

By Poyi Lee and Emily Ying Yang Chan

While China is among the countries with the most frequent occurrence of disasters, rural areas of China, where ethnic minorities reside, are always disproportionately affected. A major flood occurred on 31 August 2012 in Liangshan Yi Autonomous Prefecture in Sichuan Province and affected 218,000 local residents and destroyed 13,300 houses. A post-flooding assessment in Hongyan Village in the prefecture showed more than half of the villagers regarded a disaster preparedness kit as important but only around 25% had taken action to prepare it at home.

In March 2014, a face-to-face intervention-based study was conducted to evaluate the impact of the disaster preparedness intervention implemented at Hongyan Village, a rural community with high illiteracy rate. A survey of 40 questions was designed to examine participants' awareness of, and knowledge about, the tangible items and their use in a disaster preparedness kit, as well as the importance of preparing oral rehydration solution (ORS) in a resource-deficit setting.

A total of 102 households (around half of the village) participated in the disaster preparedness intervention and completed the pre- and post-questionnaires. Over 80% of the participants regarded a disaster preparedness kit as necessary but less than half of them knew what tangible items should be included. Important knowledge gaps included the necessity of preparing long-term medication in a disaster preparedness kit and the awareness of ORS's potential use for diarrhoea which is common after flooding. After the health intervention, over 70% of the participants showed improvement in awareness and knowledge of both the disaster preparedness kit and ORS. This project provides evidence that health education campaigns in disaster preparedness can empower communities with a high illiteracy rate in China to engage in self-help and household-based preparedness. Policymakers might consider applying this programme model for other remote, ethnic-minority-based communities to improve household-based resilience and self-efficacy in disaster preparedness (Chan, Zhu, Lee, Liu, & Mark, 2014, September).

KNOWLEDGE BOX 8.2   AN EXAMPLE OF A DISASTER PREPAREDNESS KIT AND THE FIVE BASIC SURVIVAL NEEDS IN THE RURAL COMMUNITY

What should be put in a disaster preparedness kit? CCOUC recommends the following items, which cover the five main core functions of maintaining health (see Figure 8.4): non-perishable food, emergency blanket, first-aid kit and simple medication, torch, whistle, fire starter, multipurpose knife, thermo-durable bottle, copies of personal documents (e.g. identity card and medication list), family pictures, medical records and information cards (carrying information like the procedure for making ORS and key messages in post-disaster health management).

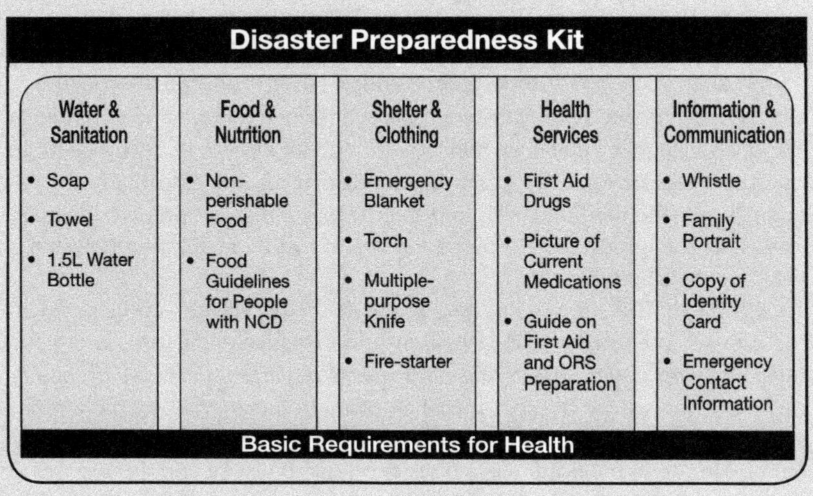

Disaster Preparedness Kit

Water & Sanitation	Food & Nutrition	Shelter & Clothing	Health Services	Information & Communication
• Soap • Towel • 1.5L Water Bottle	• Non-perishable Food • Food Guidelines for People with NCD	• Emergency Blanket • Torch • Multiple-purpose Knife • Fire-starter	• First Aid Drugs • Picture of Current Medications • Guide on First Aid and ORS Preparation	• Whistle • Family Portrait • Copy of Identity Card • Emergency Contact Information

Basic Requirements for Health

FIGURE 8.4   Disaster preparedness kit

Preparedness at the community level: training and education

Education and training are important strategies to promote preparedness in civil society. Case Boxes 8.6, 8.7 and 8.8 show some examples of how community preparedness can be enhanced by training and education.

CASE BOX 8.6   COLLABORATIVE TRAINING OF COMMUNITY MENTAL HEALTH WORKERS

By Elizabeth A. Newnham

Populations affected by war and disasters are at increased risk of psychological disorders. Yet, the significant need for psychological care in regions affected by natural disasters is largely unmet (Kohn, Saxena, Levav, & Saraceno, 2004). A number of treatments for depression and post-traumatic stress reactions in post-emergency settings have demonstrated their effectiveness (Tol et al., 2011). However, for evidence-based psychological practice to meet the vast needs of war- and disaster- affected populations, extensive training of lay mental health workers combined with ongoing supervision is needed.

Collaboration was vital to successful training. To implement the Youth Readiness Intervention in post-conflict Sierra Leone, the team utilised a model of collaborative training (Betancourt et al., 2014). Local Sierra Leonean mental health workers with various levels of education and experience were employed as facilitators. Training occurred over two weeks, and comprised a dynamic mix of didactic learning, role play and constructive feedback on trainees' practice. The expert opinion of local teams thus guided a process of ongoing refinement and cultural adaptation of the intervention, with targeted examples and exercises to engage group members.

The trainee team developed a range of strategies for using everyday materials (including chairs, stones, fruit), active demonstrations (of communication techniques, interpersonal issues), and drawing with figures rather than words. Creativity and flexibility in both training and implementation thus enabled a stronger and more suitable treatment that will promote engagement without marginalizing youth who had not had access to schooling postwar. For training outcomes to be sustainable, ongoing supervision both in the field and via regular phone calls (or Skype) was critical. A weekly supervision structure that provided support, professional development, access to scientific literature and assessments of fidelity to treatment might enhance programme sustainability (Newnham et al., 2015). Ultimately, collaborative capacity-building was vital to delivering an effective treatment that resulted in significant improvements in emotion regulation, functioning and schooling outcomes for war-affected young people (Betancourt et al., 2014).

CASE BOX 8.7   COMMUNITY PARTICIPATION ENSURING DISASTER RISK MANAGEMENT, LIVELIHOOD AND FOOD SECURITY OF THE COMMUNITIES IN LAOS

By Provash Mondal

Oxfam's Community-based Disaster Risk Management (CBDRM) projects have been implemented in collaboration with the Government of Lao People's Democratic Republic (LPDR). The projects' main focus is to mitigate the negative impact of disasters on rural communities by promoting community-based disaster risk reduction (DRR) using participatory approaches to identify local hazards (such as floods), including those that impact on livelihoods (such as droughts and animal diseases) and health (such as waterborne disease outbreaks). The overall project strategy is to change the knowledge, attitude and practice (KAP) relating to disasters at the community and government levels to focus on risk reduction, preparedness and mitigation of the impact of disasters rather than the passive acceptance of disasters or a focus only on emergency response. In addition, the project has resulted in positive outcomes in terms of food security and access to basic health services. Importantly, capacity has been built at the community and local government levels to plan, manage and support a wide range of activities. The projects have also developed the capacity to manage activities such as the rice banks that are contributing directly to improved food security by giving improved access to rice during the traditional rice shortage months.

Based on the outcomes and lessons learnt, the projects recommend effective engagement at the national level to influence decision-making in disaster risk management based on field-level evidence. This includes sufficient and targeted resourcing for government staff and community members to strengthen their capacity to effectively implement national policies. This will require effective collaboration and coordination mechanisms between non-government and government partners, including a clear definition of roles and responsibilities.

CASE BOX 8.8   HONG KONG JOCKEY CLUB DISASTER PREPAREDNESS AND RESPONSE INSTITUTE (HKJCDPRI) AS AN EXAMPLE OF A COORDINATED PROFESSIONAL EFFORT TO ADDRESS DISASTER PREPAREDNESS AT THE COMMUNITY LEVEL

By Donald KT Li and Kevin KC Hung

Hong Kong is a Special Administrative Region of China and one of the major global cities in Asia. It ranks 13th out of the 187 countries and territories in the world, according to the UNDP Human Development Report 2013 (Hong Kong Special Administrative Region [HKSAR], 2015). Hong Kong had a population of 7.24 million in 2014 (HKSAR, 2015, May 15). With an average of 6,690 persons per km^2, Hong Kong is one of the most densely populated places in the world. Of the total land area of 1,104 km^2, 6.9% of the land was being used for residential purposes (United Nations Development Programme [UNDP], 2013). As a densely populated city, Hong Kong is vulnerable to epidemics and infectious diseases, technological accidents, as well as tropical cyclones. In the 1960s and 1970s, Hong Kong used to have tremendous loss of life and infrastructure damage caused by the landslides and flooding triggered by tropical-cyclone-related rainstorms (Ho, 2003). With the improved infrastructure building codes and slope safety measures, cyclones are no longer perceived as major disaster risks to the general public. Climate change, however, might bring this back on to the agenda by increasing the frequency and severity of storm surges striking Hong Kong.

HKJCDPRI is a five-year project (2014–2019) funded by the Hong Kong Jockey Club Charities Trust, aiming to build a community in Hong Kong that is ready to respond to disasters. HKJCDPRI is based at the Hong Kong Academy of Medicine, and partners with The Chinese University of Hong Kong and the University of Hong Kong, with the participation of Harvard University. Working together with its academic and community partners, the institute provides comprehensive training, research and policy exchange platform to enhance resilience in the community and employs a blended learning approach which includes using e-learning, face-to-face teaching, simulation training and field-based complex exercises. The institute is an attempt to address the community need for competencies in knowledge, skills and attitude to reduce loss and suffering in disasters.

Case Box 8.9 describes how differences in local adaptation of community drills and simulation exercises may affect human health outcomes in disasters.

CASE BOX 8.9   HOW DIFFERENT MIYAGI SCHOOLS FARED IN THE FACE OF THE GREAT EAST JAPAN EARTHQUAKE TRIPLE DISASTER IN 2011

By Makiko Kato MacDermot

In Japan, although various multi-level initiatives were implemented to enhance disaster reduction education in local communities and schools, the number of deaths varies among disaster-affected schools when north-eastern Japan was struck by "a triple disaster" with a magnitude 9.0 earthquake, tsunamis and nuclear plant meltdowns in 2011, which caused a total deaths of nearly 20,000.

After the Great East Japan earthquake in 2011, many case reports from affected elementary schools were presented. Although there were many tragedies, there were some positive results regarding drills and exercises held in school. The experience highlighted the importance of preparedness for disasters, including safe evacuation training based on active public participation and learning from past disasters.

Arahama and Tokura elementary schools (schoolchildren aged 6–12)

The Arahama area in Sendai was one of the worst affected by the tsunami. There were 704 deaths and 51 people were recorded missing. The area is situated

4 km from the coastline and had a population of around 2,700 (800 house-holds). All the houses, except the Arahama Elementary School building, were damaged or washed away. The remaining four-storey school was made of steel and reinforced concrete and, since there were no high grounds around the Arahama coastline, it was designated as one of the tsunami evacuation points. After the quake, 520 people, including schoolchildren and local residents, were evacuated to the school led by fire fighters and local leaders. The level of water from the tsunami reached as high as 4.6 m (the second floor), but everyone managed to reach the roof top so no deaths were reported from that group. It took three days before everyone was safely evacuated by helicopters from the school as all the infrastructure around was completely destroyed. The school evacuation plan was revised two years before the quake. The new evacuation protocol was based on "staying in the school and evacuating to a higher floor in case of tsunami" instead of the old "going into the schoolyard after the quake". A similar positive case was reported at Tokura Elementary School, Minamisan-riku in the Miyagi prefecture. Two months before the earthquake, the school revised the evacuation drill and safety procedures along the same principles as the Arahama school and all the children were saved. Both schools had well-planned evacuation points and conducted monthly training, including drills for children, teachers and people in the local communities. In addition, the school administrators had selected the most appropriate evacuation points based on an "all-hazard approach" (see Section 8.12 for more details on the all-hazard approach). All those who followed the plan were saved.

Ōkawa elementary school

The Ōkawa Elementary School in Ishinomaki of Miyagi Prefecture is known as one of the worst affected: 74 pupils (70% of the total) died or went missing and 10 out of 11 teachers died. The case raised questions about the school safety procedures and who was then responsible for managing the school. Four years after the earthquake, there was still an ongoing lawsuit between the deceased children's families and the city and prefecture governments over responsibility.

There are several contributors to the tragedy. According to the tsunami hazard map, the area around Ōkawa School was NOT marked as hazardous area and thus the school was designated as one of the evacuation locations for the local community. There were about 50 minutes between the start of the earthquake and the arrival of the tsunami. It is reported that the schoolteach-ers and the students stayed out on the playground, instead of evacuating to a safer place. This was mainly due to the fact that there was no "all-hazards plan" and the tsunami was NOT included as a hazard in their plan. Therefore, they could not make the correct decision before it was too late. The school was also a steel-framed, reinforced concrete building, the same as the school in Arahama, and was as high as 10 m. However, Ōkawa School did not have a rooftop, which restricted the evacuation options.

Policy and action in response to these cases

When developing safety procedures, it is important to have a basic plan for all hazards which can be modified according to the degree and type of event. These plans should be developed in collaboration with local governments, scientists and academia, and must be shared by all stakeholders including the people in local communities. The plans and drills need to be practised. Selecting evacuation and emergency points depends on many factors, such as topology, population size and the availability of resilient infrastructure. For tsunami-affected schools, positive health outcomes (minimum mortality) were associated with: i) Possession of an all-hazard approach evacuation plan; ii) Regular up-to-date, evidence-based drills, preparedness and risk perception training activities for both children and teachers; iii) Re-adaptation of preparedness actions in settings, and iv) Schools with disaster resilience structures. Future policy recommendations should thus include: i) Adaptation of an all-hazard approach which is modified according to the degree and types of extreme events; ii) Multi-stakeholder-based preparedness activities to improve coordination, communication and collaboration, and iii) Regularly organised drills and updated plans to maintain disaster risk awareness and enable spontaneous actions.

Sources: Petal (2008, November), Kikuchi (2011, July 20) and Ōkawa Primary School Incident Investigation Committee (2014, February).

Preparedness at community level: infrastructure

Strengthening of infrastructure is one of the most important approaches to reduce disaster risk. Case Box 8.10 highlights the human impact of Bam earthquake, which largely arose from suffocation as a result of collapsed housing. Examples of global efforts of infrastructure strengthening to mitigate disaster risks are discussed in Case Boxes 8.11 and 8.12.

CASE BOX 8.10   THE 2003 BAM EARTHQUAKE, IRAN

More than 30,000 people were killed and another 30,000 injured when an earthquake struck on 26 December 2003 in Bam, southern Iran. The weak infrastructure constitutes weak resilience in the community, leading to heavy casualties. A major factor contributing to the high death toll was suffocation with fallen mud bricks, which were the traditional building materials of the disaster-affected community. Post disaster, almost all of the survivors were left homeless as 85% of the city's buildings collapsed (UNISDR, 2007).

CASE BOX 8.11 THE 2010 GREAT FIRE OF BUMTHANG IN THE KINGDOM OF BHUTAN

By Rinzin Jamtsho

On 26 October 2010, a fire disaster occurred in Chamkhar town in Bumthang, Bhutan. The fire, which started in a mobile phone shop, claimed two lives, destroyed 59 shops and hotels, and rendered 267 residents homeless. The psychological symptoms reported by the affected population include mood swings, sleeplessness and anxiety. The socio-economic impact included the loss of most of the victims' life savings.

Risk, hazard and vulnerability

Fires are a frequent occurrence in Bhutan. This is due to the heavy reliance on wood for building houses and as fuel so that the town burnt down in a matter of hours. The houses in Bumthang, as elsewhere, were built closely together and lack electricity supply. Those that have electricity supply sometimes install faulty wiring which increases the risk of fire.

Realising the risk of disasters and its impacts, the government of Bhutan has adopted a proactive strategy, beginning with upgrading the Disaster Management Division under the Department of Local Governance to a full-fledged department under the Ministry of Home and Cultural Affairs in 2008. Despite the detailed planning and the formation of the organisational framework for disaster response, Bhutan continues to suffer from inadequate fire management, emergency service equipment and technologies. According to the Fire and Rescue Services Division of the Royal Bhutan Police, by 2014 the response capability had been improved with the addition of 56 fire engines to provide fire-fighting services to the capital city Thimphu and all the towns of the 20 dzongkhags of the country. Twenty-seven were donated by Japan and 19 by India. However, indigenous fire-fighting methods are still in use for many of the forest fires due to the limitation of equipment availability. The equipment currently provided to Bhutanese villagers/foresters includes walkie-talkie handsets, knife spades, rakes and backpack pumps for fighting fire, but the supplies are inadequate.

Sources: Dorji (2006), Royal Bhutan Police (2008), Chan, Hung, Cheung, Koo and Wong (2012, April), Dema (2013), Chan, Lee and Tam (2014), Pokhrel (2014) and Dargye (2004).

CASE BOX 8.12 DISASTER-RESILIENT COMMUNITIES: PREPARED TO COPE WITH DISASTERS IN VIETNAM

By Provash Mondal

Vietnam's Hà T nh Province is regularly hit by natural disasters, especially flash floods and landslides. In 2007 and 2010, devastating floods struck the area and caused heavy losses. After providing emergency relief, Oxfam implemented Community-based Risk Reduction projects in three districts of the province and then replicated these in other provinces. Communities analysed their own economic, social and motivational vulnerabilities, risks and capacities, and then developed a Community-based Disaster Risk Management Action Plan. The objective of the action planning is to ensure that communities play a key role in reducing vulnerability, increasing capacity and taking appropriate measures for household-level preparedness.

In these projects, households have gained an understanding of emergency preparedness measures to be taken before, during and after emergencies. Many disaster-prone communities have been advised about how to protect livelihoods, repair houses, store emergency food, identify safe places to relocate their livestock, poultry and household materials, safeguard agricultural seeds and fertilisers, protect fishponds and fingerlings, fruit orchards and vegetable gardens, seedlings and plants, etc. Sources of pure drinking water have been identified, wells and other water sources repaired or maintained as necessary, and water for drinking and domestic use collected and preserved. Toilets were improved before the disaster season, and arrangements made for toilets to be available in evacuation centres and the introduction of better hygiene practices.

The government has committed to include the community-based disaster risk reduction (DRR) approach into their National Strategy for Disaster Management and integrating gender issues into their strategy. Community leaders supported households to implement risk reduction measures and methodologies and Oxfam has replicated its experiences in six provinces to work with communities and the leadership. Other organisations have also received information, methodologies and methods for community-based DRR. Disaster-affected communities in the selected districts have become well prepared to cope with natural disasters.

However, Oxfam believes that the implementation of these risk-reduction measures is only in the initial stage and initiatives must be continuously monitored and maintained. The Community-based Risk Reduction process is fully linked with ongoing development activities and good governance. Greater efforts are needed by the government, international organisations and UN organisations to integrate risk reduction processes with livelihood and other development initiatives.

Preparedness at the community level: risk communication

Effective communication during a disaster can significantly reduce the impact on human health, can empower and mobilise communities as well as build community resilience and may reduce public anxiety during a disaster. For effective communication during a disaster, the communication strategy should be planned ahead. Proactive and interactive communication with a wide range of communication channels and media coverage will be essential. The World Health Organization (WHO) has proposed seven steps (namely assessing media needs, developing goals, plans and strategies, training communicators, preparing messages, identifying media outlets and activities, delivering messages and evaluating messages and performance) for effective communication during public health emergencies (Hyer & Covello, 2005).

Early warning system (EWS)

Mitigating disaster risk is possible with good preparedness and disaster risk literacy. Early warning, as a disaster preparedness intervention, may provide timely and effective information to support actions and decision making in emergency situations (UNEP, 2012). Early warning systems are applicable to various hazards, such as geophysical and biological hazards, as well as complex sociopolitical emergencies (Phaiju, Bej, Phokharel, & Dons, 2010). An effective EWS provides people with information that is relevant to their needs and is sensitive to their available resources. It saves lives and reduces economic and material losses from disasters.

In general, **early warning systems** should include the following four elements (UN, 2006): **risk knowledge** – collecting data and undertaking risk assessments systematically; **monitoring and warning service** – developing hazard monitoring and early warning services with a sound scientific basis; **information dissemination** – communicating risk information and early warnings to populations at risk; and **building national and community response capabilities** through conducting systematic education and preparedness programmes for communities. Case Box 8.13 describes the successful EWS in Cuba to reduce disaster risk. Case Box 8.14 discusses cold warning in a subtropical urban Chinese city and Case Box 8.15 explains how rural communities are engaged in flash flood warning in Iran.

CASE BOX 8.13   DISASTER RISK REDUCTION BY EWS IN CUBA

Cuba is one of the best-prepared countries in the Caribbean for the hurricane season. The national media issue alerts 72 hours before a storm makes landfall and civil protection committees check evacuation plans. The authorities also target warnings for high-risk areas 48 hours ahead of landfall and 12 hours before landfall to allow securing of homes, clearing of loose debris and evacuation of people. This EWS has proven its effectiveness. In 2004, when Hurricane Charley hit, 70,000 houses were severely damaged but only four people were killed. When Hurricane Ivan struck the following month, over 2 million people were evacuated and there were no deaths (UNISDR, 2007).

CASE BOX 8.14   TEMPERATURE WARNING IN URBAN COMMUNITY: THE CASE OF TEMPERATURE WARNING IN AN URBAN CHINESE CITY

By Janice Ying-En Ho and Emily Ying Yang Chan

The majority of studies on temperature warnings were conducted in western developed countries and most of them were related to heatwave warning. The findings indicated that warning effectiveness does not only depend upon the warning system and the detection of natural hazard, but also the community utilisation of the warning service. For example, a study in the United States (Kalkstein & Sheridan, 2007) identified a higher response among Hispanics resulting from their strong sense of perceived risk when compared with other ethnic subgroups.

There is currently limited study relating to the effectiveness of public communication of warnings in Asia. Hong Kong, a humid sub-tropical city in East Asia, experiences many extreme weather events every year. Despite locating in a sub-tropical area, cold weather spells occur periodically in the winter and cause unseen casualties. A study estimated that for every 1°C drop in daily mean temperature during the cold season (November–March; average: 18.9°C, range: 16.5–20.9°C), there was a 3.8% increase in mortality (or 45% increase per 10°C temperature decrease) (Goggins, Chan, Yang, & Chong, 2013).

In order to understand the effectiveness of these warnings to the community, CCOUC conducted a study in February 2016 within a week of the coldest cold wave in Hong Kong since 1957 (Chan, Yeung, et al., 2016). Through a randomised telephone survey, over 1,000 Hong Kong residents were assessed on their awareness and response to extreme temperature warnings. The study found that 98% of the respondents had heard about the "cold weather warning". Yet, awareness of the warning was not associated with the health status of the individuals. Among the 1,000 respondents, only 77% perceived their risk accurately according to their underlying health status. Those who inaccurately perceived their risk were more likely to get sick. These findings suggest that although general awareness of the warning was high within the community, better health risk perception should be promoted to enhance health protection associated with temperature warning.

CASE BOX 8.15 A COMMUNITY-BASED INITIATIVE TO ENHANCE EARLY WARNING OF FLASH FLOODS IN IRAN

By Ali Ardalan

Golestan ("land of flowers" in Farsi), a province of Iran, is infamous for deadly flash floods in rural areas where the lead time is as short as 15 minutes. An evaluation of the Golestan Early Warning System (EWS) revealed the inadequacies of top-down approaches that had put the local community at a great risk of flood damage due to delayed and imprecise warning. To address this, as suggested by the local people affected by past floods, the Village Disaster Taskforces (VDTs) were formed by including representatives from the community, the government, and the health system. The VDTs, using indigenous knowledge, establish a warning system where the trigger point is a threat of heavy rain observed and announced by villagers. A field research showed effectiveness of the VDTs on public awareness through training programmes and drills. The indigenous warning system was also found effective in timely dissemination of threats and saving lives.

Source: Ardalan et al. (2009, 2010).

Use of Internet and social media

Exposure to early warnings alone is inadequate to mitigate disaster risks. By providing well-simulated and up-to-date information, individuals can gain a good understanding of natural disasters and get enough background to make quick decisions that helps prevent and reduce damage. In addition to traditional media like television and radio. The effective and appropriate uses of mobile phones, the Internet and social media are areas of future development for disaster risk communication.

Social media platforms, such as Facebook, Twitter and Instagram, have become an essential part of human lives in the past decade. Exploring the use of new media like the Internet, SMS, Reverse 911 (call) and social media (e.g. Facebook and Twitter) might provide up-to-date information and quicker diffusion through citizen co-production (retweeting) is urgently needed. For example, the Twitter Tsunami Early Warning Civic Network used by the Indonesian government reached 4 million Twitter users in 15 minutes during an earthquake in 2012 (Chatfield, Scholl, & Brajawidagda, 2013). The United Nations "space-based information for crowd-source mapping" is an example of how the Internet and social media can be used as a tool to facilitate disaster response and build disaster resilience by disseminating information about disasters to recruit volunteers and to empower public action. For example, following the Great East Japan earthquake in 2011, many Japanese citizens used social media as a source of communication. Facebook in Japan reached over 17 million users during the disaster, and Facebook, Twitter and Mixi (a popular Japanese social media) were used to share information, spread warnings and broadcast requests for assistance.

Technology is also used to strengthen disaster resilience through online distance learning. For instance, the British Red Cross has launched an online platform named "Everyday First Aid", which aims to empower people with first-aid skills. A mobile application was also developed to provide basic first-aid knowledge to guide emergency response and preparedness for non-disaster phases. In addition, a location-based approach using satellite/GPS technology can help provide individual warnings to personal devices depending on owner location (see Case Box 8.16).

However, there are various limitations of applying new technologies in disasters. Significant portions of the at-risk population may not have regular access to new technologies, which creates digital exclusion of the most vulnerable people (e.g. the elderly) (IFRC, 2013). In addition, information accuracy and credibility on social networks remain a challenge and an important research topic for the years to come. In complex emergencies, where complex issues of security are involved, who and how information should be disseminated might be subject to major debates.

In summary, for risk communication to be effective, communities need to improve disaster literacy and preparedness in knowledge, skills, attitude and competency development.

CASE BOX 8.16   AN EXAMPLE OF GLOBAL ONLINE TRAINING

The "Public Health Principles in Disaster and Medical Humanitarian Response" online course was developed by CCOUC and launched in June 2014. The course is delivered through an online virtual learning space developed by the Technology-Assisted Lifelong Learning unit of the Department for Continuing Education of Oxford University. It comprises seven lessons, four short quizzes and one final assessment. Each lesson requires about one to three hours of study. To allow maximum flexibility, students enrolled in the course may access all learning materials and go through all learning activities online within a maximum period of seven months at their own pace. The target audience for this course is individuals studying and working in health, policy, education and humanitarian sectors. Students may be civil servants, health care personnel, frontline disaster relief practitioners and postgraduate students of closely related disciplines. More than 4,200 students from more than 120 countries in six continents enrolled within the first 30 months. The course has become more international with a decreasing proportion of students originating from Hong Kong and China.

Source: CCOUC (2016, May; 2016, November).

Preparedness at the global level: policy and contingency planning

Disaster risk management for health

In recent years, the global community has shifted its emphasis from acute response to proactive management of disasters through efforts in disaster risk reduction (DRR). DRR refers to "the systematic analysis and management of health risks, posed by emergencies and disasters, through a combination of hazard and vulnerability reduction to prevent and mitigate risks, preparedness, response and recovery measures" (World Health Organization, United Kingdom Health Protection Agency, & partners, 2011). It highlights the need for prevention, mitigation and preparedness. **Sustainable development**, **health systems** and **multi-sectoral actions** are the key underlying principles of disaster risk management in health. Disaster risk management is an essential element in sustainable development. Disasters delay development programmes as they destroy available assets and increase a population's vulnerability to health risks. The integration of disaster risk management into sustainable development is one of the key strategies to develop the post-2015 international DRR framework.

The health care system is a core element of disaster risk management for health. Well-organised and managed systems of primary health care could improve the health status of a community and increase its resilience. Safe-hospital programmes encourage the building of health facilities that can withstand disasters (WHO, 2015) (see Case Box 8.17). The health care system also needs to develop an adaptable and resilient system to maintain health services in emergency situations. The health system could not function properly without the support of other systems, such as water and sanitation, food and nutrition, logistics, communication and security. Multi-sectoral action is necessary to ensure the continuity of health services. Cross-sectoral collaboration is also required to reduce the health risks of disasters at all levels (see Case Box 8.18).

International Health Regulations and disaster risk management

The International Health Regulations (IHR) are "an international legal instrument that is binding on 194 countries across the globe, including all WHO Member States". They aim to "prevent, protect against, control and provide a public health response to the international spread of disease in ways that are commensurate with and restricted to public health risks, and which avoid unnecessary interference with international traffic and trade" (WHO, 2016, p. 10).

Before 2007, IHR covered only a limited number of diseases (e.g. cholera, plague, yellow fever, smallpox, relapsing fever and typhus) and policies. However, the revision and implementation of the IHR post 2007 has expanded the coverage to include

CASE BOX 8.17   THE COMPREHENSIVE SAFE HOSPITAL FRAMEWORK

By Carman Mark

Health facilities are essential assets for communities especially at times of emergencies and disasters. However, they often encounter major damage and casualties and thus fail to provide life-saving and support services during crisis. Damaged hospitals also result in a loss of a large portion of a ministry of health budget and may undermine the trust in local authorities. It is apparent that there is a pressing need to incorporate the framework as an essential element of a national strategy for DRR.

The Safe Hospital Framework strengthens the safety and resilience of hospitals and health facilities that are subject to a spectrum of hazards. The framework aims to ensure the functionality of health facilities throughout the disaster cycle – at its catchment area, the broader health system and the societal system. There are four components under the framework: i) policy, norms and legislation, ii) coordination and service delivery, iii) resources management, and iv) knowledge and information management.

As of 2015, 77 countries had reported their adoptions of the safe hospital strategies. Assessments on the safety of existing facilities have been widely conducted. However, there is a need to ensure there are adequate resources and active multi-sectoral engagement to implement recommendations of the assessments. This could be especially challenging for countries with limited resources and those that are under the constant threat of disaster and other emergency situations. There are three proposed targets related to the framework.

i) By 2030, all new hospitals and 80% of other new health facilities are built to withstand hazards, in accordance with the safety and building codes of the country.

ii) By 2030, 50% of existing hospitals and health-care facilities requiring improved safety are retrofitted, in accordance with the safety and building codes of the country.

iii) By 2030, all hospitals and health facilities have emergency response plans for continuing health care in disasters.

The momentum for implementing the framework is building around the globe. It is essential that the resilience of health facilities be recognised and enhanced as part of the global effort in DRR.

Source: WHO (2015).

any diseases that present or could present significant harm to humans. The regulation introduces the concept of public health emergencies of international concern, which refers to "any event that affects the public health of more than one WHO member state" (WHO & Pan American Health Organization [PAHO], 2008). This set of regulations is also applied as an instrument to reduce the spread of inaccurate information (i.e. rumours and speculations).

All-hazard approach

"Eighty per cent of what we do in emergencies is generic – we do it in every emergency in the same way."

(Rockenschaub, 2008)

While different hazards might be associated with different health outcomes in emergencies, common traits might be found in operational planning, coordination, evacuation, health service arrangement and community recovery. WHO introduced the concept of an all-hazard approach to facilitate disaster preparedness and response planning (WHO, 2007a). It is

an approach to emergency management based on the recognition that there are common elements in the management of responses to virtually all emergencies, and that by standardizing a management system to address the common elements, greater capacity is generated to address the unique characteristics of different events.

(Rockenschaub, 2008)

The all-hazard approach, along with the "whole-health" approach, maintains that coordination, information tools and basic health services (including environmental health, management of chronic diseases, maternal and child health, communicable diseases control, nutrition, pharmaceuticals and health care delivery services) must be included in any emergency preparedness plan. Of note, these approaches also recognise the specific health and medical needs related to specific hazards (e.g. chemical, biological, radiological and nuclear [CBRN] hazards). Supporters argue hazard-specific medical- and health-related responses need specific technical protocols and additional guidelines to support the preparedness and response efforts.

Human security argument

Human security argument is an important theoretical debate that has affected health and disaster responses in recent years. There are seven dimensions to **human security**: economic, food, health, environmental, personal, community and political. The human security approach to natural disasters allows the consideration of three main areas for further policy development: (1) a multidisciplinary human security platform, (2) assessment of needs and identification of vulnerabilities, and (3) thresholds for action and measurement of human security. These conceptual

CASE BOX 8.18   WHAT'S NEXT? BOTTOM-UP RESILIENCE AND DISASTER HEALTH RISK REDUCTION AFTER THE DUAL EARTHQUAKES IN NEPAL IN 2015

By Emily Ying Yang Chan, Carman Mark, Carol Ka Po Wong and Gloria Kwong Wai Chan

The international community has increased the effort to integrate the UNISDR Sendai Framework for Disaster Risk Reduction 2015–2030 in the post-disaster recovery effort of the health sector. The goal of these activities is to strengthen health systems and empower communities who might be affected by recurrent disasters, so as to build emergency health risk resilience (Aitsi-Selmi & Murray, 2015).

The dual earthquakes in Nepal in 2015 were evidence of human vulnerability in the face of disasters. One month after the first quake struck on 25 April, more than 8,500 had died, 4.2 million had been affected and 1,085 health care facilities had been destroyed (WHO Country Office for Nepal, 2015, May 26). Although relief response from 341 agencies was recorded within three days of the second earthquake (12 May 2015) (United Nations Office for the Coordination of Humanitarian Affairs [OCHA], 2015, May 16), there was no information about whether any of the 2,591 officially recorded relief activities (7% were related to "health") had incorporated in future DRR and health risk preparedness.

Seven weeks after the April earthquake, through the Oxford-CUHK-CCOUC global online training network, the CCOUC team provided a 1.5-hour technical training session in Kathmandu. The session focused on the design, monitoring and evaluation of post-disaster public health and medical interventions, and was attended by 59 representatives of local and international non-governmental organisations (NGOs). A pre-training survey (CCOUC, 2015, June 25) of this group offered some insights about their pre-disaster health preparedness, training needs and future plans: 60% had been active in relief efforts since the April earthquake and all intended to continue their on-site work for at least another two months; only 30% reported having access to at least one relevant technical support channel; 10% were aware of international relief standards and guidelines (such as The Sphere Project [2011] and WHO Disaster Risk Management for Health). Those with health response mandates reported that around 51% and 26% of their staff had received physical or psychological first aid training respectively.

Considering the pre-disaster health situation, recent health risks reported and post-earthquake health experiences in a similar regional context, local capacity building is needed urgently for the management of paediatric malnutrition, hepatitis E (Basnyat et al., 2015), non-communicable diseases (NCDs), the health of older people and people with disabilities, and gender-sensitive mental health issues. Local clinical guidelines, programme management training and technical communication platforms should be built to allow the transfer of international knowledge and enable DRR through the building of true bottom-up community resilience (Chan, 2013).

TABLE 8.1 Comparison of "human security" characteristics and public health principles

Aspects of human security framework	Public health principle	Public health tools used in practice
The four characteristics of human security		
People-oriented	People-oriented at the population, community and individual levels	Health promotion models, behaviour change models, measurement of social capital
Universality	Access to care for all	Health service delivery models, health equity audit
Multidisciplinary	Multidisciplinary approach	The pathway of care model, the primary care approach, stakeholder analysis
Early prevention	Prevention-based (3 levels of prevention: primary, secondary, tertiary)	Health education and coaching, subsidisation, taxation and legislation
The seven key components of human security		
Economic security	The social determinants of health, the hierarchy of needs	Health needs assessment of vulnerable groups, health impact assessments, quality of life scales, epidemiology & biostatistics
Food security		
Health security		
Environmental security		
Personal security		
Community security		
Political security		
The three phases of human security		
Prevent	The public health "disaster cycle"	Emergency/major incident plans, business continuity plans, training & exercising
Respond		Health needs assessments
Rebuild		Recovery plans
Other key principles of public health		
Gaps in the human security concept	Cost-effectiveness	Economic evaluations – e.g. cost-benefit analysis
	Evidence-based interventions	Research – e.g. randomised control trials, cohort studies
		Data observatories

Source: Adapted from Chan and Southgate (2014, p. 76).

developments would enhance current disaster relief and preparedness processes by breaking down barriers between disciplines and prompting a holistic consideration of well-being. While employing differing approaches, human security analysis pro-vides an important platform to highlight how health problems in disasters might be addressed within a human security paradigm (Chan & Southgate, 2014). The human security approach to natural disasters allows the consideration of three main areas for further policy development: (1) a multidisciplinary human security platform, (2) assessment of needs and identification of vulnerabilities, and (3) thresholds for action and measurement of human security. These conceptual developments would enhance current disaster relief and preparedness processes by breaking down barriers between disciplines and prompting a holistic consideration of well-being.

Human security and public health share many core principles and are both concerned with human well-being in crises (WHO, 2007b).For example, despite the health security threat posed by the increasing chronic disease burden as a result of demographic and epidemiological transitions, disaster-prone, middle-income countries like China, India, Indonesia and the Philippines seem to be almost unaware of this threat and spare only a limited effort and resources to address chronic diseases associated with disasters. Table 8.1 shows the comparison of "human security" characteristics and public health principles.

The cross-disciplinary nature of the human security approach and its corresponding assessment tools with their wider range of outcome indicators could improve the allocation of resources for addressing service gaps associated with disasters (e.g. mental health needs of victims and aid workers), as well as the overall efficacy of the humanitarian relief to address other emerging health needs in disasters (see Case Box 8.19).

CASE BOX 8.19 HUMAN SECURITY APPROACH TO POST-DISASTER CHRONIC DISEASE NEEDS

Clear overlaps can be found between the three temporal phases of human security and the public health disaster cycle (Figure 8.5), making these useful entry points for the integration of the two disciplines.

Convergence of the two concepts, demonstrated in Figure 8.6, highlights how the human security framework can add value to the public health approach by insisting that, at every stage of the disaster cycle, public health responders should: i) uphold the tenets of living in freedom from want, freedom from fear and in dignity, and ii) consider the interaction between an individual's health and other areas of their functioning and welfare, using the "7 key components" as a framework for analysis. Through this lens, several interventions enhancing the public health response to disasters could be identified; some of these are listed in Table 8.2.

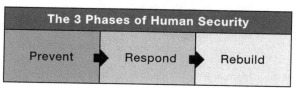

FIGURE 8.5A The three temporal phases of human security.

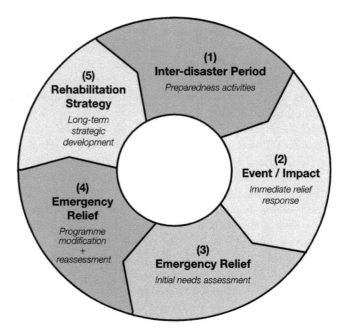

FIGURE 8.5B The public health disaster cycle

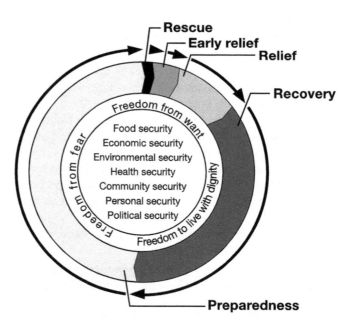

FIGURE 8.6 Human security-aligned public health disaster cycle

TABLE 8.2 Post-disaster chronic disease interventions suggested by the convergence of the human security approach and the public health disaster cycle

Aspect of human security	Stage of the public health disaster cycle	Intervention
Freedom from want (W) Freedom from fear (F) Freedom to live with dignity (D) 7 key components	Non-disaster (Preparedness)	• Provide chronic disease education and simple healthy lifestyle education. (W) • Provide disaster response training to those with chronic diseases as well as the wider community. (F) • Provide "disaster preparedness kits" containing a supply of regular chronic disease medications. (W) • Develop a measurement system for human security and set thresholds for action. (F)
	Event/impact	
	Early relief	• Develop a human security needs assessment to identify vulnerable groups (W) and determine the actions required to assure their human security during crises. (F) • Establish a multidisciplinary human security platform to coordinate assessment and action in response to disasters. (W&F) • Respect individuals' right to refuse care or medical evacuation. (D) • Ensure the provision of end-of-life care to those with severe chronic diseases and others. (D)
	Relief (Needs assessment and programme modification)	• Ensure access to chronic disease services. (W) • Maintain medical record confidentiality (especially for those with HIV/AIDS). (F&D)
	Recovery/ rehabilitation	• Establish systems for long-term care and treatment within a sustainable local health service. (W) • Ensure adequate income for purchase of appropriate healthy diet and long-term medications. (W)

Source: Adapted from Chan and Southgate (2014, p. 84).

Note: Each intervention is mapped with the three aspects of human security. Please also refer to the section on "Disaster response cycle" in Chapter 2.

Hyogo Framework for Action 2005–2015

The Hyogo Framework for Action (HFA) was adopted in January 2005 by 168 governments to explain, describe and detail the work that is required from all different sectors and actors to reduce disaster losses. Its goal was to reduce disaster losses substantially by 2015 through building the resilience of nations and communities. The framework sets priorities for states, regional organisations and international organisations to reduce disaster risk. The HFA outlines five priorities for action and offers guiding principles and practical means for achieving disaster resilience (see Table 8.3). Collaboration is crucial to the process and the framework identifies civil societies, including volunteers and community-based organisations, scientific communities, media and private sectors as vital stakeholders. Health is considered as a core component for action within the HFA (UNISDR, 2007) (see Case Box 8.20).

TABLE 8.3 HFA's five priorities in building the resilience of nations and communities to disasters

---

1. **Make disaster risk reduction a priority**
   Ensure that disaster risk reduction is a national and a local priority with a strong institutional basis for implementation.

2. **Know the risks and take action**
   Identify, assess and monitor disaster risks – and enhance early warning.

3. **Build understanding and awareness**
   Use knowledge, innovation and education to build a culture of safety and resilience at all levels.

4. **Reduce risk**
   Reduce the underlying risk factors.

5. **Be prepared and ready to act**
   Strengthen disaster preparedness for effective response at all levels.

Source: UNISDR (2007).

CASE BOX 8.20   HFA AND RESILIENCE BUILDING

Priority 4 of the HFA suggests that countries can build resilience to disasters by investing in simple, well-known measures to reduce risk and vulnerability. By applying relevant building standards to protect critical infrastructure, such as schools, hospitals and homes, vulnerable buildings can be retrofitted to a higher degree of safety. Protecting precious ecosystems, such as coral reefs and mangrove forests, could turn them into natural storm barriers. Effective insurance and microfinance initiatives can help transfer risks and provide additional resources. Although the framework does not specifically adopt public health-related concepts and theories in disaster preparedness, it is a central flagship initiative of the international community in reducing disaster risk and could be used for enhancing public health emergency preparedness.

2015 and beyond: Sendai Framework for Disaster Risk Reduction 2015–2030

The Sendai Framework for Disaster Risk Reduction 2015–2030 was adopted in March 2016, following discussions during the HFA period. This international strategic framework has been given a much more enthusiastic welcome by the health sector. The Sendai Framework is a perfect illustration of the all-hazard approach to DRR. Agreed commitments include the improvement of health systems and infrastructure resilience, the implementation of the International Health Regulations (2005) and the provision of psychosocial support for those who are in need. The four priorities for action include: 1) understanding disaster risk; 2) strengthening disaster risk governance to manage disaster risk; 3) investing in disaster risk reduction for resilience; and 4) enhancing disaster preparedness for effective response and to "Build Back Better" in recovery, rehabilitation and reconstruction. The Sendai Framework aims at achieving the following outcome: *the substantial reduction of disaster risk and losses in lives, livelihoods and health and in the economic, physical, social, cultural and environmental assets of persons, businesses, communities and countries.* To succeed, it requires an orchestrated effort beyond the health sector and across different levels. It is urged that synergies between DRR, climate change and sustainable development be better recognised and that more efforts should be dedicated to address underlying inequity and the associated problems that might arise (see Case Box 8.21).

CASE BOX 8.21   AN EXAMPLE OF HOW "HEALTH" MIGHT BE INTEGRATED INTO INTERNATIONAL POLICY FRAMEWORKS: THE SENDAI FRAMEWORK FOR DISASTER RISK REDUCTION 2015–2030, BANGKOK PRINCIPLES (MARCH 2016) AND NEW DELHI DECLARATION (NOVEMBER 2016)

By Sharon Tsoon Ting Lo, Gloria Kwong Wai Chan and Emily Ying Yang Chan

While the relevance of health is clearly described within the HFA (see Section 7.14), the United Nations General Assembly Resolution 66/199 requested that UNISDR facilitated the development of a post-2015 framework for DRR. The two-phase consultation process began in March 2012 and the consultations culminated at the 3rd World Conference on Disaster Risk Reduction in 2015 in Japan (UNISDR, 2012). In March 2015, the Sendai Framework for Disaster Risk Reduction 2015–2030 (SFDRR) was adopted by UN member states, replacing the previous Hyogo Framework for Action 2005–2015 (HFA). The SFDRR represents a landmark agreement, which prioritises DRR and resilience building within the international community, creating a 15-year roadmap to enable countries to reduce disaster risk, and losses in lives, livelihoods and health. Following its adoption, the UNISDR Science and Technology Conference, held in Geneva, Switzerland in January 2016, identified how science and technology should be leveraged to implement the Sendai Framework. Health is an expected outcome and goal of the Sendai Framework: four out of the seven global targets directly relate to health, including reducing disaster mortality and the number of affected people.

The Sendai Framework aims at achieving the following outcome: the substantial reduction of disaster risk and losses in lives, livelihoods and health and in the economic, physical, social, cultural and environmental assets of persons, businesses, communities and countries. To succeed, it requires an orchestrated effort beyond the health sector and across different levels. It is urged that synergies between DRR, climate change and sustainable development be better recognised and that more efforts should be dedicated to address underlying inequity and the associated problems that might arise.

An International Conference on the Implementation of the Health Aspects of the Sendai Framework for Disaster Risk Reduction 2015-2030 was held in Bangkok in March 2016 to promote the systematic integration of health in DRR national policies and strategies, and to mainstream DRR within health systems and policies. The Bangkok Principles for the implementation of the health aspects of the Sendai Framework for Disaster Risk Reduction 2015-2030 (2016), the outcome of this conference, recommend enhancing cooperation between stakeholders to strengthen countries' capacity for disaster risk management for health; stimulating public and private investment in DRR; integrating DRR into health education and training; incorporating disaster-related mortality and morbidity data into early warning systems and national risk assessments; and advocating for a cross-sectoral and trans-boundary collaboration for an all-hazard approach to DRR.

In early November 2016, Asian Ministerial Conference for Disaster Risk Reduction (AMCDRR) 2016 was held in New Delhi, India. The New Delhi Declaration, a joint inter-governmental statement was the outcome of this meeting, wherein the ministers and heads of delegation to the conference reaffirm the commitment of governments in the Asian region to the Sendai Framework and to prioritise its meaningful realisation within their national contexts. The Declaration was complimented by the Asia Regional Plan for Implementation of the Sendai Framework for Disaster Risk Reduction 2015-2030. Consisting of a broad policy direction, a long-term roadmap and a two-year action plan, the Asia Regional Plan seeks to guide and support the national implementation of the Sendai Framework by identifying priorities, enhancing exchange of good practice, knowledge and information amongst governments and stakeholders, and strengthening regional cooperation to support this work.

Source: New Delhi Declaration 2016.

Conclusion

For the twenty-first century, rapid global climate change, unplanned urbanisation, increased income disparities and exacerbating environmental degradation are all factors that will increase the economic cost of disasters. To manage the impact of natural disasters cost-effectively, DRR must be made a priority for policy.

Disaster preparedness activities might be organised at the individual, household, community and global levels. In recent years, strategies and policies to address disaster preparedness have evolved from pure "top-down" to increasingly "bottom-up" approaches. While the Hyogo Framework for Action and the Sendai Framework are examples of top-down approaches to resilience building at the global level, promotion of community disaster health risk literacy and implementation of early warning systems are examples of community-based, bottom-up disaster preparedness activities.

The notion of disaster health risk management for health proposed by the WHO highlights the need for proactive management and prevention of the health impact of disasters by both health and non-health sectors. The all-hazard approach encourages the formulation of a standard, comprehensive emergency management system that would address the health needs common to all types of emergencies. The introduction of the "public health emergencies" concept by the International Health Regulations in 2005 signifies the formal and legally binding regulation of natural and man-made hazards that is of unique significance to disaster preparedness at the global level. It attempts to minimise unnecessary loss of health that results from service gaps and the lack of coordination of relief assistance in more fragmented, hazard-specific, emergency response systems. Last but not least, the human security approach to health provides a highly relevant paradigm for conceptualising public health emergency and disaster preparedness in the development of global policies that have direct influence on the allocation of relief resources, and the rights of states to claim such resources to meet the rising challenges in medical and humanitarian response in the decades to come.

References

Aitsi-Selmi, A., & Murray, V. (2015). The Sendai Framework: Disaster risk reduction through a health lens. *Bulletin of World Health Organization*, 93(6), 362.

Ardalan, A., Holakouei Naieni, K., Mahmoodi, M., Zanganeh, A. M., Keshtkar, A. A., Honarvar, M. R., & Kabir, M.-J. (2010). Flash flood preparedness in Golestan province of Iran: A community intervention trial. *American Journal of Disaster Medicine*, 5(4), 197–214.

Ardalan, A., Holakouei Naieni, K., Honarvar, M. R., Kabir, M.-J., Zanganeh, A. M., Keshtkar, A. A., . . . Khodaei, H. (2009). [The early warning system for flash floods in Golestan province: The model of village disaster taskforce]. *Payesh* [The Journal of Health Research Institute], 8(2), 147–154.

Bangkok Principles for the implementation of the health aspects of the Sendai Framework for Disaster Risk Reduction 2015-2030. (2016). Retrieved from the website of the World Health Organization: http://www.who.int/hac/events/2016/Bangkok_Principles.pdf

Basnyat, B., Dalton, H. R., Kamar, N., Rein, D. B., Labrique, A., Farrar, J., & Piot, P. (2015). Nepali earthquakes and the risk of an epidemic of hepatitis E. *The Lancet, 385*(9987), 2572–2573.

Benson, C., & Clay, E. J. (2004). *Understanding the economic and financial impacts of natural disasters.* Washington, DC: World Bank.

Betancourt, T. S., McBain, R., Newnham, E. A., Akinsulure-Smith, A. M., Brennan, R. T., Weisz, J. R., & Hansen, N. B. (2014). A behavioral intervention for war-affected youth in Sierra Leone: A randomized controlled trial. *Journal of the American Academy of Child & Adolescent Psychiatry, 53*(12), 1288–1297.

Bethel, J. W., Foreman, A. N., & Burke, S. C. (2011). Disaster preparedness among medically vulnerable populations. *American Journal of Preventive Medicine, 40*(2), 139–143.

Chan, E. Y. Y. (2013). Bottom-up disaster resilience. *Nature Geoscience, 6,* 327–328.

Chan, E. Y. Y., Chan, G. K. W., Wong, C. K. P., Wong, C .S., Liu, K. S. L., Huang, Z., & Yan, M. W. L. (2016). *Globalisation – Climate change and human health.* Hong Kong, China: Collaborating Centre for Oxford University and CUHK for Disaster and Medical Humanitarian Response.

Chan, E. Y. Y., Hung, K. K. C., Cheung, E. Y. L., Koo, S., & Wong, A. H. (2012, April). *Disaster case study on health impact of the 2010 fire disaster in Bhutan.* Paper presented at the 13th World Congress on Public Health, Addis Ababa, Ethiopia. Abstract retrieved from https://www.researchgate.net/publication/268133874_Disaster_Case_Study_on_Health_Impact_of_the_2011_Fire_Disaster_in_Bhutan

Chan, E. Y. Y., Kim, J. H., Lin, C., Cheung, E. Y. L., & Lee, P. P. Y. (2014). Is previous disaster experience a good predictor for disaster preparedness in extreme poverty households in remote Muslim minority based community in China? *Journal of Immigrant and Minority Health, 16*(3), 466–472.

Chan, E. Y. Y., Lee, P. P. Y., & Tam, G. (2014). *The 2010 great fire of Bumthang in Bhutan* (Disaster Case Studies series of CCOUC). Hong Kong, China: CCOUC.

Chan, E. Y. Y., & Southgate, R. J. (2014). Responding to chronic disease needs following disasters: A rethink using the Human Security approach. In C. Hobson, P. Bacon, & R. Cameron (Eds.), *Human security and natural disasters* (Routledge Humanitarian Studies series, pp. 74–93). Tokyo, Japan: Routledge.

Chan, E. Y. Y., Yeung, M. P. S., Liu S., Huang, Z., Ho, J. Y., & Wong, C. K. (2016). *Do socioeconomic factors have an effect on cold-related health outcomes in sub-tropical cities? The case of Hong Kong* (CCOUC Working Paper Series). Hong Kong, China: CCOUC.

Chan, E. Y. Y., & Yue, J. S. K. (2012). *Mapping out the concept of "Disaster Health Risk Literacy"* (CCOUC Working Paper Series). Hong Kong, China: CCOUC.

Chan, E. Y. Y., Yue, J., Lee, P., & Wang, S. S. (2016). Socio-demographic predictors for urban community disaster health risk perception and household based preparedness in a Chinese urban city. *PLOS Currents Disasters.* Jun 27. Edition 1. doi:10.1371/currents.dis.28 7fb7fee6f9f4521af441a236c2d519

Chan, E. Y. Y., Zhu, C. Y., Lee, P., Liu, K. S., & Mark, C. K. M. (2014, September). *Impact of disaster preparedness intervention in Yi minority community in Sichuan Province, China.* Paper presented at the 12th Asia Pacific Conference on Disaster Medicine, Tokyo, Japan.

Chatfield, A. T., Scholl, H. J. J., & Brajawidagda, U. (2013). Tsunami early warnings via Twitter in government: Net-savvy citizens' co-production of time-critical public information services. *Government Information Quarterly, 30*(4), 377–386.

Collaborating Centre for Oxford University and CUHK for Disaster and Medical Humanitarian Response (CCOUC). (n.d.a). Ethnic Minority Health Project [Internet]. Retrieved from http://www.ccouc.ox.ac.uk/home-5

Collaborating Centre for Oxford University and CUHK for Disaster and Medical Humanitarian Response (CCOUC). (n.d.b). Ethnic Minority Health Project: Project details [Internet]. Retrieved from http://ccouc.org/project-details

Collaborating Centre for Oxford University and CUHK for Disaster and Medical Humanitarian Response (CCOUC). (2015, June 25). *Technical assessment report on 2015 Nepal earthquakes.* Hong Kong, China: Author.

Collaborating Centre for Oxford University and CUHK for Disaster and Medical Humanitarian Response (CCOUC). (2016, May). Online course – Public Health Principles in Disaster and Medical Humanitarian Response [internet]. Retrieved from http://www.ccouc.ox.ac.uk/public-health-principles-in-disaster-and-medical-humanitarian-response-2

Collaborating Centre for Oxford University and CUHK for Disaster and Medical Humanitarian Response (CCOUC). (2016, November). *CCOUC online course interim report: Public Health Principles in Disaster and Medical Humanitarian Response.* Hong Kong, China: Author.

Cretikos, M., Eastwood, K., Dalton, C., Merritt, T., Tuyl, F., Winn, L., & Durrheim, D. (2008). Household disaster preparedness and information sources: Rapid cluster survey after a storm in New South Wales, Australia. *BMC Public Health, 8*(195), 1–9.

Dargye, Y. (2004). A brief overview of fire disaster management in Bhutan. In C. Menegazzi (Ed.), *Cultural heritage disaster preparedness and response* (International Symposium Proceedings, Salar Jung Museum, Hyderabad, India, 23-27 November 2003, pp. 111–116). Paris, France: International Council of Museums. Retrieved from http://archives.icom.museum/disaster_preparedness_book/country/dargye.pdf

Dema, P. (2013). Japan donates two more fire engines. *Kuensel online* [Internet]. Retrieved from http://kuenselonline.com/archive/japan-donates-two-more-fire-engines/

Dorji, T. (2006). Bhutan: Fire situation in Bhutan [Internet]. *International Forest Fire News (IFFN), 34.* Retrieved from http://www.fire.uni-freiburg.de/iffn/iffn_34/07-IFFN-34-Bhutan.pdf

Goggins, W. B., Chan, E. Y. Y., Yang, C., & Chong, M. (2013). Associations between mortality and meteorological and pollutant variables during the cool season in two Asian cities with sub-tropical climates: Hong Kong and Taipei [Internet]. *Environmental Health, 12,* 59. doi:10.1186/1476–069X-12–59

Ho, P. (2003). *Weathering the storm: Hong Kong Observatory and social development.* Hong Kong, China: Hong Kong University Press.

Hong Kong Special Administrative Region (HKSAR), Census and Statistics Department. (2015, April). *Hong Kong: The facts* [Internet]. Hong Kong, China: Information Services Department, HKSAR Government. Retrieved from http://www.gov.hk/en/about/abouthk/factsheets/docs/population.pdf

Hong Kong Special Administrative Region (HKSAR), Planning Department. (2015, May 15). Planning data: Land utilization in Hong Kong 2014 [Internet]. Retrieved from http://www.pland.gov.hk/pland_en/info_serv/statistic/landu.html

Hyer, R. N., & Covello, V. (2005). *Effective media communication during public health emergencies: A WHO handbook.* Retrieved from World Health Organization (WHO) website: http://www.who.int/csr/resources/publications/WHO%20MEDIA%20HANDBOOK.pdf

International Federation of Red Cross and Red Crescent Societies (IFRC). (2013). *World disaster report 2013: Focus on technology and the future of humanitarian action* [Internet]. Retrieved from the website of IFRC: https://www.ifrc.org/PageFiles/134658/WDR%202013%20complete.pdf

Kalkstein, A. J., & Sheridan, S. C. (2007). The social impacts of the heat-health watch/warning system in Phoenix, Arizona: Assessing the perceived risk and response of the public. *International Journal of Biometeorology, 52,* 43–55.

Kikuchi, M. (2011, July 20). なぜ大川小学校だけが大惨事となったのか (Japanese) [Why did the tragedy happen at Ōkawa Primary School?] [Internet]. 中央公論 *[Chuokoron]*. Retrieved from http://www.chuokoron.jp/2011/07/post_87_2.html

Klein, R.J.T., Huq, S., Denton, F., Downing, T. E., Richels, R. G., Robinson, J. B., & Toth, F. L. (2007). Inter-relationships between adaptation and mitigation. In M. L. Parry, O. F. Canziani, J. P. Palutikof, P. J. van der Linden, & C. E. Hanson (Eds.), *Climate change 2007: Impacts, adaptation and vulnerability.* (*Contribution of Working Group II to the Fourth Assessment Report of the Intergovernmental Panel on Climate Change*) (pp. 745–777). Cambridge, UK: Cambridge University Press.

Kohn, R., Saxena, S., Levav, I., & Saraceno, B. (2004). The treatment gap in mental health care. *Bulletin of the World Health Organization, 82*(11), 858–866.

New Delhi Declaration - 2016. (2016). Retrieved from the website of Asian Ministerial Conference on Disaster Risk Reduction (AMCDRR) 2016: https://www.amcdrrindia.net/wp-content/uploads/2016/11/Final-NEW-DELHI-DECLARATION-05-November-2016.pdf

Nutbeam, D. (2000). Health literacy as a public health goal: A challenge for contemporary health education and communication strategies into the 21st century. *Health Promotion International, 15*(3), 259–267.

Ōkawa Primary School Incident Investigation Committee. (2014, February). 大川小学校事故検証報告書 (Japanese) [Report on Ōkawa Primary School Incident] [Internet]. Retrieved from http://www.mext.go.jp/b_menu/shingi/chukyo/chukyo5/012/gijiroku/__icsFiles/afieldfile/2014/08/07/1350542_01.pdf

Petal, M. (2008, November). *Disaster prevention for schools: Guidance for education sector decision-makers* (Consultation version) [Internet]. Retrieved from United Nations International Strategy for Disaster Reduction (UNISDR) website: http://www.unisdr.org/files/7556_7344DPforSchoolssm1.pdf

Phaiju, A., Bej, D., Phokharel, S., & Dons, U. (2010). *Establishing community based early warning system: Practitioner's handbook.* Nepal: Mercy Corps and Practical Action. Retrieved from http://www.preventionweb.net/files/19893_19866cbewspractionershandbooktraini.pdf

Pokhrel, N. (2014). *Japan donates fire engine and truck pump* [Internet]. *Kuensel online.* Retrieved from http://kuenselonline.com/archive/japan-donates-fire-engine-and-truck-pump-2/

Ratzan, S., & Parker, R. M. (2000). Introduction. In *Health literacy: January 1990 through October 1999* (Current Bibliographies in Medicine series No. 2000–1) [Internet]. Bethesda, MD: National Library of Health. Retrieved from https://www.nlm.nih.gov/archive//20061214/pubs/cbm/hliteracy.pdf

Rockenschaub, G. (2008). *Support health security and preparedness planning and crisis management in EU, EU-accession and neighbouring (ENP) countries* (Presentation on behalf of WHO Regional Office for Europe (WHO/EURO)). Retrieved from http://ec.europa.eu/chafea/documents/news/technical_meetings/WHO_health_security_collaboration.pdf

Royal Bhutan Police, Royal Government of Bhutan. (2008). *Fire and rescue services division* [Internet]. Retrieved from http://www.rbp.gov.bt/fire.php

The Sphere Project. (2011). *Humanitarian charter and minimum standard in humanitarian response* [Internet]. Retrieved from http://www.sphereproject.org/resources/download-publications/?search=1&keywords=&language=English&category=22

Tol, W. A., Barbui, C., Galappatti, A., Silove, D., Betancourt, T. S., Souza, R., . . . van Ommeren, M. (2011). Mental health and psychosocial support in humanitarian settings: Linking practice and research. *The Lancet, 378*(9802), 1581–1591. doi:10.1016/S0140–6736(11)61094–5

United Nations. (2006). *Global survey of early warning systems: An assessment of capacities, gaps and opportunities towards building a comprehensive global early warning system for all natural hazards*

[Internet]. Retrieved from the website of UNISDR: http://www.unisdr.org/2006/ppew/info-resources/ewc3/Global-Survey-of-Early-Warning-Systems.pdf

United Nations Development Programme (UNDP). (2013). *Hong Kong, China (SAR): HDI values and rank changes in the 2013 Human Development Report* (Explanatory note on 2013 HDR composite indices) [Internet]. Retrieved from http://hdr.undp.org/sites/default/files/Country-Profiles/HKG.pdf

United Nations Educational, Scientific and Cultural Organization (UNESCO). (2004). *The plurality of literacy and its implication for policies and programmes.* Paris, France: Author.

United Nations Environment Programme (UNEP). (2012). *Early warning systems: A state of the art analysis and future directions.* Nairobi, Kenya: Division of Early Warning and Assessment (DEWA), UNEP.

United Nations International Strategy for Disaster Reduction (UNISDR). (2007). *Hyogo Framework for Action 2005–2015: Building the resilience of nations and communities to disasters* (Brochure). Retrieved from http://www.preventionweb.net/files/1217_HFAbrochure English.pdf

United Nations International Strategy for Disaster Reduction (UNISDR). (2009). *2009 UNISDR terminology on disaster risk reduction* [Internet]. Retrieved from http://www.unisdr.org/files/7817_UNISDRTerminologyEnglish.pdf

United Nations International Strategy for Disaster Reduction (UNISDR). (2012). *Towards a post-2015 framework for disaster risk reduction* [Internet]. Retrieved from http://www.unisdr.org/files/25129_towardsapost2015frameworkfordisaste.pdf

United Nations Office for the Coordination of Humanitarian Affairs (OCHA). (2015, May 16) *Nepal: Who does what where when (4W) – as of 15 May* [Internet]. Retrieved from http://reliefweb.int/report/nepal/nepal-who-does-what-where-when-4w-15-may

Vorhies, F. (2012). *The economics of investing in disaster risk reduction* [Internet]. Retrieved from http://www.preventionweb.net/posthfa/documents/drreconomicsworkingpaperfinal.pdf

World Health Organization (WHO). (2007a). *Risk reduction and emergency preparedness: WHO six-year strategy for the health sector and community capacity development* [Internet]. Retrieved from http://www.who.int/hac/techguidance/preparedness/emergency_preparedness_eng.pdf

World Health Organization (WHO). (2007b). *The world health report 2007 – A safer future: Global public health security in the 21st century* [Internet]. Retrieved from http://www.who.int/whr/2007/whr07_en.pdf?ua=1

World Health Organization (WHO). (2014). *World Health Organization Conference on Health and Climate Change: Conference report.* Retrieved from http://www.who.int/globalchange/mediacentre/events/climate-health-conference/whoconferenceonhealthandclimatechangefinalreport.pdf?ua=1

World Health Organization (WHO). (2015). *Comprehensive safe hospital framework.* Retrieved from http://www.who.int/hac/techguidance/comprehensive_safe_hospital_framework.pdf

World Health Organization (WHO). (2016). *International Health Regulations (2005)* (3rd ed.) [Internet]. Retrieved from http://apps.who.int/iris/bitstream/10665/246107/1/9789241580496-eng.pdf?ua=1

World Health Organization (WHO) & Pan American Health Organization (PAHO). (2008). The new international health regulations: What they mean for disaster managers. *Disasters: Preparedness and Mitigation in the Americas, 109* [Internet]. Retrieved from http://www.paho.org/disasters/newsletter/index.php?option=com_content&view=article&id=98%3Athe-new-international-health-regulations-what-they-mean-for-disaster-managers&catid=69%3Aissue-109-march-2008-editorial&lang=en

World Health Organization (WHO), United Kingdom Health Protection Agency (HPA), & partners. (2011). *Disaster risk management for health: Overview.* Retrieved from http://www.who.int/hac/events/drm_fact_sheet_overview.pdf?ua=1

World Health Organization (WHO) Country Office for Nepal. (2015, May 26). *Nepal earthquake 2015* (Situation report # 19). Retrieved from http://www.searo.who.int/entity/emergencies/crises/nepal/who-sitrep19–26-may-2015.pdf?ua=1

9
CONCLUSION

Reviewing the deadliest disasters in recent decades would indicate humans are at least in part culpable for contributing to the risk factors, such as environmental degradation, global warming and urbanisation, that can result in catastrophic events. Proactive engagement of disaster stakeholders in preparedness, emergency responses and recovery can save thousands of lives. This book examines natural disaster preparedness and responses from a public health perspective. It shows how public health tools can be used to support preparedness and response. Better disaster preparedness and response might not only support community recovery but also contribute to the cost-effective use of resources, which, in turn, might advance the social and economic development of communities.

INDEX

Academy of Agricultural Science 71
acute respiratory infections, shelter/clothing and 135
acute risk from release of hazardous materials 67, 68
acute stress disorder 158
Adam, H. 169
adaptive capacity, temperature-related events and 108
Alexander, D. E. 30
all-hazard approach to disaster preparedness 232
anaemia, drought and 105
ashes 90
asphyxiation 90
authority failure 40, 41

baseline average mortality rate 56
Bayer, C. P. 169
Bethel, J. W. 215
biological hazards 33, 110–13; *see also* epidemics
biostatistics, defined 7
blunt trauma 90
Bolton, P. 125
bottom-up resilience 212, 213, 233
Brown, L. R. 104
Brunei Darussalam floods and landslides 96
Burke, S. C. 215
bystanders, public health impacts of natural disasters on 62

case boxes: Aceh, Indonesia tsunami 197–8; Bam, Iran earthquake, 2003 223; Bangladesh sea level rise 193; bottom-up resilience 213, 233; Brunei Darussalam floods and landslides 96; Bumthang, Bhutan great fire 224; Chernobyl accident 35–6; child-friendly spaces 172; children in Bangladesh floods 168; child soldier 169; chronic disease care, post-disaster Asia 138; chronic non-communicable disease care post-disaster 155; climate change, Hong Kong and 192; cluster approach, West Sumatra earthquake 186–8; cold waves in Hong Kong, 2008 109; collaborative training of community health workers 218–19; Community-based Disaster Risk Management (CBDRM) 219–20; Community-based Disaster Risk Management Action Plan, Vietnam 225; cyclone Nargis in Myanmar 63–4; Democratic People's Republic of Korea (DPRK) droughts and floods 70–1; disaster preparedness 209; disaster preparedness, in Yi minority community 216–17; disaster preparedness, rural settings 215–16; disaster preparedness, urban settings 215; disaster tourism 141; Dutch famine tragedy 13; Eastern Horn of Africa drought, 2010-2011 103; Ebola, cost of 200; Ebola epidemic, West